Build Your Own Car Dashboard with a Raspberry Pi

Practical Projects to Build Your Own Smart Car

Joseph Coburn

Apress®

Build Your Own Car Dashboard with a Raspberry Pi: Practical Projects to Build Your Own Smart Car

Joseph Coburn
Alford, UK

ISBN-13 (pbk): 978-1-4842-6079-1   ISBN-13 (electronic): 978-1-4842-6080-7
https://doi.org/10.1007/978-1-4842-6080-7

Managing Director, Apress Media LLC: Welmoed Spahr
Acquisitions Editor: Aaron Black
Development Editor: James Markham
Coordinating Editor: Jessica Vakili

Distributed to the book trade worldwide by Springer Science+Business Media New York, 233 Spring Street, 6th Floor, New York, NY 10013. Phone 1-800-SPRINGER, fax (201) 348-4505, e-mail orders-ny@springer-sbm.com, or visit www.springeronline.com. Apress Media, LLC is a California LLC and the sole member (owner) is Springer Science + Business Media Finance Inc (SSBM Finance Inc). SSBM Finance Inc is a **Delaware** corporation.

For information on translations, please e-mail rights@apress.com, or visit http://www.apress.com/rights-permissions.

Apress titles may be purchased in bulk for academic, corporate, or promotional use. eBook versions and licenses are also available for most titles. For more information, reference our Print and eBook Bulk Sales web page at http://www.apress.com/bulk-sales.

Any source code or other supplementary material referenced by the author in this book is available to readers on GitHub via the book's product page, located at www.apress.com/978-1-4842-6079-1. For more detailed information, please visit http://www.apress.com/source-code.

Printed on acid-free paper

I'd like to dedicate this entire book to the Raspberry Pi Foundation and the Pallets team. Without the Pi Foundation, there would be no Raspberry Pi at all, and their continued hard work to ensure that computer science is not forgotten in UK schools is something we should all strive to emulate. The Pallets team developed Flask, which is the Python framework upon which this whole book is based. Not only that, but Pallets developed many more incredibly useful Python packages, including Flask-SQLAlchemy, Click, ItsDangerous, and more. These free tools make it easy to spin up an entire Python application, and the team works tirelessly to maintain their projects to a very high standard.

Table of Contents

About the Author

Joseph Coburn is an experienced computer science teacher, writer, editor, and software developer. His work has been shared by Adobe, Lifehacker, and the Arduino Foundation. His code is used by thousands of people daily. And he is well versed with designing, implementing, and troubleshooting complex software systems.

About the Technical Reviewer

 **Massimo Nardone** has more than 22 years of experiences in security, web/mobile development, cloud, and IT architecture. His true IT passions are security and Android.

He has been programming and teaching how to program with Android, Perl, PHP, Java, VB, Python, C/C++, and MySQL for more than 20 years.

He holds a Master of Science degree in Computing Science from the University of Salerno, Italy.

He has worked as a project manager, software engineer, research engineer, chief security architect, information security manager, PCI/SCADA auditor, and senior lead IT security/cloud/SCADA architect for many years.

Preface

Back in July of 2018 I wrote an article for MakeUseOf titled "How to Add Smart Features to Your Old Car with These 10 DIY Projects." It was a fairly standard article for us at the time; a list of ten cool car projects using the Raspberry Pi and links to the tutorials and YouTube videos – a fairly normal article of 1000 words or thereabouts. I don't remember anything special about this article, and my editor requested no changes at the time of submission – which was great to hear. I'd written several Pi articles at the time, along with several Python tutorials, but my main focus was on product reviews. At that time, I'd just started a partnership with *BenQ*, and published several fun reviews on their 4K projectors and LCD gaming monitors.

Toward the end of June 2019, Aaron Black (senior editor at Apress) reached out to me regarding the article and enquired as to my interest in writing a book on the Raspberry Pi. Up until that point, I hadn't, but I remember thinking "is that all it takes to kick off the process?" I followed up on Aaron's email, and after some correspondence and a pitch, I signed the contract to deliver this book in nine months. I certainly learned a lot writing this book, and it's my hope that you will learn a lot by reading it.

While I had a clear structure of the book layout and managed to write the first 12,000 words within a week in August, it was certainly a huge effort that took many writing sessions, head-scratching coding sessions, and self-editing sessions locked away in my office. You sometimes wonder if it's worth it at all, but having finished the book now as I write this preface, I can say unequivocally "yes."

With several hundred articles under my belt with both MakeUseOf and Blocks Decoded publications, I was well practiced in juggling multiple jobs, pitches, authors, and editors, yet a minimum of 55,000 words seemed far more achievable *in theory*. In practice, it felt like the final 10% took 90% more effort than the first 90%. It seems the software development aphorism *the ninety-ninety rule* holds true for books just as much as software development. "The first 90 percent of the code accounts for the first 90 percent of the development time. The remaining 10 percent of the code accounts for the other 90 percent of the development time" – Tom Cargill.

Introduction

The modern computer is a revolutionary device. In less than 100 years, society has changed, with computers running almost every aspect of our lives. The mobile phone is a futuristic science fiction–like gadget, with instant access to almost all the information ever created. We live in an unparalleled age of technology, one in which you can book a train, video-chat with friends, or earn money from the comfort of your own home.

In 1957, computers were the size of a bus, with each component requiring a team of people and a crane to unload. Now 63 years later, the Raspberry Pi can fit into your pocket and costs less than a takeaway. In November 2015, the Raspberry Pi Zero launched for a price of $5, and a promotional campaign saw it attached to the front of a magazine.

Few could have predicted the enduring popularity of the Raspberry Pi. With over 25 million units sold and no end in sight, it's safe to say that the humble Pi has become legendary. Its low barrier to entry helped spawn a new industry. Now in its fifth generation, the Pi has been to the International Space Station in low Earth orbit. Pis can control home lighting, 3D printers, drones, security systems, arcade machines, and many more projects.

This book will teach you how to use the Raspberry Pi and the Python programming language through a practical car-based project. Not only will you learn how to build your own hardware connected to the Pi, but you'll learn how to write software and the industry-standard best practices which keep your software running smoothly. These will keep you safe as a software developer. This book may not be like others you read. I want you to question everything. It's hoped you will learn how the circuits work, and why the code looks like it does, instead of copying the code and hoping for the best. By doing this, you'll gain a solid foundation in both the Raspberry Pi and software development.

Throughout this book, I encourage you to hand-type every line of code. It will be tedious, and the temptation to grab the code from GitHub and paste it into your work will always be present. I promise you that by really understanding every line, and each and every word by reading, understanding, and typing it yourself, you'll become a better programmer. I'm a big fan of simple code – and hopefully the projects contained in this book are manageable. Each project starts small and then builds in complexity as your confidence grows – each chapter expanding on concepts learned in the previous chapter.

Remember – code is for you (or other developers) to read and understand. Computers will interpret almost any valid code, no matter how complex, slow, inefficient, or hard to read. Other developers understanding the code are far more valuable than a *clever* solution which is convoluted, or confusing to get your head into.

My hope is that you'll complete this book and know *how to program*. Not knowing how to write Python code, or use the Raspberry Pi, rather you have the skills to quickly pick up (almost) any programming language. The skill of problem solving is an integral part of software development, and code is the medium through which we as developers can express our solutions.

All you need to build these projects yourself is a little equipment, and a desire to learn more. A constant burning question of *why* and an insatiable appetite for answers are more powerful than any number of degrees or years of experience. In my career as a software developer, I'm fortunate enough to occasionally have the need to interview developers for midlevel to senior developer positions. I'd rather employ someone who has a willingness to learn and a desire to better themselves than someone who can code the pants off a donkey, but is stuck in their ways, or even worse, unable to acknowledge the fact that they don't know everything.

I'll guide you through the process of developing software and hardware for the Raspberry Pi, but that doesn't mean the solutions presented here are *the best*. By the time you read this (given the rapidly advancing nature of technology), some of these techniques may have fallen out of favor. New technologies may exist, or better techniques and algorithms arrive to make your job easier. Bring it on I say! The day you stop learning as a developer is the day you stop growing.

If you think there's a better way to solve some of the problems in this book, or you just want to say "hi," then drop me a line on GitHub, or even better, open a pull request and start a discussion in this project's repo at `https://github.com/CoburnJoe/Pi-Car`. I'll maintain a branch which mostly matches the code in this book, but I'm more than willing to open this project to the open source community.

Last of all, remember to have fun. Coding should be fun, and nothing compares to that feeling of elation after fixing a bug or getting something working. On more than one occasion, I've spent *days* diagnosing or troubleshooting systems, only to find a missing comma, semicolon, or bracket. It's such a good feeling that I'd happily continue to track bugs down over weeks or months if the need arises.

CHAPTER 1

Raspberry Pi History

Chapter goal: Learn about the main Raspberry Pi boards and their (brief) history. Understand the key differences between different Pi models, and why certain features were introduced.

First introduced in 2012, the Raspberry Pi has seen five major version releases across 13 form factors. Dozens of derivatives and knockoff clones exist, and a huge number of different modules, accessories, cases, and projects exist to help you use the ultimate tech tool. I've personally used Raspberry Pis to build business operation dashboards and display real-time server statistics and for face recognition and identification with OpenCV, retro gaming stations with RetroPie, video streaming, CI/CD deployment servers, and much more. Their small form factor, cheap price, and modest energy consumption features lend themselves perfectly to these kinds of projects – and many more besides.

A Brief History of Pi

The idea for the Raspberry Pi came about after computer scientist Eben Upton grew concerned that college students lacked the necessary skills to work with computer hardware, instead focusing on software and online interactions. While working for the University of Cambridge, UK, in 2006,

© Joseph Coburn 2020
J. Coburn, *Build Your Own Car Dashboard with a Raspberry Pi*,
https://doi.org/10.1007/978-1-4842-6080-7_1

Eben along with colleagues Rob Mullins, Jack Lang, and Alan Mycroft developed a hand-soldered prototype which was a far cry from today's credit card–sized computers. It wasn't until February 2012 that Eben et al. managed to release the affordable yet powerful computer we know and love.

The Pi was developed with support from Broadcom, who designed and developed the SoC (system on a chip) processor used to power the Pi. Almost everything the Pi needs to work is built in to the system. The memory, GPU, CPU, I/O, and more are soldered into place. It's not possible to upgrade the Pi's components, but with regular new releases increasing the Pi's power and usefulness, and a sale price of less than $50, few can complain about planned obsolescence.

Originally marketed with modest sales expectations, the Pi took the world by surprise, eventually going on to sell more than 30 million units. As a computer science student at the University of Lincoln, UK, I (along with all the other students on my course) was gifted a first-generation Pi by the university, with no expectation or pressure to use it and no mandatory modules requiring ownership of one. Perhaps it was hoped the Pi would spark a revolution in computer hardware design, or more likely my university wanted to support a cool project. The Pi has since become the best-selling UK computer of all time.

Figure 1-1. *Raspberry Pis, from left to right: Pi 1, Pi 2, Pi Zero, Pi 3, Pi 4*

While there have been five main models of Pi release thus far (shown in Figure 1-1), each series saw several variations and minor specification changes – either as a midlife refresh or at launch. This allows the Pi to cater to a huge number of budgets, users, and projects. Models such as the Pi Zero are tiny, while the Pi 4 comes in three variants, each one with more RAM (and a larger price) than the previous model.

This huge flexibility helps to keep the Pi affordable, while offering higher-end features for those with the larger budgets. Note that lacking the funds to purchase a "faster" Pi doesn't exclude someone from the best experience – most Pis retained the same processor and basic specifications across models, meaning the incremental upgrades are limited to changes such as total memory, I/O ports, and other small improvements. The Raspberry Pi has never seen an Apple style price gouge, instead opting to keep the Pi affordable. Figure 1-2 shows the Pi 4, with USB power, USB devices, and HDMI cables connected.

Figure 1-2. *Raspberry Pi 4 wired up*

3

Today, the Pi is managed by two organizations. The *Raspberry Pi Foundation* is a charity that exists to promote the study of computer science in education. It's a registered charity, with a board of trustees. It's supported both by Broadcom and the University of Cambridge, UK. After the initial success of the Pi, a limited company called *Raspberry Pi (Trading) LTD* was created to handle the research, development, and production of all future Pis. Eben Upton is still a key driving force in both organizations today.

Raspberry Pi 1

The original Raspberry Pi was introduced in 2012 as the *Pi 1 Model B* (Figure 1-3). It measured 3.37 x 2.22 inches and cost $35. It didn't have wireless networking built in, but it has one USB 2.0 port, an Ethernet port, an analog video out, 3.5mm audio out, and a full-size HDMI port. Powered by MicroUSB, this Pi has 26 GPIO (general-purpose input/output) pins for interfacing with the real world, the now standard CSI camera connection, and a DSI interface, to connect LCD displays to (in addition to the HDMI port).

Figure 1-3. *Raspberry Pi 1*

The Model B is powered by a single-core Broadcom BCM2835 SoC processor running at 700MHz, with 256MB of RAM (shared with the GPU). The *Pi 1 Model A* arrived in 2013, which removed the Ethernet port. By 2014, the *Model 1 A+* and *B+* arrived, with a modest bump up to 512MB of RAM, a slightly lower price, and a doubling to two USB 2.0 ports, along with several miscellaneous component changes. The B+ increased the GPIO layout to the now standard 40 pins.

Raspberry Pi 2

After three years, the Raspberry *Pi 2* arrived in February 2015 (Figure 1-4). Boasting four USB 2.0 ports, a slight reshuffle of the layout, and dropping the component video out, this model is the simplest in the range, simply sold as *Pi 2 Model B*. While there is still no support for Wi-Fi, this model quadrupled the power with a quad-core Broadcom BCM2836 SoC running at 900MHz, and another doubling of the RAM to 1GB. The form factor remained unchanged. This model was a significant step-up on the now slow and clunky Pi 1, yet kept the same $35 price.

Figure 1-4. Raspberry Pi 2

Raspberry Pi Zero

In November 2015, the *Pi Zero* arrived and once again revolutionized the market (shown in Figure 1-5). This dropped the price to $10 per unit and drastically reduced the size to a new form factor measuring 2.59 x 1.20 inches. This model switched back to the BCM2835 SoC from the Pi 1 along with 512MB of RAM. The processor came pre-overclocked to 1GHz. This Pi saw minor I/O changes to accommodate the smaller form factor. You had to solder the GPIO header yourself, and mini HDMI and micro-USB ports kept the size small.

The revolutionary device was given away for free on the cover of *The MagPi* magazine – another first for the Pi Foundation. I remember the launch day well, as it was a complete surprise to everyone. I managed to get a copy of the magazine and a Pi Zero on launch day, but only by pure chance. My then boss got a tip off to go buy *The MagPi* before work and he bought one for me – there were only two left on the shelf!

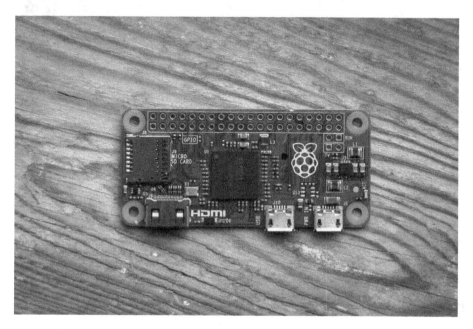

Figure 1-5. *Raspberry Pi Zero*

In February 2017, the Pi Zero was updated to include Wi-Fi and sold as the *Pi Zero W*. Since release, various combinations of Wi-Fi and pre-soldered headers arrived, offering you total flexibility in your style of pocket computer.

Raspberry Pi 3

The *Pi 3 Model B* launched in 2016 (Figure 1-6) saw a return to the "traditional" credit card–sized form factor. By now, the layout has stabilized with 40-pin GPIO, Ethernet, and 4x USB 2.0 ports as standard. The Pi 3 used a BCM2837 quad-core processor running at 900MHz, with

1GB of DDR2 RAM. For this first time, the Pi featured a built-in Wi-Fi receiver and a gigabit Ethernet port. This was the first model to support a 64-bit architecture.

Figure 1-6. *Raspberry Pi 3*

The *Pi 3 A+* and *B+* arrived in 2018, once again bringing with them the standard removal of Ethernet, and minor spec shuffling. These models saw a slight processor change to the BCM2837B0 quad-core chip, running at 1.4GHz – a worthwhile upgrade for those craving speed.

Raspberry Pi 4

The *Pi 4 Model B* (Figure 1-7) is surprisingly consistent so far. Granted, it only arrived in June 2019, so it's yet to see a minor spec bump and *A+/B+* release. The Pi 4 upgraded two of the USB ports to USB 3.0 and provided *two* mini HDMI outputs, capable of driving 4K displays. It sports a 1.5GHz SoC in the form of the BCM2711. Three variations of the Pi 4 are available, with 1GB, 2GB, and 4GB of RAM – for an increased price of $34, $45, and $55, respectively.

Figure 1-7. Raspberry Pi 4

The Pi 4 builds upon the vast Pi heritage curated over eight years of production, and many more of development. The Pi 4 is seriously powerful, and it starts to dwarf the earlier models – especially the *Pi 1 Model B*. Be it video encoding, building files from source, and any other intensive task, the Pi 4 significantly speeds up the job. The king is dead, *long live the king!*

Pi Cameras

Every model of the Pi (with the exception of the Zero) features a *camera serial interface*, or CSI port. This allows the connection of the Pi Camera – which you'll use in the completion of the car project in this book.

The original Pi camera launched in May 2013. It measures 1 x 0.78 inches, with a flat ribbon cable, which connected to the CSI port. Priced at roughly $20, the camera was expensive when compared to the Pi itself, but it did (and still does) provide a fascinating insight into computer vision and image processing. Capable of a maximum resolution of 5MP for photos, or 1080p video at 30 frames per second, it was "good enough" for most projects.

It was shortly followed by the Pi NoIR camera – an infrared variant designed for night vision with IR lighting.

Figure 1-8. *Raspberry Pi Camera V2.1*

By 2016, the successor to the Pi camera arrived in the Pi Camera V2 (Figure 1-8) – with the same dimensions and connection, but a significantly better 8MP sensor. The V2 camera was a huge upgrade in quality. A V2 NoIR version followed shortly after.

In 2020, a $50, 12MP model was announced, with support for interchangeable lenses. This modern lens mount will let you connect DSLR lenses – some of which cost several hundreds or thousands of dollars more than the sensor itself!

Chapter Summary

In this chapter, you learned about the five main Raspberry Pi boards, along with the Pi camera, and the history behind the Pi and the Pi Foundation. You learned about the various different form factors and revisions of the Pi itself, and the different CPU and I/O configurations, along with the pricing model and publicity stunts (such as giving away the Pi Zero on the cover of *The MagPi* magazine).

The next chapter is a software development primer. In it, you'll learn some basic computer science theory, along with some historical case studies. You'll gain an understanding of how software works, and how you can use the lessons from history to make your code better.

CHAPTER 2

Software Development Primer

Chapter goal: Learn some of the fundamental computer science terms, techniques, and best practices. Learn a brief history of Python, and read case studies to understand how to improve software.

This book covers a multitude of software development tools, techniques, and best practices. The aim of this chapter is to upskill you on the core fundamentals necessary to follow along with the projects. While anyone can write code, it takes skill to write *software*.

Do you ever get frustrated by a software package that crashes every time you use it? Or what about a magical button that crashes every time you press it? All software has to run under a huge variety of conditions. The operating system, installed drivers, hardware, accessories, other software, and many more conditions make it impossible to test every different computer configuration.

By employing industry-standard best practices for software development, it's possible to develop applications and tools that are resilient to an unexpected error or condition. While it may not always be possible to carry on normal operation if a critical error happens, you'd

© Joseph Coburn 2020
J. Coburn, *Build Your Own Car Dashboard with a Raspberry Pi*,
https://doi.org/10.1007/978-1-4842-6080-7_2

hope that the software in question will not crash when it gets unexpected data or a strange and unusual operating environment.

By writing automated tests for your code, you can be confident that each component is working both as an individual module and in the context of the system as a whole. Version control tools help keep your code organized and backed up, and object-oriented programming ensures you don't waste time writing the same code over and over again.

- While these primers are necessary for you to understand the why behind the code explained in the later chapters, I hope that you, the reader, will learn these principles and apply them to other projects you work on. Whether it's a remote-controlled robot, desktop software package, or even a spreadsheet macro, almost any project benefits from "software hardening" and defensive programming.

Types of Programming Languages

When working with programming languages, you may have heard the terms "static" and "dynamic." These terms refer to the type checking. Before digging into type checking, it's necessary to understand interpreting and compiling.

Compiled languages need converting into machine code through a process called "compiling." This makes them very fast to run, as all the instructions have been "figured out" before the application runs at all. You don't need any expensive or hard-to-find tools to compile your code, as the compiler is a core part of the language. Any syntax errors or invalid code will not compile, reducing (but not eliminating) the possibility of bugs getting introduced to your system. Examples of compiled languages include C++ (`https://isocpp.org/`), Rust (`www.rust-lang.org/`), Go (`https://golang.org/`), and Java (`www.java.com/`).

Here's a basic "Hello, World" application in C++:

```
#include <iostream>

int main() {
    std::cout << "Hello, World!";
    return 0;
}
```

Here's the same application in Java:

```
public class HelloWorld {

    public static void main(String[] args) {
        System.out.println("Hello, World");
    }

}
```

Notice how both applications use a "main" function. This is required as a starting point – when executed, the language interpreter looks for a function called main as the place to start running the code. Notice how both languages specify a data type. The C++ example returns an integer status code, whereas the Java example uses considerably more words to state that its main function does not return any value.

The alternative to compiled languages is interpreted languages. These do not need compiling, as their instructions get followed line by line as they execute. Sometimes they get compiled on-demand through just-in-time compilation. Interpreted languages can be slower to run than compiled languages, but they offer smaller file sizes and dynamic typing, and can be quite fast to write. Interpreted languages include PHP (www.php.net/), Python (www.python.org/), and Ruby (www.ruby-lang.org/en/).

Here's "Hello, World" in PHP:

```
echo "Hello World!";
```

The Python example is almost exactly the same, replacing "echo" with "print":

```
print("Hello, World!")
```

These interpreted language examples are considerably less wordy than the compiled language examples earlier. Python does have a "main" function, but it's not always required. PHP does not have one at all. Don't be misled; however, as while some interpreted languages are quicker to write, they can be much slower to execute than compiled languages.

Back to type checking, in some languages, if you tell the code you want to store an integer, it's not possible to store a string in that same variable. Programming languages reserve space in memory to store your data. If you change that data, it may not have enough room to store the new data. Sure, you could reserve more memory, but the simplest thing to do is raise an error, and let you, the programmer, fix the problem. All languages check the type of data, whether you know about it or not. Not all languages will even raise an error, however.

Statically typed languages need you to specify the data type of all your variables. They won't work without doing so and will crash if you try to store the wrong data in your variables. Examples of statically typed languages include C++ (https://isocpp.org/), C# (https://docs.microsoft.com/en-us/dotnet/csharp/), and Java (www.java.com/).

Dynamically typed languages are the alternative to statically typed languages. With dynamic typing, the types of your variables get checked at runtime. The disadvantage here is that you have to run your program to find the error. Dynamically typed languages include PHP (www.php.net/), Python (www.python.org/), and Ruby (www.ruby-lang.org/en/).

Note   Interpreted languages often use dynamic typing, and statically typed languages are often compiled. It's possible to have a dynamically typed compiled language, but they are not very common.

Python uses a simpler attitude toward type checking. Python uses "duck typing." This is like dynamic typing, but with one big difference. Duck typing does not care how you use your objects, providing the operation, command, or attribute is valid for that object. You can mix up your strings and integers all you like, and it will only become a problem once you attempt to perform string-specific operations on integers, or vice versa.

Data Types

Understanding data types is crucial to programming in any language. You can write code without understanding them (and as you gain more experience you'll begin to understand them more), but knowing why they exist and which ones to use is a fundamental basic step to learning to program. Everything you store (even in volatile memory such as RAM) is specific by your programming language. Even if you don't explicitly specify a data type, somewhere along the chain, a software tool or package will reserve sufficient space in memory to store a specific piece of data. It doesn't make sense to always reserve as much memory as possible, in case you want to store really big data (even if you only want to store tiny data), so specifying a data type helps your computer to save memory and perform its tasks faster. Data types underpin everything your computer and software applications do, so having a basic understanding of them is crucial.

Data types let you tell the code how you intend to store a piece of data. This allows type checking (discussed in "Types of Programming Languages"). This also lets the code know what operations you can perform on your variables. For example, you can't divide "potato" by five, but you can add five to six. Some popular basic data types are

- Integer
- Boolean
- String

Integers let you store whole numbers (1, 5, 451, etc.), Booleans are true or false, and strings store words or single characters ("hello", "apples", etc.), including numbers. There are many more data types such as signed and unsigned integers (unsigned ints store positive numbers and zero), complex objects, floats, and decimals (for storing really precise numbers), along with abstract data types. I cover more of these as you need to know them later on in the project chapters.

Python 2 vs. Python 3

In February 1991, Guido van Rossum (`https://twitter.com/gvanrossum`) released Python 0.9.0 to the wild. Known as the benevolent dictator for life, Guido took Python from nothing to the powerful tool it is today. Once Python version 2.0 came out in October 2000, Python's community and popularity soared. For a large percentage of Python's life, Python version 2.x was the only choice if you wanted to code in Python. It had its flaws but it did a good job at the time. Many minor version releases added powerful new features, and Python's popularity went from strength to strength.

Fact   "Benevolent dictator for life" (BDFL) is a title sometimes given to leaders of open source software projects. This is often the project founders who have the final say in any disagreement. Guido was the first benevolent dictator for life of any software project in 1995! Guido retained the BDFL moniker until July 2018, when he resigned the title stating, "I'm tired, and need a very long break." There are no plans for a successor to the throne.

December 2008 saw the release of a new major version 3.0. This version altered how the language worked and meant code written in Python 3.0 was not compatible with code written in Python 2.0. This change aimed to fix major design flaws with Python, guided by the overarching mantra "reduce feature duplication by removing old ways of doing things."

Due to these breaking changes, it wasn't until Python version 3.6 released in December 2016 that developers finally started jumping ship from the old version to the shiny new version. One of the reasons for such a slow adoption rate is that it takes a long time to write software, and having to rewrite that software in a similar but different language isn't always an easy or quick task to do. The other reason is that the 3.6 release introduced enough desirable features to make upgrading worthwhile, and even fun.

Python versions 2.6 and 2.7 released in parallel with the newer versions, and these "old" versions introduced several changes to encourage users to upgrade. These included warnings about deprecated features, along with several "taster" features. Several features added in Python 3.1 were also released in 2.6 and 2.7 as a way to help developers still on Python 2. Python 2.7 support existed until 2020, but as of November 2014, users are heavily encouraged to use Python 3.

It's foolish to begin any new Python project in Python 2, and as Python version 3.7 introduces significant memory management and speed improvements (alongside all the other Python 3 improvements), all the code and examples in this book are written in Python 3.

Object-Oriented Programming (OOP)

Object-oriented programming is a paradigm based around objects and data. By creating common blocks of code, you can share data around, reduce code duplication, and keep your code neat and tidy. This makes it easier to use, easier to troubleshoot, and easier to test. Not all languages follow all "the rules" of OOP, and Python is notorious for its laid-back approach to enforcing the rules and how it implements certain features. Python has a saying "we are all consenting adults." In the context of

Python, this means it won't stop you from doing bad things or breaking the rules, trusting that you understand the consequences if it all goes wrong.

When a language is said to be OOP, that doesn't mean it abandons its feature set. OOP languages still use variables, loops, and many of the other features you may expect from the language. OOP languages provide features and tools to work with objects. This may be support for classes, functions, inheritance, and more. Python is mostly a pure OO language, as it treats everything as an object.

Classes

Classes are one of the core building blocks of OOP. Classes are containers that store information. They have attributes, which are often variables that store data. They also have functions (sometimes called subroutines or methods), which perform a specific task. Classes are like a recipe. They are a set of instructions to complete a specific task. For a cake recipe, the attributes could be the quantity of each ingredient or the total baking time. The functions could be helpful utilities such as mixing or baking.

Classes are a template (the recipe), but they don't do anything on their own. For a class to be useful, it needs to be instantiated. This creates an object based on the template. Objects that get instantiated from a class are instances. They are individual instances of a class.

For the cake recipe, the objects are the finished cakes. This could be a blueberry cake or a chocolate cake. Each cake is its own entity (object), but both are based on the original recipe (class). Both of these cakes followed the instructions in the recipe but turned out differently. These objects started in the same class, but are not tied to each other at all. You can cook them independently, change the ingredients or the quantity, or delete one or both cakes – either by eating them or throwing them in the bin!

Everything in the core library for a programming language is a class. Even if you've never written a class before, you've used them. In Python, the *for* loop is its own class, as is the *print* function, or the *string* type.

Inheritance

Inheritance is a way of creating a new type of class based on some other class. Looking at the previous cake example, you have a cake recipe class. This is good for making cakes, but what if you wanted to make muffins? Muffins are a type of cake, but does the cake class need muffin-specific tooling? If it's all clogged up with functions and attributes for all the different types of cakes, it may become large and cumbersome.

By creating a new class that inherits the parent class, your new class gains access to all the attributes and functions in the parent but can add extra attributes and functions. This new class that inherits from some other class is a subclass, while the parent is a superclass. If you subclass the cake recipe as a muffin recipe, you can still mix and bake the muffin objects, only now you may be able to pour the muffins into muffin tins, distribute many small muffins, or anything else you add to your muffin recipe. Subclassing/inheritance is the same as photocopying your recipe and writing a note on the bottom!

Note   Not all attributes are accessible to subclasses and objects. This is explained in the class protection section. Python ignores these rules, however!

Encapsulation

As you've learned, classes have different kinds of data. They can store variables, and they can store functions, to execute specific code. These can all have different return types, and different accessibility levels. If your class contains a piece of code that only you should use, then any objects created from your class should not be able to access this. The way to do this is through access modifiers. The three access modifiers are

1. Public

2. Private

3. Protected

Public members are accessible by anyone and anything. As the name implies, there is no restriction on these. Instantiated objects can all freely access this data. For the cake recipe, this could be bake or mix functions, or this could be the total baking time.

Private members are only accessible by code inside the class. The recipe class can change these, but any objects created from the class cannot even see these members. This is useful for code that's only used internally. For your cake class, the baking method may be accessible to everyone, but what if it stores an internal baking temperature? If other people can access and change this value, the cake may burn. Making this private means only you (or other developers working on the class itself) can work with this.

Finally, there are protected members. This is like private, in that only members of the class can access this data, but is extended to any subclasses. If you create a protected member, the main class can access it, and so can any subclasses (such as muffins). Objects instantiated from the cake class cannot see or access this.

Many languages use tools such as getters and setters. These are often simple public functions that regulate access to private members. This is a good practice. Going back to the oven temperature example, it may be useful to let objects change the temperature, but suppose every time the temperature changes, you need to adjust the cooking time. If objects have access to the temperature, they could change it without adjusting the cooking time. They may not even know the cooking time should change. By using a setter, you can ensure the cooking time gets readjusted anytime the temperature changes. Besides this, you can change how data gets stored in your class, and any objects using the getter or setter do not need to change. This makes your code less fragile and easier to change in the future. This is encapsulation, and it's a very important aspect of OOP. Only you, the developer, get to decide the rules and regulations around your code.

Unfortunately, Python does not have access modifiers. This can make Python code challenging to work with at times. While there are some pseudo-workarounds and Python best practices you'll see in the project code, most of these revolve around trust. There's nothing stopping you from accessing private data in classes, but don't expect any help if things start going wrong. For the reasons mentioned earlier – sometimes data needs changing in a specific way, or other attributes calculated at the same time. For small projects or instances where you are the sole developer on a code base, you'll often have enough working knowledge to know where potential hazards reside.

There are other access modifiers, but these vary between languages and are often an amalgamation of the main three.

The final type of class protection is that of the method type. When working with methods, you need to define how the function can interact with the object and the class. The three types are

1.   Static

2.   Instance

3.   Class

The default method type varies per language, as does the need to specify one at all. In Python, instance methods are the default modifier, but in Java, it's common to use static methods.

Static methods do not need access to any other class information. They don't need specific object data such as ingredients or cooking time. Everything these need to run is self-contained in the function. A good example of this is a multiplication function. You give it two numbers, and it returns the product. This is what happens in any programming language when you use the asterisk sign. The reason you don't need brackets or to instantiate the function is because special math symbols are designed for use as we've come to expect, but the language itself still stores this as a function.

Instance methods have full access to everything in the class. These get tied to the object itself. If your cake recipe has an instance method to get the weight of the ingredients, then this will change for every object. A cake may need 10 ounces of flour, whereas muffins may need 11 ounces. Instance methods can call both static methods and class methods, and each method is only aware of the data for that object.

Class methods can only call static methods in the class. They cannot access object-specific data, but they are not stand-alone functions like static methods. These are useful when you need to access other class utility functions, but don't need specific data every time they run. If you don't have any static methods, you won't often need a class method. Only once you have static methods will you need to even consider a class method, and even then you'll only need it if you want to access other static methods.

Note   Python uses the decorator pattern for its methods. If you don't specify the method type, it will be an instance method by default. Look out for the decorator pattern in the "Design Patterns" section.

Polymorphism

As you may guess from the name, polymorphism refers to many forms. Polymorphic code is code that can handle many different uses or data types. Polymorphism in Python is another interesting topic, because

Python doesn't work like other languages, but I'll get on to that shortly. Polymorphism is often divided into two categories:

1.   Compile-time polymorphism

2.   Dynamic method dispatch (runtime polymorphism)

Compile-time polymorphism (sometimes called overloading) is only possible with statically typed languages. This can be very fast as the compiler does all the work. The most common compile-time polymorphism technique is function overloading.

Function overloading lets you use different data types or even parameters in a function. Suppose you have a function called bake. It takes one parameter, an integer called duration. Without function overloading, you couldn't create another function in the same class with the same name. By overloading this function, you can. You can create functions with different data types, or a different number of parameters. For example, you could change the bake function to take a single string called duration. You could also change it to accept two integers, duration, and temperature. When you compile your code, the compiler will choose which function to use, based on the supplied arguments.

You can also change the return type, but you can't only change this, you'll need to change the signature as well. The code for these functions can be different, or one can change the data and call the other one. By overloading functions, you can make your code flexible, and able to handle a variety of different parameters and data types.

Operator overloading is similar, but it lets you define custom functions to extend the built-in operators. A good example of this is the *addition* symbol. This works fine for integers but will crash if you try to add strings or custom classes. By overloading this operator, you can create custom functions to add your own data types or classes.

Dynamic method dispatching resolves references when the code gets run, instead of at compile time. This approach is more flexible than compile-time polymorphism and is useful when it's not possible for the compiler to figure out the function you need. The outcome is the same as compile-time function overloading. It may not be possible for the compiler to decide what to do for many reasons. Perhaps one or both of your overloaded functions extend the other, or perhaps you base the function on user input, which is not known at compile time.

Note   Python does not support function overloading in the traditional sense, but it's still possible. By using inheritance, your subclasses can contain functions with the same name as their parent class. These subclass functions override the superclass functions. Generally, you'll want to keep the purpose of these functions similar (a function called bake shouldn't launch a missile, for example, unless you want to bake your enemies). This is useful because the parent classes can implement functionality which your subclasses can change if it's not quite right. Anything using objects of these instances won't have to change their calls.

Design Patterns

Design patterns are blueprints in the sense that they describe how to solve a problem. They are not quite the same as classes (which are also blueprints). Design patterns give you a handy way to describe a solution. When you bake cookies, you don't say to your friends "hey, want some round baked goods, made with chocolate chips and dough?", you use their name – cookies! Design patterns can help you to communicate with your team. Design patterns consist of a name, a problem, a solution (ideally language agnostic), and an outline of the possible side effects of this solution (if any).

Creating a new design pattern is possible, but improbable. Design patterns arose out of engineers designing similar solutions to problems, so unless you can get your code written into thousands of different code bases, and set the world alight with your unique solution, it probably won't become a new pattern.

Design patterns evolved in the late 1970s, but they rose to popularity after the famous gang of four (Erich Gamma, Richard Helm, Ralph Johnson, and John Vlissides) held a workshop in 1991 and then published their book *Design Patterns: Elements of Reusable Object-Oriented Software*. Their book documents 23 different design patterns. Some common patterns are as follows:

The Adapter Pattern acts as an interface between incompatible objects. An example of this would be calling the baking method on a roast chicken. It still needs baking, but chickens are not part of the cake class. By writing an adapter to interface the two, you can make it work.

The Decorator Pattern is one of the most well-used patterns in Python. This lets you extend classes through subclassing but dynamically at runtime. This pattern is very powerful, and happens per object, independently of any other class instances.

The Facade Pattern provides an interface to a class or piece of code. If you need to call ten different functions in a specific order to use your class, a facade pattern can wrap these into one simple-to-use function, which performs all the work in the correct order.

The Factory Pattern delegates the creation of objects to a centralized entity. This is useful for letting subclasses define which superclass to use, without getting bogged down in the details.

This is only a small fraction of all the possible design patterns. The 23 documented patterns in the GoF's book have achieved almost legendary status – and for good reason. Next time you're looking to solve a software problem, check that a design pattern doesn't already exist.

SOLID Principles

SOLID is a mnemonic for five object-oriented design principles introduced by Robert C. Martin in his 2000 paper titled "Design Principles and Design Patterns." These principles exist to make software easier to develop, easier to fix, and easier to understand.

The five principles are

1. Single responsibility

2. Open-closed

3. Liskov substitution

4. Interface segregation

5. Dependency inversion

The single responsibility principle states that each individual component of a code base should have sole responsibility for one piece of functionality. The reason for this is to limit the work required to make a change. If you're making doughnuts and decide to change the filling from jam to custard, you shouldn't have to change how you mix the batter. If there is only one place in your code that handles a requirement, it becomes very easy to change this and the code. If one part of your code handles several different operations, or several different pieces of code involve the same operation, it becomes a confusing mess to change any code.

This doesn't mean your code should be tiny and only perform one task. It's fine to have different functions grouped together, but they should be loosely related. Code for icing cakes can all live together, and code to dust doughnuts with sugar can live here as well – both are a type of glazing. Code to fry doughnuts belongs somewhere else.

The open-closed principle is the idea that software components should be "open for extension, but closed for modification." Through this, it should be possible to extend the functionality of a component without changing its original source code. In simpler terms, your code should need few changes to meet a new or recently changed requirement. This is often carried out through inheritance or polymorphism.

Say you have a function to calculate the surface area of a doughnut (very useful to know how much icing to make). This works very well, but it's not very flexible. If you want to calculate the surface area of a cake or even a square cake, you need to change the code. By writing this function to calculate the surface area of any baked good, you can be confident your code can handle any future confectionery requirements. Don't get too carried away though, as YAGNI.

YAGNI stands for you ain't gonna need it. It's a reminder to only put in place features you need right now, and not start coding things nobody has asked for. If nobody wants a feature, or you start coding features you think people will want, that's a lot of wasted effort for little reward. With a new code base, startup company, or code following the open-closed principle, it can be a fine balancing act between flexible code and worthless features, but taking the time to think through your solution can make a big difference.

Liskov substitution suggests that subclasses should be direct substitutes for their superclasses. In other words, you should be able to swap a parent instance for a child class and nothing changes in the code. It's fine for your subclasses to extend the behavior of their parents, but if a subclass is fundamentally different or incompatible with its parent, you should redesign your solution.

Here's an example. Suppose you have a class for cakes. Your code follows the open-closed principle and allows for all kinds of extensions. This works great for a variety of cakes: cupcakes, muffins, Victoria sponges – yum. Then, along comes a pastry chef with some fresh doughnut batter. It's possible to subclass the cake class as a doughnut, but doughnuts are usually fried, not baked. All the cake-specific functions and attributes don't work on doughnuts.

You could create new functions to fry or override the bake function to perform frying duties on the subclass, but this starts to get confusing. Even with a highly modified doughnut subclass, anything or anyone using instances of these objects will get themselves into all kinds of trouble. Doughnuts need a deep fat fryer or at least a frying pan – will the pastry chef have one available if the function is called "bake," and the documentation says it requires an oven?

By following the Liskov substitution principle, it should be very clear what your objects are, how they work, and the functionality they implement. It's fine to extend classes, but drastically changing how they work, or implementing "quick fixes," "hacks," or other nasties is a bad idea.

Interface segregation states, "No client should be forced to depend on methods it does not use," and is summarized as splitting large modules and classes into smaller and easier-to-use pieces. This applies to huge modules more than smaller projects, but it's still worth considering.

Here's an example. Your cake class wasn't useful for all cases (such as doughnuts), so you modified it to become a generic confectionary class. This class can do everything – baking, frying, mixing, icing, and more. While it's a good class, written using the other four SOLID principles, it's massive. It's thousands of lines long, and developers dread working on it. By moving pieces out into their own classes, you can reduce the size of this mega-class and make the code easier to understand, read, and use.

You could have individual classes for baking, frying, and icing. You could have a utility class for common functions. Now, the confectionary class implements the other classes through its own instances.

The final principle is dependency inversion. High-level modules should not depend on low-level modules. Both should talk to each other through abstractions. High-level modules should provide complex business logic and be easy to reuse and change. Low-level modules should provide operations such as network or disk access.

Without following this principle, tightly coupling business logic to a file handler means that changes to the file handler (such as using a different library or function) need changes to the business logic.

Here's an example. Your high-level cake classes handle the production of cakes – mixing, baking, stirring, and so on. These classes shouldn't care about how the oven produces the heat. They put cakes in, set the temperature, and then remove them after a set period of time. If the cake class had to call an oven function such as "heat up coil for 15 minutes," then this is very tightly coupled. What if you get a new oven? What if it's gas-fired, or charcoal? Suddenly the cake class needs updating to call the appropriate functions to light the gas or empty a new bag of charcoal. If these classes talk to each other through an abstraction, only one piece of code has to change.

This may seem complex, but by following the Liskov substitution and interface segregation principles, you almost get dependency inversion as a by-product.

Event-Driven Programming

When developing any system, it's a good idea to plan the architecture, and the events. How will your system work? When you press a button, what logic will route you to the appropriate piece of code to perform some work?

Event-driven programming is a paradigm in which actions happen in response to events. It's used frequently with JavaScript, but many languages support it. Event-driven programs often use a loop to listen for events and then trigger the appropriate action in what's known as a "callback." While you can write this loop yourself, a framework or other suitable tooling may tool it for you. Event-driven programming is often used for graphical user interface (GUI) applications.

Any code you write to respond to events is an "event handler" because it handles the appropriate event. These event handlers subscribe to each event, so they get notified when it fires through the callback. There are no rules around how much or how little work event handlers can perform, and you can have as many as you like (even for the same event). Generally sticking to one task for each event handler is a good idea. It makes your code easier to test and easier to understand and maintains a good separation of concerns.

Event-driven programming is flexible, but there is room for improvement. The publish-subscribe (pub-sub) design pattern is an often used pattern for event-driven systems. Rather than have the event triggers call the subscribers, publishers publish to specific channels, of which subscribers subscribe to. Publishers do not need to know about all their subscribers, they publish to these channels, regardless of whether anyone will act upon the messages.

The pub-sub approach to system architecture is very flexible. Events don't need to know about any event handlers, and you can add, remove, manipulate, or otherwise alter event handlers without having to rework any event or callback logic.

Subscriptions can be topic-based or content-based. Topic-based subscribers join areas of interest. This may be cakes for a cooking platform or wheels for a car system. The publisher sends out a notification to this specific topic. Anything subscribed to this topic will begin handling the event. This is akin to a public channel or group chat in systems such as IRC, Slack, or WhatsApp.

With content-based subscriptions, callbacks get tagged with attributes, and subscribers are only notified if their subscription settings match the attributes in the callback. Both content-based and topic-based pub-sub event handling are a form of message filtering. Some systems even combine the two for a more flexible approach.

Defensive Programming

Defensive programming is a big part of this book. Learning what it is and why it's necessary can make you a better programmer. The subsets of offensive programming and secure programming can mean that defensive programming covers a vast range of topics.

In short, defensive programming (or defensive design) is a way of developing software such that it can still function under impossible or unexpected circumstances. Can you imagine what would happen if your email client could not handle an incoming email while you were writing an email? Or what about a video game that doesn't work without the Internet? Sometimes developers (or sales and marketing) make deliberate decisions about functionality, but it's often unexpected conditions that cause problems. By anticipating the worst, and preparing your code to handle all eventualities, you can be confident your code can survive the worst possible scenarios.

Many coding projects don't experience any ramifications from services becoming unavailable or unexpected circumstances arising. This doesn't mean defensive programming is redundant. History is full of tragic examples of impossible situations that became possible and caused real harm. If something is impossible, or will never happen, then Murphy's Law says that it will happen. It's how your code handles the impossible that matters.

Murphy's law is an adage summarized as "anything that can go wrong will go wrong." If you're optimistic, then the variation known as Yhprum's law states that "anything that can go right, will go right."

This historical example highlights just how badly things can go wrong if you don't expect the unexpected.

1992 London Ambulance Service Computer-Aided Ambulance-Dispatch System

On 26th October 1992, the London Ambulance Service deployed a new computerized system to dispatch over 300 emergency ambulances to 7 million people living in a 600 square mile area of London. This was a brand-new computerized system designed to replace the fully manual process.

Within hours of launching, the system was unable to keep track of ambulances. As many as 46 people died because an ambulance did not arrive in time, never arrived at all, or in some cases, more than one arrived. For one patient, by the time the ambulance arrived they had already died, and been that way for quite some time.

There are many reasons why this system failed on that fateful day. Two significant failures were

- Imperfect data

- A memory leak

The ambulance-dispatch system failed to function when given incomplete data about ambulance locations. As the system didn't know where ambulances were, it attempted to reroute or dispatch vehicles currently in use.

This memory leak retained event information on the system even when it was no longer necessary. Over time (and compounded by the excessive call volume due to the early failures), the memory filled up, and the system failed.

By defensively programming this system from the beginning, some of these problems may have been avoided. While testing and deployment all work together for the benefit of the customer (and this project has far greater deep-rooted problems), by assuming the worst will happen and preparing your code to handle it, you can start to stem the flow of a problem before it even arises.

You've read how badly things can go wrong, but that can never happen right? Sitting at home coding your small little system can never kill anyone? Perhaps not, but you don't know where your code will end up if you share it online, or what projects you might pull your code into in the future, because you have a working solution.

That's enough of the bad news; here are some tried and tested areas to safeguard your code against:

- Never trust user input – Always assume users are out to get you. Use whitelists for allowed characters or valid file extension types. Never allow users access to your database through text input boxes – use prepared statements and sanitize user input before it touches your database.

- Don't assume a service will always be there – If you are using another service such as an API, there could be many reasons why you can't reach it. Perhaps the service is unavailable, or there is a problem with their domain. Your device could be offline, or the payload comes back in a different format to that you expected. Assume the worst and prepare your code to handle missing or invalid services and data.

- Raise and catch exceptions – Many languages will raise exceptions when errors happen. Catch these and then implement code to handle the failing condition. Equally, if your code fails, raise an exception of your own.

- Keep code clean – Each piece of your code should have a specific and defined task. A function to get the temperature should not alter the speed. Clearly defined expectations and doing one thing well ensure your code is small, easier to test, easier to understand, and easier to defensively program.

35

- Testable code – As you'll learn shortly under the
  "Testing" section, small chunks of code are easy to test.
  By writing tests to run code under unusual conditions,
  you can be confident you can handle strange and
  unexpected edge cases.

Note   Whitelists are lists of allowed things. Whitelists state what
is allowed and block anything else by default. Whitelists are like the
bouncers at a posh party or nightclub – if your name is not on the list
you're not getting in!

Blacklists are less secure than whitelists, but they have their place.
Blacklists are the opposite of whitelists – they specify what to block,
and anything else is allowed by default. Blacklists are like a poster
of banned people at a gas station. All customers can buy gas, apart
from known bad people on the poster.

The final aspect of defensive programming is that of security. Secure
programming is a subset of defensive programming. By writing your code
to expect vulnerabilities, and never trusting anything or anyone, you'll
be in a much better place from a security perspective. The OWASP Top
Ten Project is a curated list of the ten biggest security threats facing any
application today. Security mitigations follow some of the advice already
mentioned. Deny everything by default. Validate all input, and keep it
simple. While this project has limited interaction with users and the
outside world, it's still vulnerable.

During development with your Raspberry Pi on the Internet, it's
common for automated systems to access (or attempt to access) your Pi
in unexpected ways. Perhaps you have default passwords set or services
enabled and running on default ports. If you take the pessimistic approach
that everyone is out to hack you, and never assume anything will always be
available, you'll end up with a far better system, which provides the user
(you!) with a very pleasant experience, even if the worst happens.

Testing

Software testing is a vast and broad area of study, one that is far bigger than this chapter allows. Many books can and have been written on the topic, so this subchapter will serve as a loose starting point, from which you can research further if you so desire. If you're interested in testing and testing with Python, I can highly recommend the following books:

- *Python Testing with Pytest* – Brian Okken

- *Clean Code: A Handbook of Agile Software Craftsmanship* (Chapter 9, "Unit Tests") – Robert C. Martin

- *Python Unit Test Automation: Practical Techniques for Python Developers and Testers* – Ashwin Pajankar

Testing exists to ensure that a piece of software is free from defects and works as expected and required. No software will ever be 100% defect-free, but with a bit of thought, and some good testing, you can be confident your code generally works as expected.

Joke   "99 little bugs in the code, 99 little bugs in the code. Take one down, patch it around 117 little bugs in the code." – @irqed

---

There is no one way to test or a five-step plan to follow. If you do these steps in this order, you'll have perfectly tested software. In reality, software testing is a broad spectrum, covering a vast range of different techniques. These all work together to ensure code is the best it can be. Automated tests give you the best repeatability and consistency between test runs (especially with arduous testing), but manual testing still has its own valuable place.

To understand why testing is so important, let's look at another tragic example from history.

Therac-25 Radiation Therapy Machine

The Therac-25 was a software-controlled radiation therapy machine released in 1982. Through this machine, hospital operators treated cancer patients with radiation. Hospital machinists programmed the dosage, duration, and location of the beam, and the machine handled the rest. Between 1985 and 1987, the Therac-25 caused at least six accidents, with some patients receiving over 100 times the normal dosage of radiation. These patients either suffered serious injury or death. The US Food and Drug Administration (FDA) issued a mandatory recall on all Therac-25 machines due to their potential for serious harm.

This is an interesting and popular case study in computer science. Before looking at the root cause of the failures, it's necessary to understand how the machine worked, and the history of its predecessors.

The Therac-25 was a two-in-one radiation therapy machine. It used magnets to deliver direct electron-beam therapy. This is used for treating cancer near to the surface of the skin. The other mode of radiation therapy was a megavolt X-ray. This delivered radiation doses 100 times higher than direct electron-beam therapy, and as a result, the beams had to pass through both a filter and a combiner to ensure precise and accurate delivery. These extra tools were not needed for the other beam, and due to its increased power, the megavolt X-ray was mainly used for deep-tissue treatment such as lung cancer.

In summary, the Therac-25 used two radiation beams: a low-power beam and a high-power beam, which needed filtering and focusing. It also had a patient light, used to help position the patient without delivering any radiation.

One of the major flaws in this machine was the ability to select and use the high-power mode without the necessary filter and focusing components in place. This happened due to a software bug caused by rapidly switching from the low-power to the high-power mode. This meant patients received a lethal dose of radiation in a large area due to the lack of filtering and focusing devices. Another flaw allowed the low-power electron beam to activate when in patient-light mode.

Previous models of the Therac used hardware to ensure that these conditions could never happen. The Therac-25 removed these to reduce the cost and used a software version, which failed.

There are many reasons why this machine failed, including many bugs. Some of the serious issues were as follows:

- The developers failed to consider what might happen if the software fails.

- In any error, the system presented an error code that was not explained in the manual. The users ignored this.

- The machine was not tested until assembly at a hospital.

- Overconfidence led developers to ignore bug complaints.

From a testing perspective, you can write all the automated tests you like, and you won't catch these issues. Many of these arose out of the reuse of a previous generation model. The developers assumed that because this machine has been running for a long time, it must be good and safe, and so they can rush out this upgraded model. This was not the case and the significant software upgrades necessitated significant new testing. Onto the testing failures:

The testers did not understand how hospital staff used the machine, or the speed at which they changed programs.

- A set of nonstandard keystrokes produced a set of errors.

- A variable overflowed causing the machine to skip safety checks.

There are so many problems with this machine that not all would have been solved by testing, yet it remains my opinion that good testing, defensive programming, and code audits would have saved the lives of everyone harmed by this machine. That said, the benefit of hindsight is a wonderful thing. After the incident investigation, International Electrotechnical Commission (IEC) 62304 was introduced to specify the design and testing required for medical devices.

As this example shows, any testing is better than no testing, and don't make assumptions. Testers love testing edge cases but thinking about the possible ramifications of your code (especially code that can so easily injure or kill people) is a step in the right direction.

Joke   "A QA engineer walks into a bar. Orders a beer. Orders 0 beers. Orders 99999999999 beers. Orders a lizard. Orders -1 beer. Orders a ueicbksjdhd.

The first real customer walks in and asks where the bathroom is. The bar bursts into flames, killing everyone." – Brenan Keller

---

Now you know what can happen when testing fails, let's look at how to avoid big problems such as these. It's important to have a common understanding of the tools at your disposal. First, don't think of yourself as a developer and someone else as a tester. Testing is the responsibility of everyone involved in developing software! Testing can be loosely split into three categories.

Functional testing aims to assess whether the software meets the predefined requirements or specifications. The first step is defining these specifications! When functional testing, systems should provide a fixed output with a fixed input. For example, with a calculator, feeding in "1 + 1" should output "2".

Performance testing looks to assess the speed, responsiveness, and stability of a system. If you're building the next Facebook, then you'll want to know the system can handle more than a handful of users at the same time. When you press a button, how long does it take before you get a response? Your acceptance criteria may vary depending on the project and the deployment. If you're writing a script for your own use, then you may have simpler requirements than a system processing thousands of transactions per second.

Finally, there is regression testing. Regression testing helps ensure that new features and changes have not broken existing features. If you're working on a legacy system, a big project, or generally playing "whack a mole" with a spaghetti code base, then regression testing couldn't be more important.

As for specific ways of testing, the following snippets cover some of the over 150 different testing techniques, skills, tools, and processes available to modern-day developers.

Unit testing exists to test a specific piece of code in isolation. By writing small, single responsibility functions, you can unit test that a function performs as intended. Say you have a function to add two numbers together. If you input 5 and 6, you should get 11. You can test edge cases for this. Should it throw an exception if you pass a string? What about fractions, or will it only work with whole numbers? Unit testing should give you confidence that each piece of code is working as designed. Returning to the tasty cakes analogy, unit tests could cover breaking the eggs, measuring the flour, and setting the oven temperature. Unit tests wouldn't usually cover if the cake tastes nice or even looks like a cake after following all the steps.

Integration testing tests how individual components interact with each other, and with the whole system. It can only happen when two or more distinct parts of a system are ready. So often it happens right at the end of development after everything has been produced (if it happens at all). While this is better than no integration testing, the sooner you can run integration tests, the sooner you can get feedback on if your solution works or not. By shortening this feedback loop, you can get into a position where customers get new features faster, and with fewer defects.

If unit tests test you can break the eggs, integration tests verify that the eggs get mixed correctly with the flour, the cake starts to rise in the oven, and the icing sticks to the top of the finished cake.

System testing helps developers and testers gain confidence in the nearly finished product. This is often performed by independent testers – people who were not involved with the development of the system. Integration testing happens on two or more different components, whereas system testing happens on the whole system. System testing could test that the cake looks like a cake, it takes nice, is chocolate, and has icing and sprinkles. This involves evaluating the system against the supplied requirements.

Acceptance testing exists to ensure the system meets the business or client requirements, and if it's ready to release, or needs more work. The business may decide that the system is brilliant, but it's missing this amazing feature that it must have before it is ready to release to the wild. For a birthday cake, no matter how amazing it tastes and looks, it must have candles. Cupcakes should be small and there should be many of them. Acceptance testing happens toward the end of the process, but it doesn't have to. By getting feedback on small individual features as they are ready, you can assess their suitability.

Internal acceptance testing (or alpha testing) happens internally with people not involved in the development process. This could be customer support teams or sales teams. User acceptance testing (UAT) or beta testing involves getting the system into customers' hands. By getting real customers to use the system, you gain new and exciting insights. Is it really what they want, or does it need a little more work?

Load testing ensures the performance of a system is adequate when running under its anticipated load. It can be difficult to predict the demand for your product if it's a simple app that solves a simple problem.

By load testing the system to its breaking point, you can figure out its maximum load, and extrapolate that to give you a rough idea of future scaling requirements.

Back to cakes, load testing cakes is quite simple. You hand them all out and count how many people get one. If you're a good baker, you may want to factor in the fact some people will eat more than one muffin or a slice of cake.

Load testing sometimes emulates the load from a known or expected quantity of users. It can also serve to stress test the entire architecture to find its breaking point. Tools such as JMeter or Gatling can spin up users to an almost unlimited number, depending on your requirements.

Black-box testing happens from a user's point of view. The tester has no knowledge of how the system works or if you need to perform any special steps to get a feature to work. This testing does not prod the delicate internal organs of your code. By using testers with no knowledge of the code, black-box testing avoids the developer bias and tunnel vision sometimes present when working on a big project. Black-box testing can happen for integration, system, and acceptance testing.

White-box testing involves studying the code in question and determining both the valid and invalid operations expected of it. By assessing the outcomes of both these types of operations, white-box testing is excellent at determining if a system is working, and which edge cases it is unable to handle. White-box testing can happen with unit, integration, and system testing.

Mocking works alongside unit tests. Its main purpose is to imitate a different part of the system or an external resource which is not under test at that moment in time. Suppose you make a call to an external API, but every time you do so it costs you $1. Making this call in your unit tests could end up costing you a lot of money, so how can you run unit tests? By imitating this external API call, you can replicate the result without spending a cent.

Test-Driven Development (TDD)

Test-driven development operates around a very short feedback cycle. It starts by writing a very simple test. You then write just enough code to pass the test. After the test passes, it's time to refactor the test to include a basic requirement. Now back to the code to pass the test, this process repeats several times until all the requirements are met.

By writing the tests first, you're forced to consider how your code will work, rather than sitting down and writing whatever code comes to mind. If your test only includes one basic requirement, you're less likely to develop features you think will be needed in the future, which wastes time and resources. This all comes back to the SOLID principles discussed earlier in this chapter.

There are many benefits to developing a module with test-driven development. The biggest of which is a complete set of (unit) tests! At any point in the future, you can come back and rework, refactor, implement new features, or otherwise change your code, safe in the knowledge that your unit tests cover all the conditions required to continue working. Naturally, there may be new requirements and changes needed to the unit tests themselves, but generally, you should avoid changing both the test and the code at the same time, as you may not be able to trust that either component is working.

Some developers slide back into old habits after trying test-driven development – either through familiarity or because it involves too much effort. Some teams only work in a TDD way, and others may develop a hybrid system, encompassing a little TDD. Providing you have a good amount of unit test coverage encompassing many of the possible edge cases and error conditions, it probably doesn't matter too much how you got there.

Note   Software development legend Kent Beck is credited with test-driven development's rise to fame. Kent is an American software engineer who is one of the original signatories of the Agile Manifesto and the creator of extreme programming. Kent's top tips for test-driven development are as follows:

1. Never write a single line of code unless you have a failing automated test.

2. Eliminate duplication.

Debugging

"Debugging is like being the detective in a crime movie where you are also the murderer." – Filipe Fortes

Debugging is a general term related to finding and removing bugs in software. It can be very rewarding to fix a bug, but it can also be a cause of frustration. Spending a whole day or more tracking down a missing comma is not everyone's idea of fun.

There are many different ways to track down a bug. Your go-to technique may differ from mine, and the type of bug, the environment, your programming language, or your integrated development environment (IDE) all factor into it.

To fix a bug, you need to know what the bug is. How does it think, how does it work? What exact steps do you need to take to replicate the issue? To solve the bug, you must become the bug. At times, code can work perfectly, yet a bug may only appear on the production server, or by following a very unusual and specific set of steps, or at a specific time.

I once implemented a feature and the customers complained that it didn't work on a Tuesday afternoon. Sprawling rambling spaghetti code was the culprit here. Another time customers complained that a button only worked after pressing it ten times. The problem here was an incrementing number that the original developer expected to remain under 1000. Once it got over 1000, the code used the first three digits of the number, which only changed every ten presses.

If you recall the Therac-25 case study, one problem was that the developers and the testers did not use the system as quickly as the hospital staff did. Only by pressing specific buttons within an eight-second time frame did a bug appear.

The point is, you and the code must become one. You must know your enemy better than you know yourself. Only then can you understand what is happening with the bug. Even if you think you know what's happening, it never hurts to use some of these common debugging techniques. Making assumptions about code is how bugs get missed.

Rubber Duck Debugging

Rubber duck debugging isn't as daft as it sounds – and it doesn't have to be a rubber duck. By explaining your code line by line to someone else, the problem will often materialize. The act of revisiting every line of code is often enough to cause the problem to leap out at you.

Why the rubber duck? While other developers work equally as well, it disturbs the work they were doing. If you explain the code to an inanimate object (which has no dreams and visions of its own), then you can fix the problem without disturbing a teammate.

Rubber ducks have become an iconic symbol in developer pop culture, thanks in part to the book *The Pragmatic Programmer* (Andrew Hunt and David Thomas). Anything will do, as stepping through the code itself is the solution. The ducks aren't magic.

Logging

Logging is the process of outputting descriptive statements at key points in the code. Seeing exactly where the code is or what happened at any moment in time is a crucial clue in the riddle of the code.

If you log the start of a function call, any exceptions, unexpected conditions, and the end of a function, you can begin to understand what the code is doing – which may differ from what you thought it was doing. Suppose your code crashes every time it runs. Where is the error? By implementing explicit logging, you can follow the path of the code through the logs. If you can trace the code to the last visible log, you'll know it's failed after that point – even better if your logs tell you what happened. The logs for a cake application may look like this:

1. Starting to bake the cake

2. Heating oven to 451 degrees Fahrenheit

3. Putting the cake into the oven

4. Waiting 20 minutes

5. Removing cake

6. Turning the oven off

Through these logs, you can see what the code is doing, and trace each log back to the line of code executed.

Logs are often implemented through a log handler. These log handlers often come included in many frameworks. They let you log data through logger levels. Useful debugging information could go to a debug level, while serious crashes could go to the error level. It's possible to set the logging level so you only see the errors, for example. This keeps your production logs tidy, yet still lets you enable more verbose logs as and when required. These log handlers often output the file, date, time, or any other useful information – you can configure the format.

Print Statements: The Pauper's Logging

Print statements are as simple as they sound. Print statements send output from your program to the environment it is running in. If your code is running in the command line, your print statements will appear in the command line.

Print statements are not as comprehensive as using a log handler. There's no way to group different statements or issue an error code or type of statement. Print statements are quick to write and easy to use, but they should be primarily used for quick troubleshooting when running code locally on your machine. Want to know if your new code is even running? Put a print statement in, and look out for it when the code runs.

As print statements shouldn't live for very long, and log handlers are the preferred choice for application visibility, many developers use shorthand, quick, or otherwise nonsense print statements. If you're looking to see if a new function gets called, and you will delete the print statement almost immediately, then random statements such as "I am here" or my personal favorite "potato" are commonplace. Very recently I had to *remove* a print statement that sneaked into production which simply said "one quiche."

Breakpoints

"You know nothing. In fact, you know less than nothing. If you knew that you knew nothing, then that would be something, but you don't." – Ben Harp, Point Break (1991)

Breakpoints let you stop the flow of your code. They pause execution and allow you to inspect all your variables. You can see the exact state and conditions your code is in. You can resume execution and see where the code goes next. Breakpoints are useful when debugging software. They don't make any assumptions but may highlight some odd behavior that you can fix. By inspecting the code while it is executing, you can spot anything which is not the expected behavior.

As this quote highlights, you don't know anything about your code until it runs. You may think you know how it works, and for most of the code you may be correct. When things go wrong, however, the best way to figure out the problem is by halting the code with a breakpoint.

Programming languages such as Python come with support for debugging and breakpoints. Your tooling needs configuring (often performed through your IDE), but once configured, it's often as simple as pressing "debug" instead of "run." Breakpoints specify the line of code to pause at. Once the software reaches that line, it pauses execution instead of continuing. You can add or remove breakpoints, continue execution, or cancel the debugging altogether.

Version Control with Git

Version control is one of the most powerful tools in a developer's toolkit. It tracks your changes across all files. Should your latest release break your code base or you change your mind or want to look at an older version of your code, you can do so with version control. Version control is not the same as backing up your files! Copying a file or making a backup shows how that file existed at a point in time. While this can be useful, it's not easy to manage, and it's hard to know where and when a change occurred. Version control tracks every change. You can see who made a change, and when, along with every change before and after. You can experiment in a nondestructive way, and collaboration with other developers is so much easier than without using version control.

Git (`https://git-scm.com/`) is one of the most popular version control systems on the planet, but Apache Subversion (`https://subversion.apache.org/`) and Mercurial (`www.mercurial-scm.org/`) are two alternatives. Each system works differently, but the basics remain the same. Throughout this book, I'll reference version control techniques with Git, but you can use any system. Many job adverts look for familiarity with Git, but some workplaces use very specific version control systems and tooling. Here are the basics.

Git requires any project to have a repository and a repository host. A repository (a "repo") is a place for a project to live – like a folder on your computer. You can have as many different repos as you like, but it's a good idea to keep each repo self-contained to a single code base or project. Repos need to live somewhere. This is where repository hosts come in. GitHub is a very well-known host, as is Bitbucket. You can even self-host if you'd prefer to. Repository hosting places your repos online, and accessible over the Internet. To prevent any unauthorized tampering, repositories are secured with credentials, so only authorized users can view or change code – depending on the author's preference.

Inside repositories code lives in branches. A branch is a specific version of code within your repo. Suppose you have a website in your repo. You have a branch named "master." Every time your code goes into master, the website gets updated. How would you test your code, or even store half-finished code without everyone seeing it on the website? – by using another branch. By creating a branch for work that is not yet ready, you can enjoy the benefits of Git without disrupting other people or services that rely on working code. You can have as many branches as you like, each different to the main branch.

To start working on a code base, you need to get the code from the repo to your computer. This is called cloning, or checking out. Through Git (no copy and paste required), every file in the branch gets copied to your computer. When you've made your changes, you need to get these changes back into the branch. This is a commit. A meaningful message accompanies each commit, so other developers know what happened during this commit. Finally, you need to get your committed code from your machine to the main repository. This is pushing. You push your changes to the remote repository host. You can also pull changes from the remote, if it's changed since you last pulled it.

When you're ready to get your code from one branch to another, you need to make a pull request. If you are working on your own, this may be acceptable immediately, but working in a team often necessitates an approval process. How will other developers learn that your code is available? How can your employers ensure you wrote adequate unit tests, or followed any legal requirements or obligations you may be following? A pull request is like saying "here's my latest code, I want it to go into this branch, would you mind taking a look at it." Once a pull request is open, you can decline it, or merge it. Repository hosts often offer tools to enable discussions around pull requests. Business process often dictates that a certain number of developers must look and approve a pull request before it is merged. This ensures everyone is happy with the quality before merging.

There are many more Git and version control tools and options available, but I'll cover most of these as and when you need them. The specifics of how Git works and the intricacies of these commands can get complicated, but you don't need to know everything about Git to start using it right now.

Deployments

Writing the best code in the world is no good if you can't put it anywhere, and this is where deployments come in. Deploying your code gets it in front of people, running on a server somewhere. This could be a Raspberry Pi, physical server, or cloud computing service such as Amazon Web Services (AWS) (https://aws.amazon.com/) or Google Cloud Platform (GCP) (https://cloud.google.com/). It doesn't matter where this code lives but the method to get your code from repository to host is what matters.

Little and often is the mantra here. As soon as your code reaches a specific branch (often designated as "master"), an automated system should deploy this to the server for you. It's possible to manually deploy code, but this is troublesome. You have to remember all the steps, passwords, and servers. It takes time, and it's a major effort for minimal gains. It's possible to automate the whole deployment process, including rollbacks in the event of a catastrophe. We'll build a deployment pipeline later on during the project chapters, but there are a few concepts worth considering.

To ensure a good deployment process, you need a good pipeline. Pipelines drive deployments and are crucial to ensuring strong and stable software gets released with a minimal amount of risk. Pipelines are a set of automated steps followed to deploy software. The input of each step is based on the output of a previous step. If the first step fails, there's no need to continue with future steps. A basic pipeline may look like this:

1. Run unit tests.

2. Run integration tests.

3. Run load tests.

4. Deploy.

5. Validate release.

If the unit tests fail, the software won't deploy. This keeps you safe. You need to have unit tests to begin with, but what's the point of having them if you ignore the failures? By requiring the tests to pass to deploy, you can be confident that code that fails the tests will not reach the customer.

This is a basic example, and larger code bases may have many more steps. Some pipelines automate everything. If the release fails, they roll back to the previous known working version. The Raspberry Pi pipeline you'll configure later on won't go this far, but it will check the unit tests pass before allowing you to merge. Tools such as Jenkins or Travis facilitate this pipeline process, although these are not covered in this book.

Blue/green deployment is a technique which is only cost-effective on a cloud computing platform. In the traditional server-based approach (and the pipeline discussed earlier), there's one massive server. Deployments release the change and, if it fails, revert back to a previous change. This works, but it has its flaws. There's no way to quickly revert the code back to a working state, and every user gains the new code immediately. Blue/green deployments create a brand-new server for the new code and run this alongside the old server with the old code. Once it's ready and tested, customers get moved to the new server all at once. If there's an issue once customers use it, they all get migrated back to the old server.

With physical hardware-based servers, blue/green deployments are difficult to achieve. It's possible, but not easy or cheap. Cloud infrastructure makes this so much easier to achieve. You can create new servers almost instantly, and then turn them off after the release to save money.

Canary releases are like blue/green deployments (and may work in conjunction with them). Like blue/green deployments, once the code is released on a new server, and it's available, a small percentage of traffic (perhaps 1%) moves to the new server. If it's stable, more traffic gets sent over. This continues until everyone is on the new release, and the old server gets switched off.

Should the new release fail, everyone can stay on the old release. Only a small percentage of customers get affected. These customers can move back to the old server. This has massive benefits. Fewer customers have a bad experience in the event of a bad release, and you can be confident that new code releases won't cause an outage for every user.

While a car system may not need blue/green deployments or a canary release, what about automated updates? While not used in this project, many software applications update themselves automatically. Many cars gain updates in a process known as over-the-air updating. If you're a car manufacturer, it makes sense to trial an update on a small number of cars, before pushing it out to all your customers and risk breaking every car.

Note   I haven't discussed CI/CD pipelines. CI/CD stands for continuous integration and continuous delivery (sometimes deployment). It's the process of constantly integrating and delivering code/features. If you wait until the very end of a project to start integrating it, testing it, and delivering features, you may find a large number of things which don't work, or are not to the customer's needs. By constantly integrating and getting feedback, you can adapt to changing requirements, circumstances, or errors.

Chapter Summary

Throughout this chapter you've learned the basics of computer science. You've studied how programming languages work, and how version control, debugging, object-oriented programming, and more exist to make your life as a developer easier, safer, and help to prevent bugs arising in the first place.

You've seen some tragic case studies from history which illustrate how badly things can go wrong when proper care is not taken when developing software, and used the benefit of hindsight to critique these historical events.

In the next chapter, you'll learn what the projects in this book involve. The software packages you'll use and the hardware you need to buy to follow along.

CHAPTER 3

Project Overview

Chapter goal: Understand how this project is structured and what equipment you need to follow along.

By now you should have an understanding of software development processes, tools, and best practices. Chapter 2 covered the basic building blocks needed to make you a software developer, and not just someone who can write code. With that in mind, this chapter aims to provide you with an overview of the mini-projects covered in the following chapters and explains how these projects work together to produce a complete system in the form of a smart car dashboard.

Chapter 2 is intended as both a software development primer and a beginner's reference guide. If you're unsure about an aspect of a mini-project, refer back to Chapter 2, but remember that it's a beginner's guide, so it naturally can't go into intricate details for every topic. This chapter and all those following furnish you with further information and practical examples as you need to know them.

The mini-projects encompassed in the following chapters are designed as stand-alone projects. Each one builds upon skills learned in the previous chapter, yet jumping right into a project doesn't mandate the completion of all the previous projects. By working through each chapter sequentially, you will produce a fully functional in-car computer or smart dashboard. While these projects involve electronic circuits,

© Joseph Coburn 2020
J. Coburn, *Build Your Own Car Dashboard with a Raspberry Pi*,
https://doi.org/10.1007/978-1-4842-6080-7_3

sensors, and interactive components, these are all software-heavy projects. Sensors provide data and facilitate interaction with the outside world; the Raspberry Pi and software you write does all of the hard work.

Project Structure

This smart dashboard is similar to the one you might find in your car, although it's significantly more intelligent than that of an entry-level model. The Pi drives a full-color LCD display which outputs an abundance of real-time sensor data – data such as the temperature, time, reversing status (complete with rear camera), available light, a boot sensor, fog light sensors, and more.

The Pi is connected to a series of simple electronic circuits installed in your car – although installation is optional if you'd prefer not to tinker with your pride and joy. Code developed in Python interrogates these sensors, interprets the results, and displays them to you in a functional and aesthetically pleasing way. You could run this project on any computer, but the Pi's size, price, and energy consumption make it a clear winner here.

Rather than developing a *graphical user interface* (GUI) from scratch, this project displays information to the user via a web server and basic HTML web page. This has many advantages. Primarily, it's easy to produce and fast to load. It may not be the most efficient way to design an application, but it's certainly the easiest. It's good enough for this project and is the way most applications are heading through *software-as-a-service* (SaaS) models. By letting Python handle the hard work, and limiting the client-side code (JavaScript), the main downsides of an HTML GUI are mitigated.

Note   Client-side code is code executed by your web browser. This uses the client's computer (that's you or me) to do some work. JavaScript is the language of choice for this, and it can greatly enhance the user experience of a website. The downside is that it's slow to run, and user support varies for different commands.

The alternative to client-side code is server-side code. This is code executed by a server of some kind, written in a server-side language such as Python. In this project, the Pi is both the client and the server, and as the server can execute code far faster than the client, it makes sense to restrict the JavaScript in use and let Python do all the hard work.

Once completed, you could easily extend this project. A Bluetooth module provides endless expansion options – Apple CarPlay or Android Auto support. Electronic seat driver profiles, keyless entry, or anti-theft driver photography and tracking are all very real and achievable projects building upon the skills learned here.

As with all modern gadgets, this is a software-heavy project. Python is easy to write, easy to understand, and "fast enough" for this use case. Some may argue that compiled languages such as C++ or Java are far better choices, yet their relative complexity is enough to scare most people off such a project. Besides, Python is rapidly growing as the number one choice for many different projects, and it's been around long enough now to ensure a thriving and active ecosystem exists to serve you and your needs.

If you're familiar with digital car diagnostics, you may be screaming at me right now. Modern cars equipped with OBD-2 (onboard-diagnostics) ports can provide an abundance of car data to anyone who cares to connect to the port. Statistics such as engine error codes, current revolutions per minute (RPM), engine health, fuel efficiency, and much more are available.

Here's the problem with the OBD-2 port: It's for mechanics. Sure, you or I *might* find some useful information in the torrent of data provided by the car, but its primary purpose is to aid with troubleshooting and diagnostics. It generally won't augment your experience as a driver, and it's harder to connect to and use than a home-brew solution. Granted, consumer USB or stand-alone OBD-2 modules exist, but those would boil this project down to reading in existing data and spitting it out to the screen. The Raspberry Pi presents a truly exciting opportunity to learn basic electronics skills, and really hone your software development experience skills.

The Hardware

The Raspberry Pi provides the processing power for this project. It's cheap enough to be accessible to most people and powerful enough to run a huge number of applications. It has a host of different input/output (I/O) ports and is easily extended with a variety of affordable hardware components. As outlined in Chapter 2, there are several different models of Raspberry Pis. While processing power and style of I/O ports often changes, the basic structure of the Pi itself is very consistent. These projects will work on *almost* any Pi model, although early revisions may struggle due to their limited processor speeds and the amount of RAM they use. Any model from the Model 2 B+ and above will work with these projects, providing you account for the slight changes in I/O location between models. For the purposes of consistency, I am using a Pi 4 Model B 4GB throughout this book.

You'll need a power supply to run your Raspberry Pi. During the development stage of these projects, a mobile phone charger or dedicated Pi power supply is suitable. For final installation in a car (well known for their lack of mains power sockets), you'll need a different power solution. Early Pi models require a micro-USB charger capable of providing 3A of current. For modern boards, a USB Type-C charger of the same rating is needed.

You'll also need a microSD card. This is the solid-state hard drive for your Pi. Not only does it store the entire Pi operating system, but it stores all of your settings, configurations, and application logic. These are reasonably priced (the $10–$20 range) and smaller than your fingernail. Ensure you buy a "class 10" or higher memory card, which is the speed rating of the card. These faster cards can handle the needs of a Pi with ease. As these projects don't need to store reams of data, 8GB is more than enough storage space (although larger capacity cards won't cause any problems). A 4GB memory card is not large enough.

For development at home, you may want to buy a Pi case. These pieces of plastic, wood, or metal are like phone cases or the case for your computer. They protect the hardware while still allowing easy access to the ports. They serve to protect your Pi from excess grease and grime from your fingers, along with shielding it from errant fingers and providing protection from knocks and falls. In one instance, cases protect Pis from undesirable photoelectric effects! These cost a few dollars and are available in a huge variety of shapes and styles.

Fun Fact   When released, the Pi 2 would instantly power-down when photographed with a flash! This is due to an exposed component known as the WLCSP package. This component regulates the power delivered to the Pi's processor, and the intense light delivered by a camera flash is enough to confuse this part. When confused, the WLCSP cannot function properly, so the Pi promptly turns off. This isn't dangerous, and won't damage the Pi. Using a case or otherwise obscuring this circuit prevents the problem from happening.

WLCSP stands for *wafer-level chip-scale package*. It refers to the process of packaging a component at the wafer level. In short, it's a way to produce TINY integrated circuits, found in devices such as the Raspberry Pi and the iPhone.

For the screen, you can choose any suitable display you own or have access to. The keyword here is *suitable*. It's perfectly possible to build this project with a spare 17-inch LCD from your old computer, but that's not very practical for a car. A 3.5-inch HDMI display is a good choice, and it doesn't need to be a touchscreen. These cost between $20 and $50, and you can buy them on Amazon, or any large retailer such as Walmart. Often a miniature HDMI cable to connect the Pi to the display is included, but you may need to buy a standard HDMI cable if you don't get one, or you wish to install the Pi in a different location to the screen.

Electronic Components

Aside from the Pi and associated electronic parts, you'll need a selection of electronic components. These range from tire pressure sensors to breadboards, resistors, wires, and LEDs. While covered in greater detail during the mini-projects, here are the basics.

A solderless breadboard is used to quickly construct temporary circuits. These let you rewire them in mere seconds, and greatly speed up the experimental section of a project. These are no good for permanent use, or installation in a car. Breadboards contain several power rails spanning the length of the board. These allow for easy (low voltage) power distribution to the whole board. The middle contains a gap – this is wide enough to place dual inline packages (small processors to augment the Pi, or microswitches, all of which share this common spacing). Surrounding this gap are independent rows with five holes each. Each series of five holes is connected, but each group of five is independent of the next.

This lets you wire circuits without fear of a short-circuit. Sizes are defined by the number of points (or tie points). Something in the 400–800 range is a good start.

Fun Fact   Breadboards are so named because they were literal breadboards from the kitchen! Before solderless breadboards arrived, hobby engineers used wooden breadboards with nails or thumbtacks pushed into them. By wrapping strands of wire around these ad hoc terminal points, it was possible to construct crude circuits. As you can imagine, real breadboards are hard to manage and take a lot of time to build any circuit. Thank goodness for plastic and solderless breadboards.

Breadboards are wired with solid-core wire or hookup wires. These wires connect different components to each other and the Pi. By fitting into the gaps in the breadboard, you can complete the circuit. They are often called jumper wires and are covered in plastic to prevent short-circuits.

Resistors are an essential electronic component. They *resist* the flow of electricity. This is useful to prevent components from overheating due to excessive electricity. Resistors work by converting electricity to heat. This loss reduces the voltage available to the other part of the circuit. In theory, *any* resistor will work with any voltage, but are generally sized for the job at hand, both to save money and prevent excessive heat generation and early failure.

Resistors are specified with a power rating and a resistance. This indicates the maximum load that the resistor can safely dissipate. As a loose rule, bigger resistors can handle a bigger load, but every resistor sold is designed and tested with a specific maximum load. The power rating of a resistor is measured in watts (W). The resistance is measured in ohms (Ω). Ohms specify the maximum resistance this resistor can safely provide. You don't have to max this out in your circuit, and there's a formula you can use to calculate resistance and power. Resistors don't have a polarity – they work the same backward as forward.

The physics behind electronic components such as these are fascinating, and many books can and have been written on the topic. As such, I can't dive into this topic as deeply as would be preferred – I'd be here all day!

The Dallas DS18B20 temperature sensor unit lets your Pi sense the temperature of its environment. You could use several of these to determine the temperature outside the car, inside the car, and inside the engine bay. These complete units only require one wire to operate (in addition to a power connection).

Light-dependent resistors (LDRs) or photoresistors are variable resistors that alter the resistance depending on the available light. They cost a few cents and are simple to use. They are a great way to augment your Pi with light-sensing capabilities.

Fuses exist to protect circuits in the event of a failure. If there's a short-circuit, or other failure resulting in a runway current draw, the fuse breaks and breaks the circuit. Ensure you use fuses rated for your application, and don't use a bigger fuse, or worse – replace one with aluminum foil!

A piezo is a fascinating device that converts electrical energy into sound by expanding or contracting a thin membrane. By varying the amount of time power is applied for (and sizing the membrane accordingly), you can produce a beep or buzzing sound. If so desired, you can even play a tune on one, but that's not covered in this book. These cost $1–$2.

Finally, the KY-032 infrared (IR) unit is a tiny circuit. It uses an integrated circuit (IC) to generate, pulse, transmit, and then measure IR signals bouncing off nearby subjects. Available for a few dollars, this circuit is easy to implement and is a brilliant way to enhance your car.

Equipment List

This list serves as a master list of everything you need to follow along with these projects. These are repeated during the projects, but if you'd like to buy them all in one go, then here's what you need. In some cases, it may not be possible to buy the exact item required – and that's OK. For the vast majority of items, a close enough match is almost always as good as the original item, but in circumstances where a close match is critical, these items are denoted with an asterisk (*).

Core Components

- 1 x Raspberry Pi 4 Model B (or newer)

- 1 x Pi power supply (3A, USB Type-C)

- 1 x 8GB (minimum) class 10 microSD card*

- 1 x stylish Pi case (optional)

- 1 x 3.5-inch or larger LCD HDMI display*

- 1 x micro-HDMI to full-size HDMI cable

- 1 x USB keyboard

- 1 x USB mouse

- 1 x official Pi Camera module V2*

- 1 x jewelers' screwdriver set

Electronic Components

- 1 x 830-point breadboard*

- Assorted breadboard jumper wires – male and female

- 1 x Dallas DS18B20 temperature sensor unit (with integrated 4.7k ohm, 0.25 watt resistor)

- 1 x miniature momentary tactile switch

- 1 x photoresistor/light-dependent resistor

- 2 x 23k ohm, 0.25 watt resistors

- 2 x 250mA fuses*

- 1 x 3v piezo element

- 1 x 3v KY-032 IR sensor module

Chapter Summary

This chapter presents and equips you with everything required to begin the project. You should understand the software side, how the application will be structured, and what language and frameworks you'll use. You learned the basic theory of how this application will read its sensors, and present that data to the display. Not only do you have a basic understanding of the electronic components that power this system, but you have a shopping list of exactly what you need to buy to begin construction of your own smart car dashboard.

In the next chapter, you'll learn how to prepare your computer to write Python, run unit tests, and safely store your code in a version control system.

CHAPTER 4

Local Development Configuration

Chapter goal: Configure your computer to write Python and develop the application. Set up a local development environment on your computer. Configure a Git repository to store your code, and learn how to run both your code and unit tests on your computer.

Throughout this book, you've mainly learned theoretical computer science, case studies, and best practices, along with an introduction to the Pi and an overview of the software and hardware needed to follow along with these projects. You should now know the "why," but not the "how." This practical chapter covers the first steps needed to begin building the project.

A local development environment is the first and the most important tool in your software developer's toolkit. This lets you write code, write unit tests, safely store and version your code, and rapidly make changes with instant feedback. By running the project on your computer, you can quickly iterate over new designs and features and experiment with code. You don't even need a Raspberry Pi at this stage.

© Joseph Coburn 2020
J. Coburn, *Build Your Own Car Dashboard with a Raspberry Pi*,
https://doi.org/10.1007/978-1-4842-6080-7_4

Note   Running code on your computer instead of the Pi itself provides one major benefit: speed! It's far quicker and easier to run your code locally instead of remotely. With a build pipeline hanging off your Git repo, it could take several minutes to deploy code to the Pi. This doesn't sound like a lot, but it gets tedious very quickly, especially if you change something simple like a comma or a bracket. Running code on your computer lets you instantly see the changes – it's as fast as pressing save.

There is a time and a place for running and testing code on the Pi itself, as your computer is not a Pi and behaves very differently in terms of supported hardware, processing speed, and CPU instruction set. Later on, you'll learn when and why to deploy to your Pi.

Throughout this book, the instructions given are specifically for macOS Unix and the Raspberry Pi's Debian-based Raspbian operating systems. Linux users should have no problem running the commands on a different operating system – in some cases, they are the same commands. Microsoft Windows users may struggle to complete some of the console-heavy instructions.

Despite its popularity with consumers, writing code on a Windows machine is more difficult than it should be, and the vast majority of Windows development machines are used for working with Microsoft technologies. If you're attempting this project on a Windows computer, pay special attention to the instructions. Once you know what you need to do, you may need to figure out how to achieve this in Windows. Often, a simple console command on Mac or Linux requires a GUI installer on Windows.

Getting Started with Python

Almost any current version of Python will work with these projects (although you may have to perform your own troubleshooting and investigation if certain features are not available in older releases of Python). I don't recommend you use Python version 2 releases, as discussed in Chapter 2. Many new Python modules will simply not work with old versions of Python, and it is officially deprecated – meaning you shouldn't begin new projects with it.

Other languages could work with this project. Perhaps PHP, Java, or Go would work, but at the very least, you'd need to know how to develop in those languages, and much of the guidance in the following chapters would be rendered useless by choosing a language other than Python. You'd also need to learn how to interface with the sensors, and how to read the camera stream and various other components for the projects. The Official Pi APACHE server tutorial (`www.raspberrypi.org/documentation/remote-access/web-server/apache.md`) may be a good starting point for one of these alternative languages.

Don't forget that the vast majority of Pi projects are implemented in Python. There exists a vast range of articles, papers, Tweets, and tutorials around Python on the Pi, which is significantly reduced when working in other languages.

Python is quick to learn, easy to read, and uses standard English keywords. Its popularity is going from strength to strength right now, and the Pi is perfectly paired to work with Python as the go-to language.

In order to run any Python scripts, you need to install a Python interpreter. This reads your Python code and translates it into instructions your computer can understand. This happens in real time, and a Python interpreter is often simply called Python. When you run code with Python version 3.7 (`www.python.org/downloads/release/python-370/`), you are simply using the Python interpreter, version 3.7.

macOS comes with a Python interpreter preinstalled, but it's not a good practice to use this. This Python is required by some tools used by your operating system. It can change without warning and is usually an old version such as Python 2.7. There's also the problem of dependencies. Libraries you import into your code are called modules – your code is dependent on these. If these modules are not part of the Python core library, then you need to install them. If you have two projects both using your system Python, then it's common for both projects to install modules and compete with each other. Perhaps the first project needs version one of a module, but another project needs version two. This is difficult to manage and frustrating to work with.

Solving this dependency problem is simple enough – in theory. You can install specific versions of Python, and install your modules into a virtual environment, which uses any version of Python you have installed. Virtual environments keep all your modules isolated from other projects. Everything installs into a self-contained place. You can create as many as you like – one for each project is sufficient. This ensures that changes to modules in project A don't impact project B.

This project uses Python 3.7, so get started by installing this version. Open a new Terminal either from your applications folder or by going to **Spotlight Search ➤ Terminal**.

You could immediately install Python 3.7, but there's a better way to manage Python versions. A tool called *Pyenv* lets you install, uninstall, manage, and switch Python versions on a per-project level. It's easy to use and takes away a lot of the hard work of managing multiple versions of python.

Pyenv is a free tool available on GitHub at `https://github.com/pyenv/pyenv`. A Windows fork is available at `https://github.com/pyenv-win/pyenv-win`. Pyenv provides detailed installation instructions, but installation through a tool called *Homebrew* is far simpler and is a common approach for dev tools on macOS.

Homebrew is a package manager for Mac and Linux. Available at `https://brew.sh/`, Homebrew lets you install Mac packages (such as pyenv) from your command line. It's free, and marketed as "The Missing Package Manager for macOS (or Linux)." Different packages are defined as formulas, and you can see the full list at `https://formulae.brew.sh/formula/`.

Back in your terminal, install Homebrew with the following command:

```
/usr/bin/ruby -e "$(curl -fsSL https://raw.githubusercontent.com/Homebrew/install/master/install)"
```

This uses Ruby (included with macOS) to download a build script from GitHub and then run it. This will install Homebrew on your computer, but before running, it lists what it will install and what directories will be created. Click **Return** to continue the installation. Various words, modules, and formulas will fill up your terminal, but after a few short minutes, you should see "Installation successful!" if everything went to plan. If your installation failed, then take a look at the Homebrew troubleshooting tips available at `https://docs.brew.sh/Common-Issues`.

Go ahead and use Homebrew to install pyenv:

```
brew install pyenv
```

Homebrew will update you on the status of this installation. Often it begins by downloading the code for the latest package version and then installing it, which Homebrew calls "pouring."

Once installed, pyenv needs a configuration. This is done through the **pyenv init** command. This ensures pyenv works properly when using any other Python commands. Do this by adding the command to your ~/**.bash_profile**, which this command will do for you:

```
echo -e 'if command -v pyenv 1>/dev/null 2>&1; then\n  eval
"$(pyenv init -)"\nfi' >> ~/.bash_profile
```

Now restart your shell to pick up this change:

```
exec "$SHELL"
```

Note   The *.bash_profile* is a configuration file for your bash shell (Mac Terminal). When you start a new bash session, the shell looks at this config file. It's used to configure packages and export variables. Depending on your operating system, this file works and is named slightly differently. macOS Catalina uses ZSH (*.zshrc* config file) as the default interactive shell, and Linux systems may use additional files, such as *.bashrc*. Check the pyenv installation guide at `https://github.com/pyenv/pyenv` for detailed instructions across many operating systems.

The intricacies of how pyenv works are complex, and well explained in the pyenv GitHub repo. In short, whenever your Python applications run, they specify the version of Python they need. Before this command reaches your operating system's Python interpreter, pyenv jumps in and redirects the command to the version of Python managed by pyenv. It basically intercepts Python commands and redirects them to the correct version of Python.

The projects contained in this book use Python version 3.7. You can install Python with pyenv. Pyenv has access to many different versions of Python, so run this command to list the available versions of Python 3:

```
pyenv install --list | grep " 3\.[7]"
```

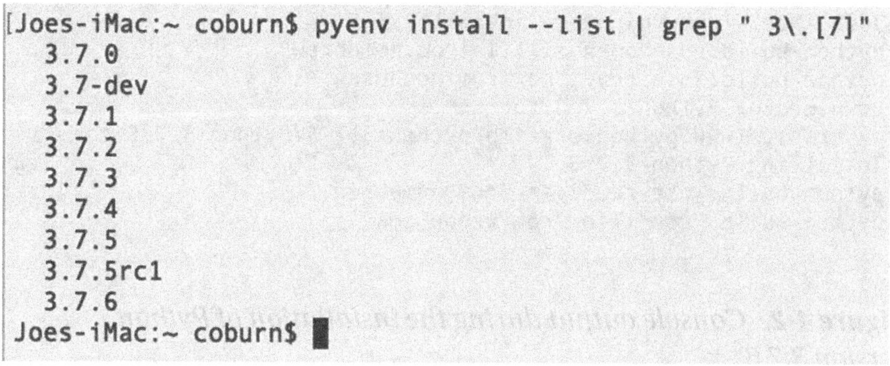

```
[Joes-iMac:~ coburn$ pyenv install --list | grep " 3\.[7]"
  3.7.0
  3.7-dev
  3.7.1
  3.7.2
  3.7.3
  3.7.4
  3.7.5
  3.7.5rc1
  3.7.6
Joes-iMac:~ coburn$ █
```

Figure 4-1. All the Python 3.7 versions listed by Pyenv

This is really two commands in one. The first half (*pyenv install --list*) lists all the versions of Python available to install with pyenv. As there are hundreds of versions, that's a bit excessive. The pipe symbol (|) instructs the shell to run another command after pyenv has finished, using the output of pyenv as the input to the next command. You can chain together as many commands as you like this way. Finally, grep filters down the list to only the Python 3.7 versions (*grep " 3\.[7]"*). You can see the output of this command in Figure 4-1.

Any version of Python 3.7 is suitable for these projects, but as a best security practice, you should generally aim to install the latest stable version unless it contains breaking changes. Python version 3.7.6 is the version used by these projects (but newer versions should work just fine). Install this Python interpreter with **pyenv install** (sample output shown in Figure 4-2):

```
pyenv install 3.7.6
```

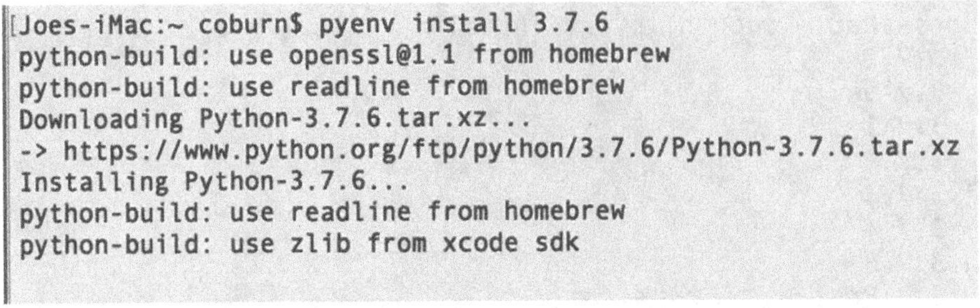

```
[Joes-iMac:~ coburn$ pyenv install 3.7.6
python-build: use openssl@1.1 from homebrew
python-build: use readline from homebrew
Downloading Python-3.7.6.tar.xz...
-> https://www.python.org/ftp/python/3.7.6/Python-3.7.6.tar.xz
Installing Python-3.7.6...
python-build: use readline from homebrew
python-build: use zlib from xcode sdk
```

Figure 4-2. *Console output during the installation of Python version 3.7.6*

Just like the previous commands, pyenv lists the various steps in this process as it goes. Once installed, you can list all the available Python versions with **pyenv versions** (shown in Figure 4-3):

```
pyenv versions
```

```
[Joes-iMac:~ coburn$ pyenv versions
 * system (set by /Users/coburn/.pyenv/version)
   3.6.6
   3.7.6
Joes-iMac:~ coburn$
```

Figure 4-3. *Installed Python versions listed by Pyenv*

Here you'll see any versions of Python you've installed with pyenv, alongside your system Python. The asterisk indicates your default Python. Despite installing Python 3.7.6, this is still your system Python. Run a Python shell to get the version and see (shown in Figure 4-4):

```
python --version
```

```
[Joes-iMac:~ coburn$ python --version
Python 2.7.10
Joes-iMac:~ coburn$ █
```

Figure 4-4. *Console output of the current system Python version*

To use the newly installed Python 3.7.6, you need to instruct pyenv to configure 3.7.6 as the default Python. You can do this with the **global** option:

pyenv global 3.7.6

Now when you get the Python version from a Python shell, it should match the version you installed. Python 3.7.6 is now installed, and you can move on to the next step.

Breaking changes are those which are not backward compatible with previous software versions. If you're upgrading to a breaking version of a package, your code may not work properly, and you may need to make changes to ensure it functions the same as it did with the previous version.

Developers try to ensure changes don't cause major issues, and you can often upgrade packages without issue. In the case of breaking changes, sometimes it's just not possible to rework the code in a way that doesn't cause an issue for someone. A good example of a breaking change is the migration from Python 2 to Python 3.

A Python package called *Pipenv* (https://github.com/pypa/pipenv) is needed to handle your virtual environment. This solves many module import issues and ensures any modules you use in this project won't interfere with other projects – either current or future.

Install Pipenv with the **pip install** command:

```
pip install pipenv
```

Pip is the default package installer for Python. In most instances, it is installed alongside Python. This command instructs Pip to install Pipenv. If you receive a warning about your version of Pip, you can install the latest version with the **upgrade** command:

```
pip install --upgrade pip
```

Pip will install Pipenv into your global system Python. This seems at odds with my recent advice to always install modules into a virtual environment and never mess with system Python. In this case, Pipenv *is* the virtual environment manager, which makes it tricky to install in its own virtual environment. As Pipenv is the basis of virtual environments across many Python projects on your computer, it receives a pardon and goes into your global Python. Once installed, all future modules can install into their own, isolated, virtual environments.

You'll revisit Pipenv later on in this chapter, so for now, all you need to do is install it.

Git and GitHub Repository Configuration

Git is one of if not the most popular version control systems in use today, and for good reason. Creating manual revisions of files may work for graphic designers or writers, but the vast number of changes made by software developers on a daily basis mandates the need for a robust code storage solution.

Git lets you store, share, collaborate, restore, undo, experiment, and back up your code easily, and it's free. GitHub exists as a web platform and remote Git host. While you may not need to share code with other people, free, secure, online code hosting is a wonderful tool to have at your disposal. Other tools exist, but GitHub is free to get started with and is very popular with the open source community.

The official Raspberry Pi Git tutorial may assist you here, available at `https://projects.raspberrypi.org/en/projects/getting-started-with-git`.

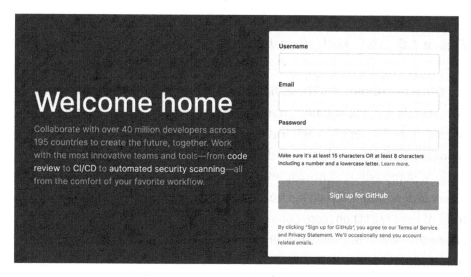

Figure 4-5. *GitHub welcome screen*

Get started by visiting `https://github.com` and creating a free account if you don't already have one. Enter a username, an email address, and a password right from the home screen (illustrated in Figure 4-5). Follow the onscreen steps to confirm your email address by clicking a confirmation link sent to you.

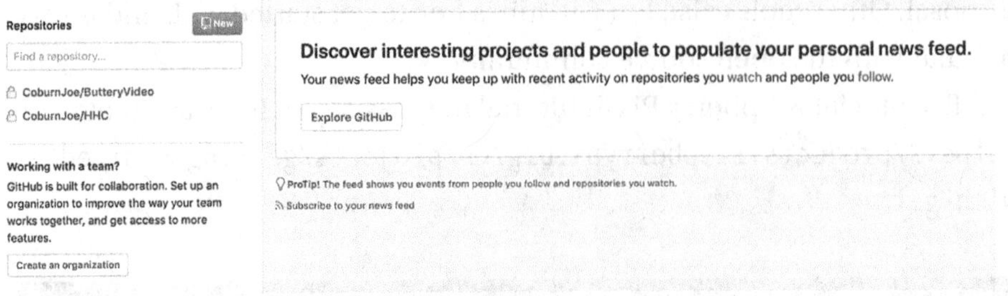

Figure 4-6. *Main GitHub dashboard*

Once registered, you'll see the main GitHub dashboard (Figure 4-6). To start this project, you need a repository, which is a place to store related code. Generally, each individual project starts with a new repository. When developing code based on another's work, it's common to "fork" a repository. This copies all the code in a repo and makes a new independent repo. Feel free to clone this project's repository from https://github.com/CoburnJoe/Pi-Car, but for the purposes of education, you'll re-create this entire code base from scratch in your own brand-new repo.

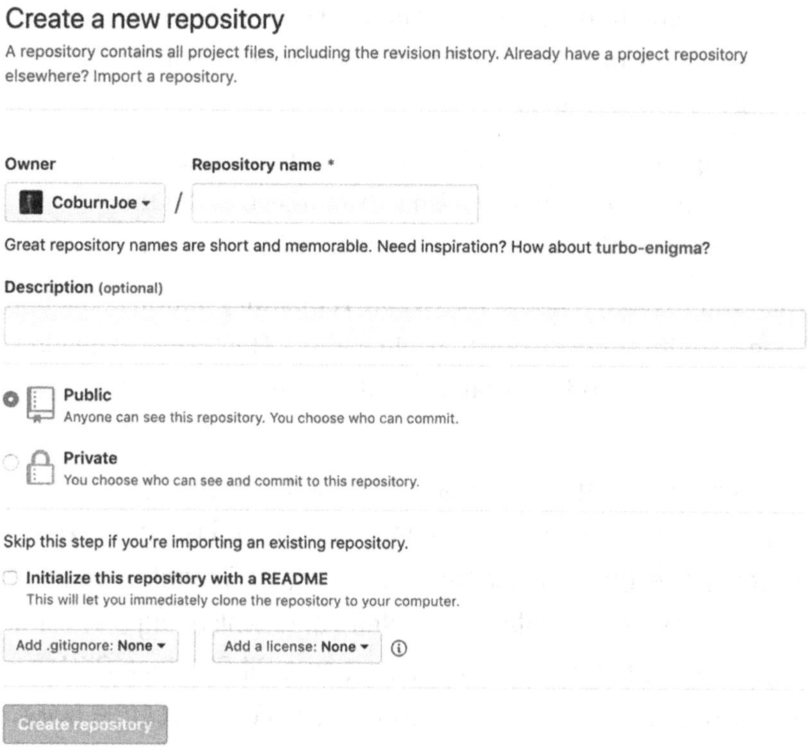

Create a new repository

A repository contains all project files, including the revision history. Already have a project repository elsewhere? Import a repository.

Owner   Repository name *

[CoburnJoe ▾] / [   ]

Great repository names are short and memorable. Need inspiration? How about turbo-enigma?

Description (optional)

[   ]

◉ Public
   Anyone can see this repository. You choose who can commit.

○ Private
   You choose who can see and commit to this repository.

Skip this step if you're importing an existing repository.

○ Initialize this repository with a README
   This will let you immediately clone the repository to your computer.

[Add .gitignore: None ▾]   [Add a license: None ▾] ⓘ

[Create repository]

Figure 4-7. *GitHub new repository screen*

From the left of the GitHub dashboard is a **Repositories** menu. Choose the green **New** button from this menu. You need to complete some basic information about your new repository (shown in Figure 4-7). These are as follows:

- Repository name – This is unique to your account.

- Optional description – A brief overview of your project.

- Visibility – Public or private. With public access, anyone can see and potentially contribute to your project. If you're not ready to share your code with the world just yet, then choose private. Only you and people you invite can see your private project.

77

- README initialization – A Git README file is where you can write a quick guide to using this code, and it's a good practice to have one.

- .gitignore – .gitignore files tell Git not to include certain files or folders when working on a project. Select the **Python** option here for a boilerplate file.

When you're ready, choose the **Create repository** button at the bottom of the page. You're almost ready to begin coding. The final step needed is to get your new code and associated Git files onto your computer.

Note   This Git configuration is all performed over the command line. If you're not comfortable with this, then various GUI Git tools exist to aid you. I'd recommend learning the basics of Git first so you can understand how these tools work instead of downloading and blindly pressing buttons in one. If you're still set on a Git GUI, then GitHub Desktop (`https://desktop.github.com/`) or Sourcetree (`www.sourcetreeapp.com/`) are both excellent choices, available for both Mac or Windows operating systems.

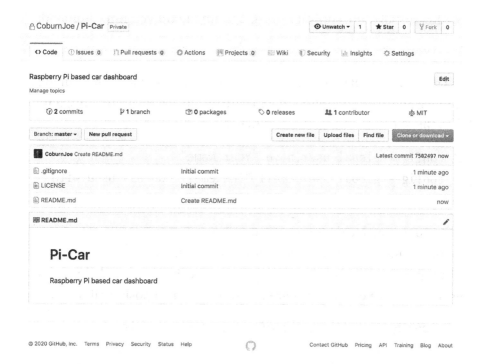

Figure 4-8. *The GitHub repository landing page*

After creating your repository (or selecting it from the repository menu on the main GitHub dashboard), you'll see the main repository overview screen, shown in Figure 4-8. Choose **Clone or download** from the top right and copy the link to the **.git** file of your repository. This lets Git know where to find your project. For my repository, this looks like this:

```
https://github.com/CoburnJoe/Pi-Car.git
```

Your repository link will contain your username and repository name. Pointing your computer to this repository is simple enough, but you need Git itself installed for this to work. Open a new Terminal and install Git with Homebrew:

```
brew install git
```

After installation, verify it is working with the **Git version** command:

```
git --version
```

This will spit out your current Git version. Finally, configure your local Git name and email address. Git and GitHub will work without this, but it helps Git associate your account with you:

```
git config --global user.name "Your Name"
git config --global user.email "The email address used with
your GitHub account"
```

You only need to do this configuration once after installing Git. Git retains this information across all projects on your computer.

Jumping back to the repository link you previously copied, download this using the **Git clone** command, followed by the repository link:

```
git clone https://github.com/CoburnJoe/Pi-Car.git
```

```
[Joes-iMac:Documents coburn$ git clone https://github.com/CoburnJoe/Pi-Car.git
Cloning into 'Pi-Car'...
remote: Enumerating objects: 7, done.
remote: Counting objects: 100% (7/7), done.
remote: Compressing objects: 100% (6/6), done.
remote: Total 7 (delta 1), reused 0 (delta 0), pack-reused 0
Unpacking objects: 100% (7/7), done.
Joes-iMac:Documents coburn$ ▮
```

Figure 4-9. *Sample console output when Git cloning a repository*

This will copy all the code from your repository onto your computer, and the sample output is shown in Figure 4-9. It will link up Git to your repo, so you can push and pull code and perform other Git associated commands. You can now begin writing code.

Integrated Development Environment Setup

Now you have a way to run Python, a place for your code to live, and a way to track changes, you need a way to write code. You may be familiar with command-line editing tools such as Vi, Vim, or Nano, but an integrated development environment (IDE) provides a wealth of useful tooling and features not possible in (some) other editors.

Subtly different to text editors such as Notepad++ or Sublime Text, IDEs let you

- Compile code without leaving the program

- Run unit tests and measure code coverage

- Debug code and halt execution at arbitrary points in time

In addition to this, IDEs often provide helpful warnings and information about your code as you write it. They point out where you may have made a typo or otherwise named something wrong. They can analyze your code and pull out docstrings, parameter names, and best practices. IDEs shouldn't be shied away from as they can greatly improve your efficiency as a developer.

My personal preference for a Python IDE is *PyCharm*, by *JetBrains*. One reason for this preference is familiarity. I know the tool well – don't underestimate the performance increase you can achieve by using tools, languages, and frameworks you are familiar with (providing they are suitable for the task at hand). PyCharm has built-in version control and conflict management tools, and a wealth of extensive tools, features, and extensions available. JetBrains (the developers of PyCharm) have a wealth of experience behind them, and continue to expand their software with useful tools, features, and bug fixes. In addition to this, there is large online PyCharm community, where you can find help to any issues you encounter. The PyCharm learning center is a good place to start (`www.jetbrains.com/pycharm/learning-center/`).

Available for free at `www.jetbrains.com/pycharm/`, PyCharm has a wealth of tools built-in to make your life easier as a developer and to save you time when writing Python. A professional version is available, but for all the projects in this book, the free community edition is sufficient.

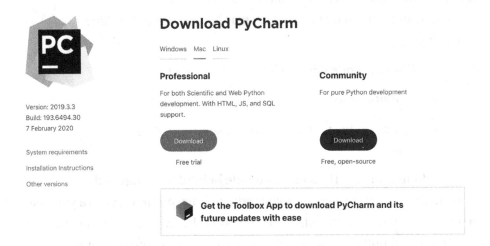

Figure 4-10. *PyCharm download screen*

Head over to the JetBrains website and download the latest version of PyCharm community edition. As of writing, this is version 2019.3.3, released in February 2020 (see Figure 4-10). JetBrains will ask for your email address, but your download will start shortly after with no requirement to provide it.

If you have a preferred Python IDE, there's no reason you can't use it to follow along with this book. Most of the examples given are executed through macOS X terminal commands, with only a small section geared toward PyCharm-specific steps.

Figure 4-11. *PyCharm Mac installation*

Once downloaded, click the Mac disk image (ending in **.DMG**). This will mount the image onto your desktop and bring up a finder window (Figure 4-11). Use this window to drag PyCharm into your **Applications** folder, thereby installing it. If you like to keep a clean computer, then unmount the volume afterward by dragging it to the trash.

Figure 4-12. *PyCharm first time landing page*

Open PyCharm, and click through their first installation steps, as shown in Figure 4-12. Accept the license agreement and use the default themes and shortcut keys (or customize how you like to work). When you get to the **Welcome to PyCharm** menu, choose **Open** and navigate to the local copy of your code which you cloned from your GitHub repository. This tells PyCharm that everything in this folder is your project. When opening a project for the first time, PyCharm needs some time to update its indexes, which you can see it doing in Figure 4-13.

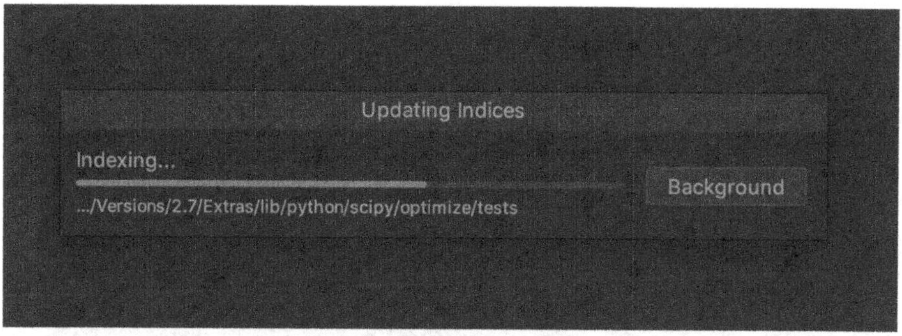

Figure 4-13. *PyCharm updating its indexes*

PyCharm consists of four main areas. You'll learn more about specific parts as you progress through the projects, but to start with, these are the following:

1. The **Project** is on the left.

2. The **Navigation Bar** is at the top, with buttons on the right.

3. The **Tool Window Bar** is at the bottom.

4. The **Main code editor** is on the right.

These four key areas are shown along with the main PyCharm screen in Figure 4-14.

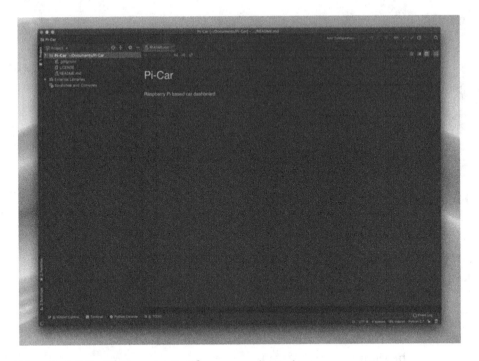

Figure 4-14. *The main PyCharm project view*

The project area lists details about your project. It lists all of your files (including hidden files used by Git). The navigation bar shows you where the current file lives in relation to the whole project. It also provides options to run your unit tests and modify your Python configuration. The tool window bar at the bottom provides lots of useful tools. A terminal is here, along with a Python console, version control options, and many more features. Finally, the main code editor is where you can read and write your code. **Double-click** a file to see it here. You can work with multiple files, split this into two or more views, and more.

You're now ready to begin writing code. By default, PyCharm will automatically save any changes for you in the background. This only happens when PyCharm loses focus – often when you click another application such as your web browser or another PyCharm tab.

Python Virtual Environment Configuration

If you look at the bottom right of PyCharm, it says **Python 2.7**. This isn't correct, as you're using Python 3.7 for this project. To fix this, you need to use Pipenv to create a new virtual environment, and then point PyCharm at that. Start with a new terminal session – either through the Mac Terminal application or by pressing **Terminal** in the **Tool Window Bar** at the bottom of PyCharm. Create a virtual environment with the **pipenv install** command:

```
pipenv install
```

This will create a new virtual environment for you using your global Python version, which is configured as Python 3.7 as per the previous instructions on Pyenv. Pipenv provides a status bar on this progress, but as you have no other modules to install yet, it shouldn't take very long.

Back in your **Project** pane, you'll notice two new files. The **Pipfile.lock** lists all the packages your project needs, and the **Pipfile** does the same but in a more human-readable way. The **Pipfile** looks something like this:

```
[[source]]
name = "pypi"
url = "https://pypi.org/simple"
verify_ssl = true

[dev-packages]

[packages]

[requires]
python_version = "3.7"
```

Let's break down these four sections. The **source** specifies where to look to find any Python packages you need. For the vast majority of projects, this is always **PyPI**, which is the de facto Python module repository. If you need to install modules not found on PyPI, you'll need to specify a different source here. The **dev-packages** area lists any packages and versions you need to write your code, but which you don't need in the final build. This is often linting tools, or a unit testing module.

The **packages** section lists any modules and versions your code needs to work. Finally, the **requires** section lists any other dependencies. Your Python version 3.7 is listed here, which outlines what version of Python is needed to run this project.

This file will grow as you build the projects and import more modules (other than those modules found in the Python core code base). This file lists the modules you need, but not necessarily specific versions. Installing modules listed as "*" will install the latest build and associated dependencies.

The **Pipfile.lock** contains mostly the same information, but it serves a different purpose. This is locked or pinned to specific versions. It's used for systems, pipelines, and automated tooling to read and install modules from. This won't ever install a newer version; it's always locked to a specific version listed when the file was last generated. It also contains hashes of modules, which allows pipenv to verify the contents are exactly the same as those it expects. This again prevents accidental upgrade of packages and protects against a polluted remote source, which may serve up poisoned or otherwise "tampered with" modules.

Let's install some basic modules and see how this file changes. Back in the terminal, install **Flask**, **Pytest**, and **Black**:

```
pipenv install flask
pipenv install pytest --dev
pipenv install black --pre --dev
```

Flask is the Python microframework which is the basis of this whole project. Pytest is a very popular unit testing framework. Notice how the **--dev** flag is used. This tells Pipenv to install this package under the dev-packages section of the pipfile. Finally, the **Black** package is an uncompromising code formatter. It reformats your code to meet the Python recommended styles outlined by the Python community. It's listed as an "uncompromising code formatter." It handles the formatting of your code, so you can think about the logic and the stuff that really matters. Black is still in prerelease, so the --**pre** flag ensures pipenv knows you really do want to install it. Using a tool such as Black is a great habit to get into, especially if you come to work with multiple developers on the same code base. You'll no longer argue over trivial semantic issues such as placement of commas, which quotes you used, or how long lines are. It sounds trivial, but everyone has a preferred style of code formatting. By using Black, it makes all the code consistent. Don't overlook how important this is.

Back in your **pipfile**, you'll see it has updated to reflect your new modules:

```
[[source]]
name = "pypi"
url = "https://pypi.org/simple"
verify_ssl = true

[dev-packages]
pytest = "*"
black = "*"

[packages]
flask = "*"

[requires]
python_version = "3.7"

[pipenv]
allow_prereleases = true
```

One final step needed in the terminal is to regenerate the **pipfile.lock**. Pipenv won't always do this for you. It doesn't want to potentially break anything upstream of your local code by inadvertently locking a newer package – maybe one that contains breaking changes. Go ahead and generate this yourself with the **pipenv lock** command:

```
pipenv lock
```

Finally, let's run some of these newly installed packages. In the terminal, you can run Black by telling it which file or folder to work on:

```
Black $PWD
```

The keyword **Black** is needed to run Black itself. The special **$PWD** statement is a bash command. It stands for "print working directory." When used with Black, this means "run Black on all the code from the folder your terminal is currently in."

Notice how this command failed? Something along the lines of "bash: black: command not found"? This is because Black is installed in your virtual environment. You need to enter this virtual environment to use the packages in it. Do so with **Pipenv shell**:

```
pipenv shell
```

Notice how your terminal now says the name of your virtual environment in brackets at the start of each line. Yours may vary slightly, but for me, my terminal now looks like this:

```
(Pi-Car) bash-3.2$
```

This is a helpful reminder that you are in a virtual environment. Go ahead and run that Black command again. If everything is working correctly, Black will say that it has nothing to do. This is perfectly fine – you have no Python files to format yet (but if you did, Black is ready to format them).

Now run some unit tests with **Pytest**:

```
pytest
```

Once again, Pytest will say there are no tests to run. This is not a problem – you simply haven't written them yet. You didn't think unit testing would be that easy, did you?

You're now all set with your virtual environment. It works. You can install packages and update your **pipfile** and **pipfile.lock**. One final step is to point PyCharm to your fresh environment. From the bottom right of PyCharm, click **Python 2.7** and choose **Add Interpreter**. Choose **Virtualenv Environment** from the left-hand menu and then choose **Existing Environment**. Find your version of Python (3.7) listed in the **Interpreter** drop-down menu and then click **OK**. This menu is shown in Figure 4-15.

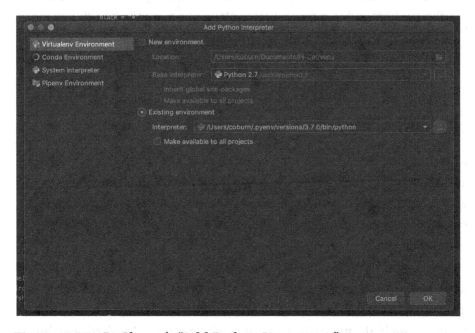

Figure 4-15. *PyCharm's "Add Python Interpreter" menu*

PyCharm will do some figuring out and perhaps recalculate its indexes. When it's ready, the bottom right of PyCharm will now say "Python 3.7," followed by the name of your virtual environment. Now you can use a virtual environment in the terminal, or with any buttons and tools within PyCharm itself.

Note   You may have noticed a Pipenv option from the PyCharm interpreter menu, so why must you select Virtualenv instead? Pipenv is really a wrapper around the Python package **Virtualenv**. By using Pipenv, it's really created your virtual environments with Virtualenv in the background (along with a few other helpful things). Feel free to select **Pipenv** and create a new virtual environment this way instead. It's not possible to point PyCharm to an existing Pipenv virtual environment without selecting Virtualenv. Knowing how Pipenv works in the background is a much better place to be in than blindly relying on PyCharm to operate it for you in either case.

Git Workflow

Now that you have two new files, let's get these into your Git repository. You could just crudely shove these into the master branch, but that's not very refined. Many businesses are not willing to tolerate code going to a customer without a code review – other developers looking and approving of the changes.

You could argue that this code is just for you, and there's no other developers working on it, so you'll shove it wherever you please. This is a valid approach, yet as you'll see shortly, your Raspberry Pi will look at the master branch. If you blindly cram unstable or even unfinished code into it, your Pi may not work until you finish the code. This may be acceptable just for you, but again, if this was a real product, website, or business, things randomly breaking is not an acceptable option.

By creating a **branch**, you can safely work and experiment on code away from the main branches, and all the other developers and systems which rely on them. A common system is a **master** branch, which is your production code. A **develop** branch is used for nearly ready or possibly unstable changes. The code goes into a feature branch (often stemming from develop) while it is developed. When ready to share, it gets **pull requested** (PR'd) to develop. You won't need to get other developer's approvals if it's just you on this project, but PRs provide an easy way to undo a whole feature at a time.

Once merged into **develop**, you can **pull request** (PR) to **master** if you're ready to go "live." A final option is that of urgent bug fixes. If there's a problem on the master branch (and therefore your production code), this can be fixed with a branch taken off master. This is known as a hotfix, and it goes back to master, bypassing develop. Once the crisis is over, you can merge it from master down to develop, to keep everything in sync.

With all that said, let's go ahead and create a **develop** branch. These projects won't use feature branches, but feel free to if you'd like the practice (the Git process remains unchanged). From the PyCharm terminal, create a new local branch with the **git checkout** command:

```
git checkout -b develop
```

This creates a new branch called develop. The **checkout** command lets you switch between local branches, and by using the **-b** flag, you can create a new branch with a name – in this case, "develop." Notice how Git confirms the command it just executed, and the bottom right of your PyCharm window shows the current branch.

Use **git status** to see a list of files that have changed and are either staged already or untracked and uncommitted, shown in Figure 4-16:

```
git status
```

This returns three files so far (or more if you've made other changes):

```
.idea/
Pipfile
Pipfile.lock
```

```
(Pi-Car) bash-3.2$ git checkout -b Develop
Switched to a new branch 'Develop'
(Pi-Car) bash-3.2$ git status
On branch Develop
Untracked files:
  (use "git add <file>..." to include in what will be committed)

        .idea/
        Pipfile
        .Pipfile.lock

nothing added to commit but untracked files present (use "git add" to track)
(Pi-Car) bash-3.2$
```

Figure 4-16. *Untracked files highlighted by Git*

The **Pipfile** and **Pipfile.lock** are expected changes, but what is the **.idea** folder, and where did it come from? This is a PyCharm folder. You don't need it in your repository, and you can safely ignore it. To ignore this folder from all your Git commands, you need to add it to your **.gitignore**. Remember, GitHub automatically generated a Python-specific .gitignore file for you. Add this folder to your **.gitignore** file with this command:

```
echo .idea/ >> .gitignore
```

This is a bash command to add "*.idea/*" to your .gitignore file. You don't need to open the file; this will append to the end of it. Now when you check the git status, you'll see three files, but with a difference. The .idea folder has gone, but it's now been replaced by your **.gitignore** file. You've modified this file, so you now need to commit it.

Committing in Git saves your changes at a point in time. This only happens to your local Git repository, so it's not the final say, but it's an important command to understand. Before you can commit changes, however, you need to tell Git which files to commit. You *could* use something like this:

```
git add .
```

But this is a bad practice. This command adds ALL changed files to your local Git. You may accidentally commit testing files, passwords, repository or access keys, or any other number of files you don't want to share. By explicitly adding the files you want to commit, you can avoid all of these issues. Use **git add** to let Git know which files you want to commit:

```
git add .gitignore
git add Pipfile
git add Pipfile.lock
```

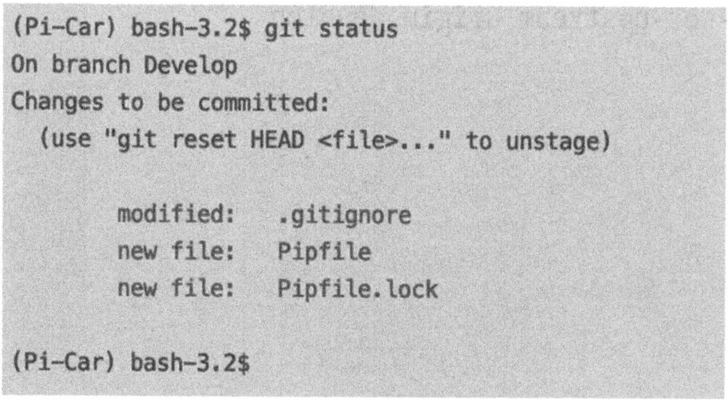

```
(Pi-Car) bash-3.2$ git status
On branch Develop
Changes to be committed:
  (use "git reset HEAD <file>..." to unstage)

        modified:   .gitignore
        new file:   Pipfile
        new file:   Pipfile.lock

(Pi-Car) bash-3.2$
```

Figure 4-17. *Tracked files highlighted by Git*

If you run **git status** again, you'll see all three of these files have turned green, indicating that they have been staged ready to commit (shown in Figure 4-17). Commit them with **git commit**:

```
git commit -m "First pipfile"
```

The **-m** option lets you type a message to accompany your commit. Make this descriptive so that you can understand what this change is, and any other developers who may look at this Git history in the future. It sounds simple but lacking the discipline to write good messages here will cause you trouble later on – either when you're trying to track down what changes occurred in a repo, or you start working with other people, who look at you quizzically as to why you let your cat walk all over your keyboard with regard to your commit messages.

The final step needed is to **push** these changes. This tells Git to get all your changes and then commit and send it to the remote repository – GitHub in this case. This gets the code off your machine. It backs it up remotely and ensures other developers can see and work with it. Without pushing to a remote repository, your code exists only on your computer.

As this branch does not exist in GitHub just yet, you need to tell Git to make the branch on the remote repository first with the **--set-upstream** option:

```
git push --set-upstream origin develop
```

```
Counting objects: 100% (7/7), done.
Delta compression using up to 8 threads
Compressing objects: 100% (5/5), done.
Writing objects: 100% (5/5), 5.68 KiB | 5.68 MiB/s, done.
Total 5 (delta 1), reused 0 (delta 0)
remote: Resolving deltas: 100% (1/1), completed with 1 local object.
remote:
remote: Create a pull request for 'Develop' on GitHub by visiting:
remote:        https://github.com/CoburnJoe/Pi-Car/pull/new/Develop
remote:
To https://github.com/CoburnJoe/Pi-Car.git
 * [new branch]      Develop -> Develop
Branch 'Develop' set up to track remote branch 'Develop' from 'origin'.
(Pi-Car) bash-3.2$ █
```

Figure 4-18. *Console output during the first push of code to a remote repository*

Providing you're not violating any repository rules configured on GitHub, and there are no surprises (such as a bad Internet connection, or an outage at GitHub), then you'll see a push confirmation message, highlighted in Figure 4-18. These may vary in time depending on the number and size of the changes you are pushing.

When pushing to a repository that already exists on the remote, you don't need to be so specific:

```
git push origin develop
```

As a good rule of thumb, you should avoid pushing without specifying where to push to. While a plain "git push" often works perfectly fine, it pushes directly to the remote branch – which may not be what you expect. By explicitly stating the branch to use, you avoid any risk of shoving your changes into the wrong place.

Pull Requests

As discussed previously, pull requests are the best way to get your code into another branch. They allow other developers to see and approve of your changes, and they provide an excellent way to discuss the merits of said code. Developers can comment on specific lines or changes, and everyone gets to see your changes with a nicely formatted output. Even if you're not working with other developers, pull requests are a great way to move code from one branch to another.

Before starting a pull request, you need to get all the changes from the upstream branch into your branch. If you're going from develop into master, then develop needs all the changes in master, plus your new additions. This places the onus of resolving conflicts and integrating all changes on the pull request author. Solo developers will rarely encounter any issues, but once you join a team, it's common for a branch to fall behind the main branch fairly quickly. Keeping your branch updated with upstream changes is a good practice to employ.

Let's merge a change from master to develop locally, and then pull request results. Begin by switching to the master branch (assuming you have no uncommitted work on the current branch):

```
git checkout master
```

Now get the latest changes from the remote master branch to your local master branch:

```
git pull
```

Switch back to your local develop:

```
git checkout develop
```

Now merge your (local) master into your (local) develop:

```
git merge master
```

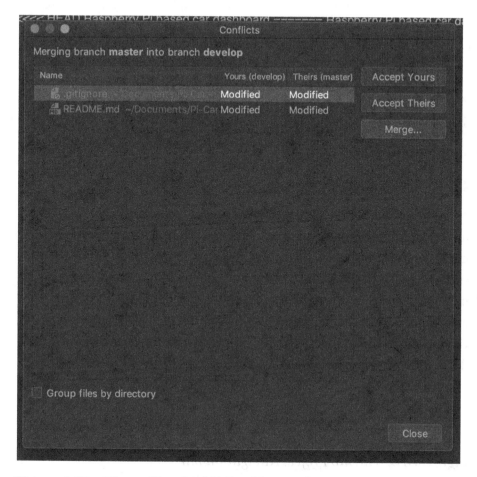

Figure 4-19. *Git conflicts highlighted by PyCharm*

If your changes are small, this merge will continue without issue.
Should there be significant changes in either branch, then you may end
up with a **merge conflict**. Merge conflicts happen when two branches
contain changes to the same file and within the same lines. Git cannot
automatically merge the files for you in some cases, so you need to
manually do so. This is easy in PyCharm. Head over to **VCS ➤ GIT ➤
Resolve Conflicts**. This brings up the **PyCharm Conflict** menu, shown in
Figure 4-19. It lists all the files that have conflicts. You can choose to accept

your changes or changes from the remote. If you need to pick and choose changes from both branches, then double-click each file and work through each change.

Once the conflicts are resolved, **commit** the changes:

```
git commit -m "Merged master"
```

and then **push** your branch:

```
git push origin develop
```

At this point in time (and providing nobody sneaks new changes into master), your develop branch contains your changes plus all the changes in master. Develop is now ready to pull request into master. This is the stage where I'll deviate from a command-line only Git tutorial. Git purists may start hating now, but creating PRs from the command line requires even more Git knowledge than is needed to start using Git right now. GitHub shows the changes between branches in a much clearer way than the stock Bash command line does, so now feels like an appropriate time to use a GUI.

Figure 4-20. *GitHub Project Navigation bar*

Head over to `http://GitHub.com` and select your project. From the **Project Navigation bar** (Figure 4-20), choose the **branches** button. This is preceded by a number, matching the number of open branches your remote repository has. This is unaffected by how many local branches you have providing they are not pushed to the remote.

Figure 4-21. *The GitHub branch overview page*

This overview lists all your branches, and is shown in Figure 4-21. Find the **develop** branch (or any branch you wish to pull request from), and click **New pull request** on the right-hand side. This loads the **Create pull request** page, shown in Figure 4-22.

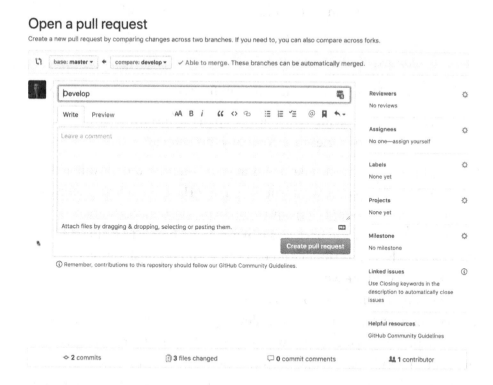

Figure 4-22. *GitHub's new pull request page*

This page is split into two sections. The top half contains details of your pull request, the number of reviewers, pull request messages, labels, assignees, and more. The bottom half outlines the number of commits made and the changes they occurred on. It highlights any additions or subtractions, along with any commit messages made on this branch.

In the top half, enter an appropriate title and description. What's an appropriate description? It is one that lets other developers know the purpose of this pull request. There are no hard and fast rules here, but a good place to start is these prompts:

1. Reason – Why are you making this PR? What problem does it solve?

2. Rational – Why did you code it this way? Was there another option that wouldn't work in this scenario?

3. Background – Other developers may not have the context of a fix that you do.

4. High-level list of changes (if significant).

5. Any future changes to follow, or pull requests in other repositories to accompany this change?

As a final sanity check, take a look at your commits and the diff. If this was someone else's code, what would you say? Have you left any debug or test logic in the code? Is it ready to run in the destination branch, or production? It's OK to go back and make changes before finishing this PR. Once ready, choose the big green **Create pull request** button to share your changes with the world.

Once opened, it's time to sit back and bask in that sweet sweet karma that comes from being an awesome developer – go you! On a serious note, it's a bad practice to merge PRs without sign-off from other developers in your team. Rules and regulations vary between businesses and teams, but it's not uncommon to face disciplinary action for failing to get enough approvals on a pull request (accidents excluded). If you're working on a personal project without any other developers, go ahead and merge this PR with the big green **Merge pull request** button. Providing there are no conflicts (there shouldn't be at this stage), your PR will merge without issue. If you do encounter any conflicts, then revisit some of the previous steps to merge and resolve them.

To keep your repository tidy, it's a good idea to close feature branches when merging PRs. This keeps branches around for a small purpose or feature. Branches cost nothing, but having lots of old ones around can clutter up your repository. Create new branches as and when you need them. Common branches **master** and **develop** (and sometimes others) rarely get closed.

Repository Rules

Any good repository needs rules. Rules stop you committing directly to the master branch, or merging a pull request without enough approvals. Once again, when working solo you may not need as many rules, but they can still keep you safe. This project uses CI/CD to automatically deploy code from the master branch to the Pi (as you'll see in the next chapter). Any changes to the master branch could result in the Pi not working properly. Sure, a home project on the Pi failing isn't a big deal, but what about a system customers are paying for, a military missile, or a medical system? Small mistakes here could cost lives (as illustrated in some of the software development case studies).

It's hard enough to write bug-free software, so save yourself the trouble and protect your branches! At the very least, branch permissions prevent you from accidentally committing work-in-progress code to the wrong branch.

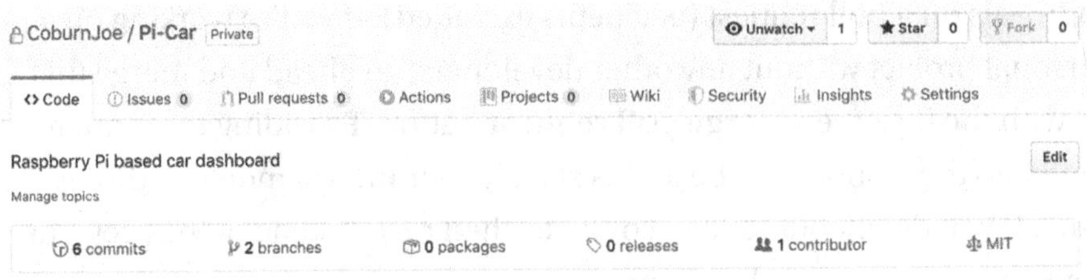

Figure 4-23. *GitHub's top navigation bar*

To add branch permissions, head over to `http://GitHub.com` and load up your repository. Choose **Settings** from the top navigation bar (as shown in Figure 4-23). From the left navigation bar, select **Branches** and you'll see the **Branch protection rules** section. Any existing branch rules will appear here. Let's create a new branch rule by choosing **Add rule**.

This add branch rule screen lets you configure in-depth rules for a branch. It's possible to have a whole host of rules for your master branch, and no rules at all for develop. It doesn't make sense to have a blanket rule policy for the whole repository. Let's add rules to the **master** branch and learn about the possible rule options in the process. Figure 4-24 shows the branch protection rules page.

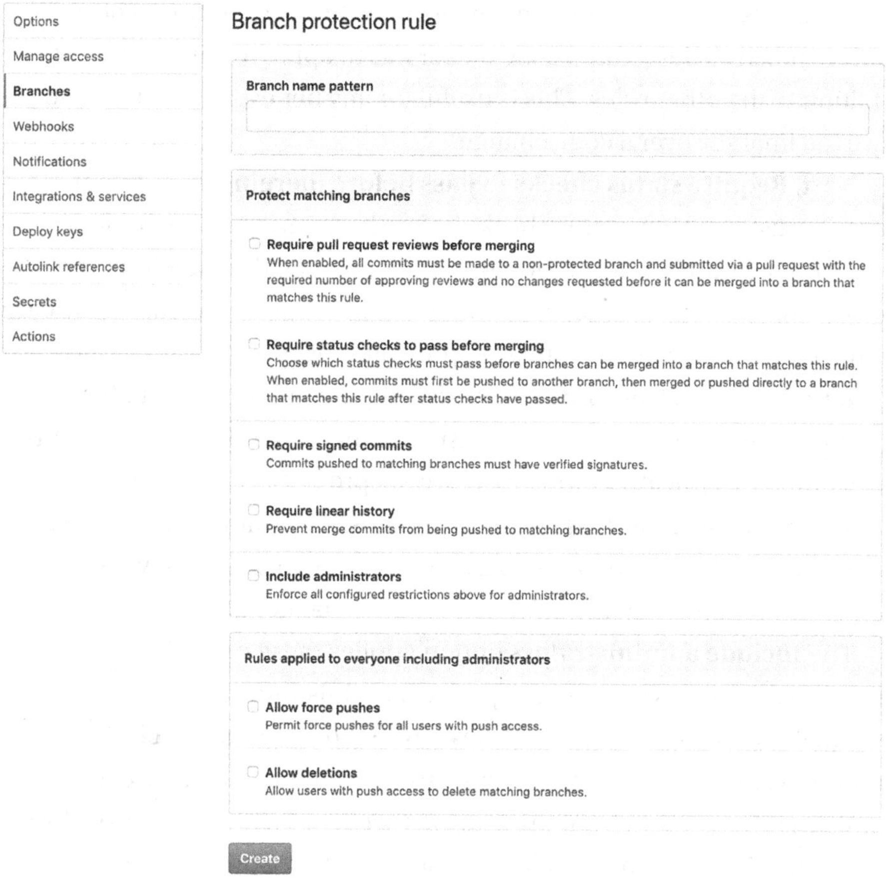

Figure 4-24. *Adding a branch protection rule in GitHub*

The **Branch name pattern** defines what branch to apply this new rule to. You can use the wildcard * operator here to match patterns, but for now, **master** is sufficient.

Require pull request reviews before merging means that any pull request must have a certain number of approvals before it can merge. Not very helpful for solo developers, but incredibly useful for a team. The **Required approval reviews** drop-down lets you specify how many reviews are needed to merge. By enabling **Dismiss stale pull request approvals when new commits are pushed**, GitHub will reset the approvals if the

105

code changes while a PR is open. Finally, **Require review from code owners** means a designated code owner has to approve any PRs in addition to the other rules. This is useful for any benevolent dictators to have the final say over a code change.

Next, **Require status checks to pass before merging** means your branch must meet any status checks before it can merge. This could be a limit on the number of conflicts present, or that all the code from the destination branch has already merged into the source branch. This is easy to meet if you follow the Git steps on previous pages.

Require signed commits enforces a cryptographically verifiable signature across all commits. This ensures users can trust project authors – not something typically enforced on private projects.

The **Require linear history** option means all commits merging in a PR go into the destination branch as one commit, instead of several. This keeps the main branch tidy if there are lots of changes going in.

The **Include administrators** option applies these rules globally to any user, or only to users who are not project administrators.

Finally, at the bottom is the **Rules applied to everyone including administrators** section. Confusingly this doesn't include the **Include administrators** option from the previous section. Inside here, **Allow force pushes** lets you allow or disable force pushing. Force pushes let you shove code into a branch that may not otherwise go. This could be commits which don't have the matching commit history or don't meet a particular rule. It's not advisable to enable this.

The **Allow deletions** option lets users delete this branch. You probably don't want this to happen on develop or master branches when using CI/CD.

As a good starting point, you should require pull request reviews before merging, with a suitable number of approvals – even one at this moment is sufficient. Enable **Dismiss stale pull request approvals when new commits are pushed**, and require status checks to pass. If these rules are too prescriptive for you, or not strict enough to prevent problems, then loosen or tighten them as you see fit once you get into the flow of Git and your project.

GitHub's **Project Administration** guide available at `https://help.github.com/en/github/administering-a-repository` goes into extensive detail with all of these options are more.

Pipeline Configuration

A pipeline or build step is an essential part of a CI/CD process. Tools such as Jenkins (`https://jenkins.io/`) or Travis CI (`https://travis-ci.com/`) exist to let you completely automate the deployment process. From running various tests and building other services to building and deploying images, and rolling back changes, pipeline automation tools can save you a serious amount of time and effort. While a large automation is little out of the scope of this book, let's discover how to run your unit tests automatically across any branch.

Before configuring a pipeline process, let's write a basic unit test first, so your pipeline has something to run. Open up PyCharm and create a new branch off **develop** with a suitable name:

```
git checkout develop
git pull
git checkout -b feat/tests
```

Create a new test folder at the top level inside your **Pi-Car** folder:

```
mkdir tests
```

Create two new files inside this folder. Pytest requires all test files to begin with the word "test", so create a **test_practice.py** file. The second file is a blank file called **__init__.py:**

```
touch tests/test_practice.py
touch tests/__init__.py
```

The **touch** command creates blank files. Why **__init__.py**? This special file tells your Python interpreter that this folder contains Python modules. You only need one per directory. They are often blank, and are an essential requirement for working with Python. Go ahead and create another __ init__.py file at the top level:

```
touch __init__.py
```

Inside **test_practice.py**, create a very basic class and test:

```
class TestPractice:
    def test_one(self):
        assert 1 == 1
        assert "banana" == "banana"
```

Black your code and then run this first test with **Pytest**:

```
black $PWD
pytest tests
```

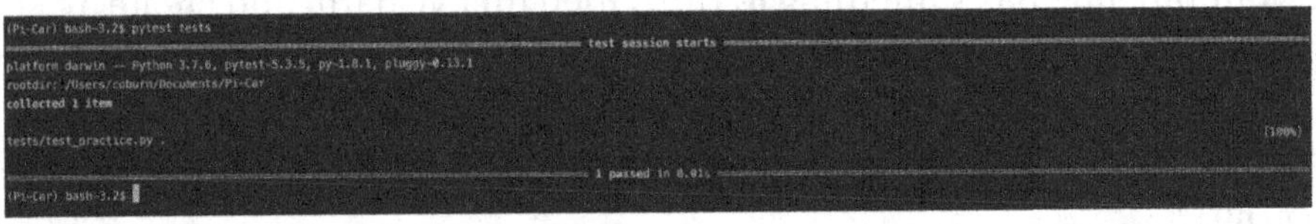

Figure 4-25. *Passing unit tests*

This command tells Pytest to run all the tests it finds in the **tests** folder, and its output is shown in Figure 4-25. You could replace this with any other folder and it will run the tests – providing the test names meet Pytest's standards. Notice how Pytest gives you a nice little test status? All your tests should pass, and Pytest should indicate so with a green bar and a 100% sign. Let's make these tests fail. The **Assert** statement is used to test that a certain condition is met. Change one of the asserts to something that is not a fact:

```
assert "apple" == "banana"
```

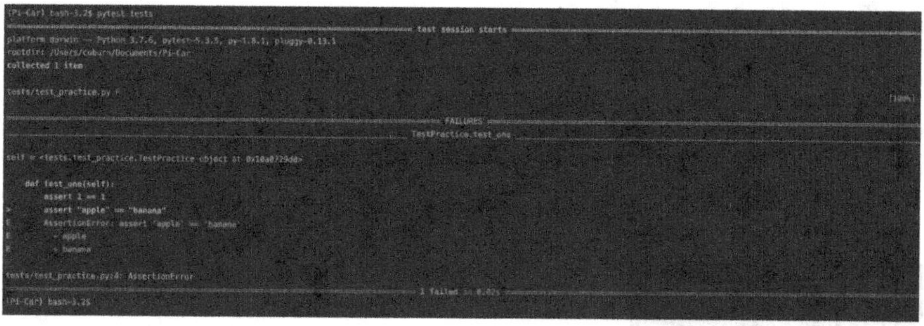

Figure 4-26. *Failing unit tests*

Now run your tests again – notice everything goes red (Figure 4-26)? Pytest highlights exactly which test failed, and why. This information is extremely useful when writing tests, or troubleshooting a failing test. Go ahead and undo this failing change. Commit your change and push your new branch:

```
git add __init__.py && git add tests/
git commit -m "Wrote a basic unit test"
git push --set-upstream origin feat/tests
```

Now you have a unit test. You have a local and remote branch called **feat/tests**, and you know how to write assertions. Pull request and merge your branch into master – you'll need it there for this next step. Let's get GitHub to run these tests in your pipeline.

GitHub's built-in pipeline process provides basic CI/CD functionality. The GitHub Marketplace (https://github.com/marketplace) is full of premium and free tools to provide extensive control over deployments, but **GitHub Actions** is the quickest way to get started with (simple) CI/CD in GitHub, and it's built in to the core offering. You can see the introductory page in Figure 4-27.

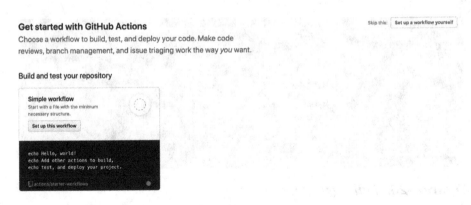

Figure 4-27. *GitHub's initial Actions page*

Head over to your repository and choose **Actions** from the top navigation bar. Here you'll find several boilerplate actions to get you started. Skip all of these, and choose the **Set up a workflow yourself** button from the top right of this page. This next interface can look daunting (Figure 4-28), but it's not as complex as it looks. This lets you configure exact actions to happen when a branch merges. This could be deploying to Amazon Web Services (AWS), sending an email, or in this case, running tests.

Figure 4-28. *Configuring a build pipeline in GitHub*

GitHub Actions are configured using a YAML file. By default, GitHub proposes you store this nested under **.github/workflows** and call it **main. yml**. You can change this name and location from the top left of this action configuration page. Alternatively, you can commit this file as is and then pull and work on it locally. For now, let's edit it online and let's leave its default file name and location. The benefit of editing this file in the GitHub Actions file editor is automatic syntax correction. If you make a mistake, or enter an invalid (but technically correct) command, GitHub will inform you of the problem.

YAML is a recursive acronym for **YAML ain't markup language**. It's a human-readable configuration language, used for config files and build pipelines. It's simple to use and nests commands through indentation, colons, and hyphens.

GitHub's actions are free (with some usage limits). You're unlikely to reach these limits for small projects or accounts where you rarely need to build multiple branches concurrently. Actions support a huge amount of customization. You can trigger builds when any code changes, or just when certain branches run. You can name your tasks, limit the execution time, run more than one in parallel, and lots more. Here's the starter code you need to run your unit tests:

```
name: Validate Build
on: [push, pull_request]
jobs:
  build:
    runs-on: ubuntu-latest
    strategy:
      matrix:
        python-version: [3.7]
```

```
  steps:
  - uses: actions/checkout@v1
  - name: Set up Python ${{ matrix.python-version }}
    uses: actions/setup-python@v1
    with:
      python-version: ${{ matrix.python-version }}
  - name: Install Dependencies
    run: |
      python -m pip install --upgrade pip
      pip install pipenv
      python -m pipenv install --dev --pre --system
      export PYTHONPATH="$PWD"
  - name: Black Check
    run: |
      black --check $PWD
  - name: Unit Tests
    run:
      pytest tests
```

Let's break this down. This **.yml** file configures your build pipeline to run in GitHub. Each individual line represents a configuration parameter. Each line starts with its name, followed by a colon, and then the value. Line breaks only exist to make it easier to read, and commands are further subdivided and nested with tabs and hyphens – a bit like Python.

It's possible to run multiple pipelines, each one performing a different task. You can name a pipeline like this:

```
name: Validate Build
```

The **on** command specifies when to automatically run this pipeline. You can put various options here. The **push** command will run the pipeline whenever code is pushed to the repo. **Pull_request** runs this pipeline whenever a pull request is made. This is a good starting point in terms of useful places and times to run this pipeline:

```
on: [push, pull_request]
```

All the following commands are nested underneath the **jobs** section. This is simply a grouping, and way to separate the pipeline actions from the configuration and metadata:

```
Jobs:
```

Everything underneath the **build** section is used to configure the prerequisites needed to run this pipeline. This is a good place to specify the operating system and Python versions you want to test with. The **runs-on** option lets you choose the operating system to test with – in this case, the latest version of Ubuntu Linux. The **matrix strategy** offers you the ability to run tests against several different versions of Python, specified by the version numbers in square brackets (**[3.7]**). This build only tests against Python version 3.7, but you can enter many different Python versions here (separated by commas):

```
runs-on: ubuntu-latest
    strategy:
      matrix:
        python-version: [3.7]
```

The **steps** section configures the build steps. This installs specific versions of Python, along with your project dependencies. It runs your unit tests and checks the code that meets Black's stringent requirements. If any of these steps fail, the build will also fail. The **uses** name configures the pipeline to require a dependency. Here's how the pipeline gets the latest version of your code:

```
- uses: actions/checkout@v1
```

The **Install Dependencies** step configures pip to install your project dependencies. It adds several options to **Pipenv** and then exports your Python path – just like you did on your computer:

```
- name: Install Dependencies
    run:
        python -m pip install --upgrade pip
        pip install pipenv
        python -m pipenv install --dev --pre --system
        export PYTHONPATH="$PWD"
```

The **Black Check** step checks your code complies with the **Black** code formatter. By using the **--check** option, Black won't actually change any of your code – it just checks there is nothing to change:

```
- name: Black Check
    run:
        black --check $PWD
```

Finally, run the unit tests with Pytest:

```
- name: Unit Tests
    run:
        pytest tests
```

When you're ready, choose **Start commit** from the right-hand side of the actions screen, and fill in the commit details, as shown in Figure 4-29. Make sure you create a new branch, instead of committing to master.

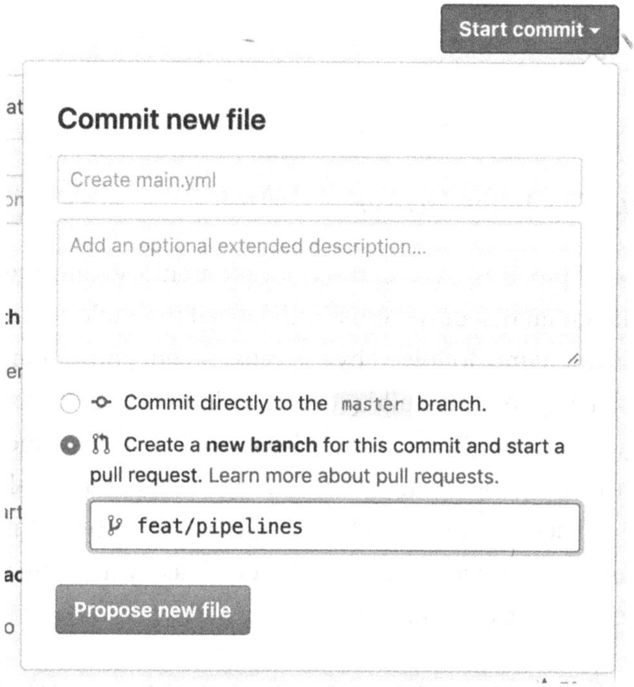

Figure 4-29. *Committing a change though GitHub's web-based interface*

To see this pipeline in action, head over to the **Actions** tab from the main repository view (Figure 4-30). Here you can see all the historical builds, their status, and any pipeline names. On the left you can filter by the pipeline names – as defined at the top of your **.yml** file. On the right are all the builds that have run in the past, ordered in chronological order. You can filter these pipelines either by their name or other search criteria or by using the predefined filters for event, status, branch, and actor (person who made a change that kicked off the build).

Figure 4-30. *The Actions screen on GitHub*

On the list of pipelines, you can see supplementary information about that build. The green tick or red cross indicates if the build was successful or not. Next is the name, followed by the most recent commit in that build. The event that triggered this build (such as pull request or code push) is listed after the words **on**. In the middle lists the branch this pipeline ran against, and the user who changed something to trigger it. Finally, the right-hand side lists the duration of this build, along with the time and date it last ran. The three ellipses on the far right will take you to the workflow configuration file once expanded.

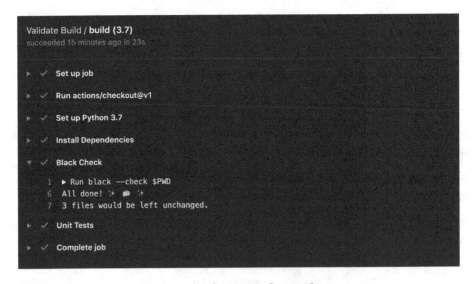

Figure 4-31. *Sample output of a GitHub pipeline*

By clicking the **build name,** you can see detailed pipeline information – shown in figure 4-31. By clicking the Python version number on the left-hand side, you can see detailed build information. Here's where you'll find the output of Black or Pytest, alongside any errors. This is a valuable troubleshooting tool when configuring a new pipeline.

When you're ready, **pull request** and **merge** this pipeline branch to the **master** branch. Congratulations! You are now well on your way to becoming an expert software developer. You'll use this pipeline regularly to assess the quality of your code. Whenever you push new code or create a pull request, this pipeline will run. It will run your latest code and tests, so you don't need to worry about updating it. You may want to regularly maintain it – adding new versions of Python as they become available, or fine-tuning it to your preferences.

Git Cheat Sheet

Now that you know enough Git to be dangerous, refer back to this cheat sheet (Table 4-1) for a helpful reminder of the basics.

Table 4-1. *A list of common Git commands*

Command	Description
git init	Initialize a new git repository in the current folder.
git add <file>	Stage a single file into your local branch.
git add .	Add ALL files recognized by Git. Localized to your current directory. Use wisely!
git commit -m "commit_ message"	Commit your staged changes with a message.

(continued)

Table 4-1. (*continued*)

Command	Description
`git commit`	Commit your staged changes without a message (opens up your default console text editor with a sample message).
`git push origin develop`	Push your staged changes and commits to a specific remote branch.
`git push`	Push your staged changes and commits to whatever your remote branch is. Use wisely!
`git push --set-upstream origin <branch_name>`	Push your staged changes and commits to a new remote branch.
`git checkout <branch_name>`	Switch to a preexisting local branch.
`git checkout -b <branch_name>`	Create a new local branch and switch to it.
`git remote -v`	List the remote branches and repositories your local branch is linked to.

Chapter Summary

This chapter has equipped you with everything necessary to write the code for this project. You used Pyenv and Pipenv to manage different versions of Python, and configure virtual environments for per-project dependency management. You created your own Git repository on GitHub, and learned how to create pull requests, and configured a build pipeline to run your unit tests automatically.

You and your computer are now fully equipped to develop any Python application you like, using industry-standard tools and best practices. In the next chapter, you'll continue this configuration by preparing the Pi itself. You'll learn how to install an operating system, install the latest version of Python, and pull your application code and run it on the Pi itself.

CHAPTER 5

Raspberry Pi Initial Configuration

Chapter goal: Configure the Raspberry Pi for basic operation. Connect your repository to the Pi and run the latest version of the code.

You have a solid code base. You can write and run unit tests and format your code with Black. You have a repo, can create pull requests, and have a build pipeline that validates your code whenever you push to a branch or create a pull request. If you don't have any of these things, I strongly advise you to go back and complete Chapter 4 before continuing with this chapter. While some of the early Pi configuration is applicable to any scenario, this chapter very quickly builds upon the artifact developed in the previous.

Providing you own a Raspberry Pi and a suitable memory card and power supply, then here's how to turn it from a shiny, pretty, paperweight into a functional minicomputer, complete with an operating system, Python 3.7, Git, and a version of your code.

© Joseph Coburn 2020
J. Coburn, *Build Your Own Car Dashboard with a Raspberry Pi*,
https://doi.org/10.1007/978-1-4842-6080-7_5

Install an Operating System on Your Memory Card

Before you can even think about using the Pi, you need to install an operating system onto its microSD memory card. The Pi is designed to let you easily swap different memory cards – it's possible to use individual cards for different projects. Before touching the Pi, let's start with the memory card and your computer.

Remember, you need an 8GB (or larger) microSD card which is a class 10 or faster. Huge storage capacities are not needed here, but high speed and reliability is. Purchase a reputable brand such as *Kingston, Samsung, SanDisk*, or *PNY*. Try to avoid second-hand cards or those of dubious origin. It's fine to recycle a known-good memory card, but buying cheap or a bargain that looks too good to be true is often a recipe for disaster.

Several operating systems exist for the Pi – including vintage remakes such as *RISC OS* and BSD derivative *FreeBSD*. *Raspbian* is the official image supported by the *Raspberry Pi Foundation*, and it's a Debian-based (free) Linux operating system. It has a graphical interface, but like most versions of Linux, its power is unlocked by the command line. The Raspberry Pi Foundation provides a free Raspbian installation tool called *NOOBS*, which stands for *New Out Of Box Software*. This free tool makes it easy to configure your Pi for the first time, so let's install it onto your memory card.

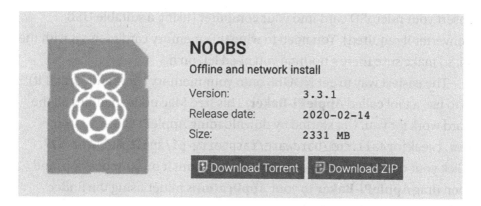

Figure 5-1. *NOOBS download buttons from the Raspberry Pi website*

Get started by downloading **NOOBS** from the Pi Foundation's website: www.raspberrypi.org/downloads/NOOBS/. Be sure to download the full-fat NOOBS, and not NOOBS Lite, which is a stripped-back version for installing over a network. You can see an example of the download buttons in Figure 5-1. Extract this **.zip** file by **double-clicking** it. Figure 5-2 shows the file extraction progress. You can delete the original file once extracted.

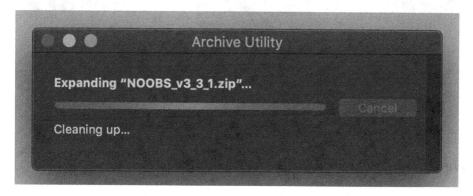

Figure 5-2. *Extracting NOOBS compressed file on macOS*

Once downloaded, you can start preparing your microSD card to work with the Pi, and install NOOBS. You can't just copy the file you downloaded, you need to prepare the memory card in a specific way.

Insert your microSD card into your computer (using a suitable USB
converter if required). You need to wipe this memory card to use it with the
Pi, so make sure there's nothing you need left on it.

The easiest way to get NOOBS onto your memory card (and format it)
is to use a tool called **AplePi-Baker**. This free Mac utility handles all the
hard work for you. Get started by downloading ApplePi-Baker v2 from
`www.tweaking4all.com/hardware/raspberry-pi/applepi-baker-v2/`.
Click your downloaded **.dmg** image file to mount it on your desktop, and
then drag **AplePi-Baker** to your **Applications** folder using the finder
dialog window – shown in Figure 5-3.

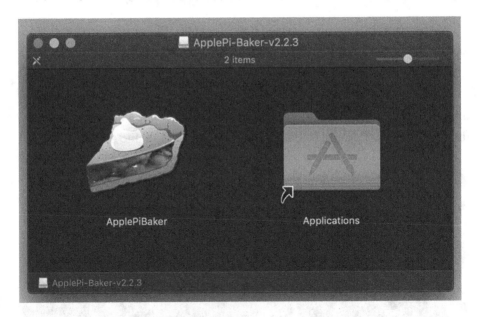

***Figure 5-3.** AplePi-Baker installation on macOS*

Go ahead and choose **Open** if macOS asks you to confirm you want to
run this file (for security reasons) – shown in Figure 5-4. Now macOS will
prompt you to enter your password – this is needed so ApplePi-Baker can
install a helper tool to read and write drives. You'll only need to do this the
first time you run AplePi-Baker.

Figure 5-4. *macOS security confirmation for ApplePiBaker*

If you're running macOS Catalina, then make sure you have all the latest operating system updates. A bug in an early version of Catalina prevents this tool from working. Newer versions of Catalina have subsequently fixed this issue.

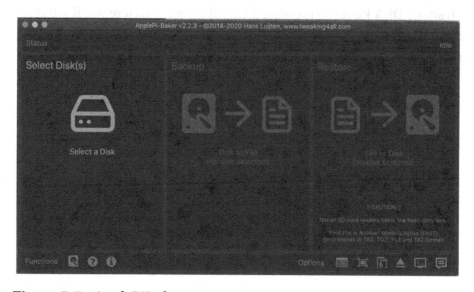

Figure 5-5. *ApplePiBaker main screen*

AplePi-Baker has a gorgeous user interface, which you can see in Figure 5-5. It supports a huge number of options, but for this project, you will use it to restore an image onto your memory card. This process will use your **NOOBS** file, and copy it to your memory card in a way that the Pi can boot and read from it.

Warning   Installing NOOBS and using ApplePi-Baker will delete ALL existing data on your memory card. Ensure you are using the correct memory card, and there is no data present you still need before proceeding.

From the left-hand side of ApplePi-Baker, under **Select Disk(s)**, click in this box and select the memory card you want to install NOOBS onto. At the very bottom left of ApplePiBaker is a **Functions** bar. Open the **Advanced Disk Panel** by pressing the hard drive icon. Here you'll see your selected memory card appear in a list on the right of ApplePiBaker. **Right-click** your memory card, and then select **Prepare Disk for NOOBS use** (Figure 5-6). This will format your memory card ready for the Pi to use.

Figure 5-6. *AplePiBaker preparing disk for NOOBS use*

The **Status** bar at the top of AplePi-Baker shows the current progress of this command, and when completed, you'll see a green **completed** message, shown in Figure 5-7. This process shouldn't take very long – less than a minute on a modern computer.

Figure 5-7. *AplePiBaker completed NOOBS preparation*

You can now close AplePi-Baker. Your memory card is formatted for use by the Pi, but it doesn't have any files on it yet. Open the memory card in **finder** (now called **RASPBERRY**). Copy the entire contents of your extracted NOOBS files to the root level of your memory card.

Your NOOBS files may be contained within a folder. Don't copy this folder; copy everything inside it, such that your memory card folder structure looks something like this:

```
RASPBERRY
     OS/
     bcm2708-rpi-b-plus.dtb
     . . .
```

Your specific files may vary depending on your version of NOOBS. When the process finishes, **unmount** your drive either by dragging it to the trash or by right-clicking and choosing **unmount**. You're now ready to get the Pi side of this project running!

Boot the Pi for the First Time

Begin by connecting the power supply to your Pi (but don't turn on the power just yet). Connect your display with the micro-HDMI to full-size HDMI cable. The Pi has two HDMI outputs, so use **HDMI0** – the one closest to the power input. Connect a USB keyboard and install your memory card. The memory card will only fit in one way – with the logo facing away from the board, which you can see in Figure 5-8. This card will appear "upside down" when the Pi is sitting the correct way up on your desk. You don't need a mouse at this stage (although one will work if you connect it).

Figure 5-8. *Underside of Pi 4 showing microSD memory card installed*

Note   Remember to always hold the Pi at the edges of the board as far as possible. Try to avoid touching the sensitive components directly, and never use it (without a case) on a conductive surface, as you may cause a short-circuit.

When you're ready, turn on the Pi by switching on the main power supply. After the Pi boots, you'll see the NOOBS main menu. Choose your language with the **L** key and your keyboard layout with the **9** key. Navigate within these submenus using the arrow keys and your enter key.

From this initial menu screen, choose **Raspbian Full [RECOMMENDED]** and then press **i** to start the installation (Figure 5-9). Confirm you really do want to install Raspbian. Now you can sit back and relax while the Pi does all the hard work of installing and configuring

Raspbian. You'll see a status bar at the bottom of the screen, and various mini-adverts and useful facts will cycle through while this happens.

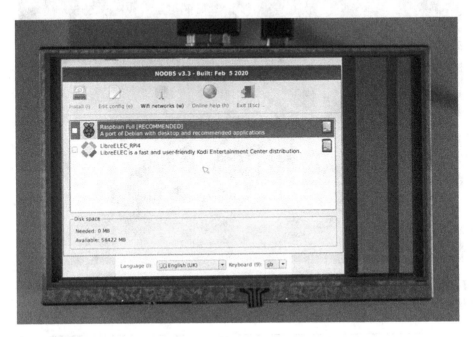

Figure 5-9. *NOOBS main installation screen*

Installation of Raspbian typically takes 20–30 minutes on the Pi 4 (although this will take longer on older models). Once installed, choose **OK** when the Pi confirms it has installed Raspbian, and wait for it to reboot.

By default, your Pi will boot into a graphical interface. You'll still use the command line for much of your configuration, but you may find it easier to connect a mouse now. Follow the introductory message and set your language preferences – shown in Figure 5-10. After setting your language preferences, follow the onscreen prompt to set your password. Right now, the default username and password on your Pi are "pi" and "raspberry". It's recommended to change these to prevent anyone accessing your Pi without your permission – either in-person or remotely.

Figure 5-10. *Pi desktop first launch screen*

Next, choose your screen options, and then move on to your Wi-Fi configuration. Choose your network and enter the password (if required). This screen is shown in Figure 5-11. You need an Internet connection to configure most of this project. Finally, perform a software update by choosing **Next** on the software update configuration page. This process may take a while (depending on the age of your NOOBS image). Anywhere from 20 minutes to two hours is not unusual. Once updated, restart your Pi by choosing **Restart** from the final screen of the introductory landing page.

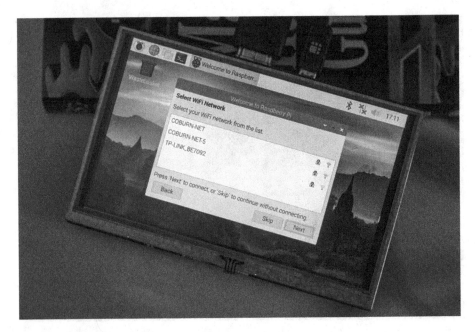

Figure 5-11. Pi first launch Wi-Fi configuration screen

Configure SSH

Now you have a working Pi; let's configure it so you can access it remotely over the command line. This lets you tinker with the Pi from your desktop computer remotely and makes it easy to write code, deploy, and then configure the Pi all from the same computer. Feel free to skip this step if you'd rather stay within the confines of the Pi itself, but remote access is a very valuable feature to have.

SSH (secure shell) is the best tool to do this. It's an encrypted protocol to communicate between a client and a server. In this project, the Pi is acting as the server, and your computer is the client. Stand-alone SSH client tools exist, but you'll use the Mac Terminal for all of these operations.

Start with the Pi itself. You need to determine the IP address of the Pi. IP addresses are like ZIP codes for computers (although they can and do often change). An *external* IP address is one used to identify your device on the Internet. You don't need one of these for the Pi unless you want to remotely tinker with it from another location. An *internal* IP address is one used only by your home network. What often happens is every device on your network gets an internal IP address, and when they reach out to the public Internet, they use the external IP address assigned to your router. You could have dozens of devices on your network, each with their own internal IP address, but all may share the same external IP address.

Open the Pi's command line by choosing the **Terminal** icon on the top left of your desktop. Use the **ifconfig** command to retrieve all the network information for your Pi – shown in Figure 5-12:

```
ifconfig
```

Figure 5-12. Output of ifconfig network command

This tool is a network administrator tool for the command line, and it's included with Raspbian. If you connected to your network over Wi-Fi, look for the **wlan0** section in the output from ifconfig. The **inet** section lists the IP address assigned to the Pi. This consists of four blocks of numbers, and will begin with the numbers **192.168**. This is the Pi's internal IP address, so it's only unique within your home network. For me, the **wlan0** section produces the following output:

```
wlan0: flags=4163<UP,BROADCAST,RUNNING,MULTICAST>  mtu 1500
        inet 192.168.1.210  netmask 255.255.255.0  broadcast
        192.168.1.255
        inet6 fe80::d2f8:a87e:49e1:6a7e  prefixlen 64  scopeid
        0x20<link>
        inet6 fd4c:fb45:dc0c:a800:c1a6:2335:ed4c:2
        ca7  prefixlen 64  scopeid 0x0
```

Within that, you can see my Pi's internal IP address is listed next to the words **inet**:

```
inet 192.168.1.210
```

Your IP address will vary, but it will begin with **192.168**. Back on your Mac, open a new terminal and use the **ping** command to send several packets to the Pi via its IP address (making sure to use your Pi's internal IP address):

```
ping 192.168.1.210
```

Ping is a tool used to test a network or network device. It sends a simple message to the IP address, and expects an explicit reply. It's a simple tool and is perfect to check everything is working on a network. You can see several ping replies in Figure 5-13. All being well, you should see a reply consisting of the payload size, duration, and some other information. Press **Ctrl+C** to stop pinging.

```
64 bytes from 192.168.1.210: icmp_seq=3 ttl=64 time=2.807 ms
64 bytes from 192.168.1.210: icmp_seq=4 ttl=64 time=521.919 ms
64 bytes from 192.168.1.210: icmp_seq=5 ttl=64 time=36.497 ms
64 bytes from 192.168.1.210: icmp_seq=6 ttl=64 time=91.413 ms
64 bytes from 192.168.1.210: icmp_seq=7 ttl=64 time=2.996 ms
64 bytes from 192.168.1.210: icmp_seq=8 ttl=64 time=1.980 ms
64 bytes from 192.168.1.210: icmp_seq=9 ttl=64 time=2.853 ms
64 bytes from 192.168.1.210: icmp_seq=10 ttl=64 time=4.472 ms
64 bytes from 192.168.1.210: icmp_seq=11 ttl=64 time=2.008 ms
64 bytes from 192.168.1.210: icmp_seq=12 ttl=64 time=2.817 ms
64 bytes from 192.168.1.210: icmp_seq=13 ttl=64 time=1.944 ms
64 bytes from 192.168.1.210: icmp_seq=14 ttl=64 time=1.721 ms
64 bytes from 192.168.1.210: icmp_seq=15 ttl=64 time=7.056 ms
64 bytes from 192.168.1.210: icmp_seq=16 ttl=64 time=2.944 ms
64 bytes from 192.168.1.210: icmp_seq=17 ttl=64 time=3.523 ms
64 bytes from 192.168.1.210: icmp_seq=18 ttl=64 time=2.780 ms
64 bytes from 192.168.1.210: icmp_seq=19 ttl=64 time=2.990 ms
64 bytes from 192.168.1.210: icmp_seq=20 ttl=64 time=3.080 ms
64 bytes from 192.168.1.210: icmp_seq=21 ttl=64 time=2.893 ms
```

Figure 5-13. *Result of a network ping to the Pi*

Keep this Pi's IP address safe for now. It might change over time, but it's unlikely to change while you're still using it. Back on the Pi, let's configure SSH.

Choose the **Preferences** menu option found by clicking the Raspberry on the top left of the screen. Head over to the **Interfaces** tab, and press **enable** under the **SSH** entry. Choose **OK** to finish the process. That's it. SSH is enabled on your Pi. It's possible to configure SSH using the command line, but until you have SSH access, it's easier to use the Pi's GUI for now.

Back on your Mac, you can now connect to your Pi in the Terminal using the **SSH** command, followed by a username and IP address:

```
ssh pi@192.168.1.210
```

Make sure you swap the IP address here for your Pi's IP address, which you previously noted down. You'll need to confirm the *ECDSA fingerprint* of the Pi. This is a calculated string of characters, which let you know the remote server really is what you think it is – as shown in Figure 5-14. Should this change the next time you connect, your Mac will flag this up to you. Enter **yes** when prompted to accept this first fingerprint. Enter your Pi's password to finish connecting.

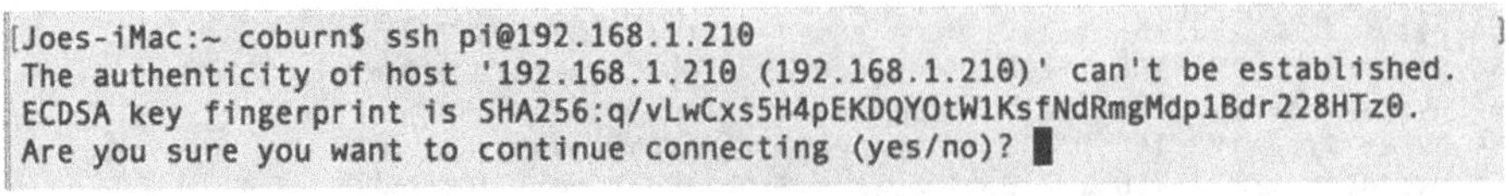

```
[Joes-iMac:~ coburn$ ssh pi@192.168.1.210
 The authenticity of host '192.168.1.210 (192.168.1.210)' can't be established.
 ECDSA key fingerprint is SHA256:q/vLwCxs5H4pEKDQYOtW1KsfNdRmgMdp1Bdr228HTz0.
 Are you sure you want to continue connecting (yes/no)? ▮
```

Figure 5-14. *First time SSH connection to the Pi verification message*

To remind you that you are connected to a remote server, the words at the start of your shell session have changed from your Mac username and computer name:

```
Joes-iMac:~ coburn$
```

to the Pi's username:

```
pi@raspberrypi:~ $
```

This is a helpful reminder that you are working on a remote system, shown in Figure 5-15.

```
pi@raspberrypi:~ $ ▮
```

Figure 5-15. *Bash SSH reminder*

Pi Python Setup

If you remember back to Chapter 4 where you had to configure Python on your computer, the same thing needs to happen on the Pi. If you look at the Python version:

```
python --version
```

this returns something like:

```
Python 2.7.16
```

As this project is developed using Python 3, you need to install a newer version of Python. These steps are explained in detail in the previous chapter, so the following commands are provided with minimal explanation except where the Pi differs from your computer. Start by installing **pyenv** directly from its repo (along with various supporting tools):

```
sudo apt-get install bzip2 libbz2-dev libreadline6
libreadline6-dev libffi-dev libssl1.0-dev sqlite3 libsqlite3-
dev -y
git clone https://github.com/pyenv/pyenv .pyenv
echo 'export PYENV_ROOT="$HOME/.pyenv"' >> ~/.bashrc
echo 'export PATH="$PYENV_ROOT/bin:$PATH"' >> ~/.bashrc
echo 'eval "$(pyenv init -)"' >> ~/.bashrc
. ~/.bashrc
```

The **apt-get** command is used to update and install packages. **Sudo** is used to run these commands with a higher security clearance for your user. The **.bashrc** file is a bash config file – this is the same as *.zshrc* or *.bash_profile* on your Mac.

```
Collecting filelock<4,>=3.0.0 (from virtualenv->pipenv)
  Downloading https://files.pythonhosted.org/packages/93/83/71a2ee6158bb9f39a90c
0dea1637f81d5eef866e188e1971a1b1ab01a35a/filelock-3.0.12-py3-none-any.whl
Collecting six<2,>=1.9.0 (from virtualenv->pipenv)
  Downloading https://files.pythonhosted.org/packages/65/eb/1f97cb97bfc2390a2769
69c6fae16075da282f5058082d4cb10c6c5c1dba/six-1.14.0-py2.py3-none-any.whl
Collecting appdirs<2,>=1.4.3 (from virtualenv->pipenv)
  Downloading https://files.pythonhosted.org/packages/56/eb/810e700ed1349edde4cb
dc1b2a21e28cdf115f9faf263f6bbf8447c1abf3/appdirs-1.4.3-py2.py3-none-any.whl
Collecting distlib<1,>=0.3.0 (from virtualenv->pipenv)
  Downloading https://www.piwheels.org/simple/distlib/distlib-0.3.0-py3-none-any
.whl (340kB)
    |████████████████████████████████| 348kB 873kB/s
Collecting zipp>=0.5 (from importlib-metadata<2,>=0.12; python_version < "3.8"->
virtualenv->pipenv)
```

Figure 5-16. *Python 3 installation sample output*

If possible, try to install the same Python version as your computer uses (this may take a long time to complete) – you can see a sample output of this command in Figure 5-16:

```
pyenv install 3.7.6
```

Now configure Python, install **Pipenv**, and upgrade **Pip**:

```
pyenv global 3.7.6
sudo pip install pipenv
sudo pip install --upgrade pip
```

Finally, check your Python version:

```
python --version
```

All being well, this should return Python 3:

```
Python 3.7.6
```

Cloning the Repository

Now that you have Python installed, it's time to get your code on the Pi. There are two approaches here. If you want to share your code with other developers, then you could publish a package on https://pypi.org/. This would let you install your code with Pip or Pipenv. For this project, you won't need a custom PyPI package. The Pi will pull the code from your repository.

To start, check your current Terminal location with **pwd**:

```
pwd
```

This should output your home folder:

```
/home/pi
```

This folder is a good place to store your code, so if you're not there, navigate to it with the **cd** command:

```
cd /home/pi
```

If you list the current directory (shown in Figure 5-17), you can see the various user files and folders that already exist in this folder:

```
ls
```

Alternatively, you can see further information about these files with the **-lah** flags:

```
ls -lah
```

```
[pi@raspberrypi:~ $ pwd
/home/pi
[pi@raspberrypi:~ $ ls
Desktop    Downloads   Music     Public   Templates
Documents  MagPi       Pictures  pyenv    Videos
[pi@raspberrypi:~ $ ls -lah
total 96K
drwxr-xr-x 17 pi    pi    4.0K Feb 29 15:45 .
drwxr-xr-x  3 root  root  4.0K Feb 13 15:55 ..
-rw-------  1 pi    pi     971 Feb 29 15:44 .bash_history
-rw-r--r--  1 pi    pi     220 Feb 13 15:55 .bash_logout
-rw-r--r--  1 pi    pi    3.6K Feb 29 15:28 .bashrc
drwxr-xr-x  6 pi    pi    4.0K Feb 29 15:20 .cache
drwx------  4 pi    pi    4.0K Feb 29 14:45 .config
drwxr-xr-x  2 pi    pi    4.0K Feb 13 16:31 Desktop
drwxr-xr-x  2 pi    pi    4.0K Feb 13 16:31 Documents
drwxr-xr-x  2 pi    pi    4.0K Feb 13 16:31 Downloads
drwx------  3 pi    pi    4.0K Feb 13 16:31 .gnupg
drwxr-xr-x  4 pi    pi    4.0K Feb 29 15:20 .local
drwxr-xr-x  2 pi    pi    4.0K Feb 13 16:03 MagPi
drwxr-xr-x  2 pi    pi    4.0K Feb 13 16:31 Music
drwxr-xr-x  2 pi    pi    4.0K Feb 13 16:31 Pictures
-rw-r--r--  1 pi    pi     807 Feb 13 15:55 .profile
drwxr-xr-x  2 pi    pi    4.0K Feb 13 16:31 Public
drwxr-xr-x 13 pi    pi    4.0K Feb 29 15:40 .pyenv
drwxr-xr-x 11 pi    pi    4.0K Feb 29 15:28 pyenv
drwxr-xr-x  2 pi    pi    4.0K Feb 13 16:31 Templates
drwxr-xr-x  2 pi    pi    4.0K Feb 13 16:31 Videos
-rw-------  1 pi    pi      56 Feb 29 15:45 .Xauthority
-rw-------  1 pi    pi    2.4K Feb 29 15:45 .xsession-errors
-rw-------  1 pi    pi    2.4K Feb 29 14:31 .xsession-errors.old
pi@raspberrypi:~ $
```

Figure 5-17. *Contents of the Pi's filesystem at /home/pi/*

Navigate into the **Documents** folder with **cd** (Linux is case sensitive):

```
cd Documents
```

Now **clone** the code base. You don't need to create a folder – Git will do this for you. Swap out the repository URL for your GitHub repository – shown in Figure 5-18:

```
git clone https://github.com/CoburnJoe/Pi-Car
```

```
[pi@raspberrypi:~/Documents $ git clone https://github.com/CoburnJoe/Pi-Car
Cloning into 'Pi-Car'...
remote: Enumerating objects: 116, done.
remote: Counting objects: 100% (116/116), done.
remote: Compressing objects: 100% (64/64), done.
remote: Total 116 (delta 39), reused 79 (delta 19), pack-reused 0
Receiving objects: 100% (116/116), 20.65 KiB | 729.00 KiB/s, done.
Resolving deltas: 100% (39/39), done.
pi@raspberrypi:~/Documents $ ▊
```

Figure 5-18. *Cloning the project's Git repository*

Verify the clone by creating a virtual environment (Figure 5-19) and running the tests:

```
cd Pi-Car/
pipenv install --dev --pre
pipenv shell
export PYTHONPATH="$PWD"
pytest tests
```

```
[pi@raspberrypi:~/Documents/Pi-Car $ pipenv install --dev --pre
Creating a virtualenv for this project…
Pipfile: /home/pi/Documents/Pi-Car/Pipfile
Using /home/pi/.pyenv/versions/3.7.6/bin/python3.7m (3.7.6) to create virtualenv…
! Creating virtual environment...created virtual environment CPython3.7.6.final.0-32 in 1130ms
  creator CPython3Posix(dest=/home/pi/.local/share/virtualenvs/Pi-Car-1r8PINZ3, clear=False, global=False)
  seeder FromAppData(download=False, pip=latest, setuptools=latest, wheel=latest, via=copy, app_data_dir=/home/pi/.lo
cal/share/virtualenv/seed-app-data/v1)
  activators BashActivator,CShellActivator,FishActivator,PowerShellActivator,PythonActivator,XonshActivator

✔ Successfully created virtual environment!
Virtualenv location: /home/pi/.local/share/virtualenvs/Pi-Car-1r8PINZ3
Installing dependencies from Pipfile.lock (c063cf)…
  ⟳ ▊▊▊▊▊▊▊▊▊                15/23 —
```

Figure 5-19. *Installing project dependencies with Pipenv*

Go ahead and deactivate the environment and traverse up a level:

```
exit
cd ../
```

You now have your code on your Pi, and it works! The next step is a way to update the code. You don't want to manually remote in and pull the latest code every time you make a change.

Keeping Code Updated

All of these methods of getting the code onto your Pi rely on some kind of Git command to perform the work. Here's how to write a script to do this for you, which you can then run whenever you'd like to update the Pi's code.

Back on your desktop computer, create a bash file at the top level of your project folder and call it **clone.sh**:

```
touch clone.sh
```

This script will handle all aspects of pulling the latest code from Git. You don't have to add it to your repo if you'd prefer not to – it can live on the Pi, no problem. Here's the code you need:

```
#!/bin/bash
# Update to the latest code
git checkout master && git pull
```

You can see this combines two Git commands, but what's that confusing first line? This convention lets your shell know what this script is. It tells your shell that this is a bash script, with a helpful link to bash on the machine itself. This could be a Python interpreter, or almost anything else, depending on your code. This file would not work without this.

Hashes are used to denote comments, and here you can see a helpful note left to future you, should you revisit this script in the future and wonder as to its purpose.

Save this file, and head back to your terminal. Run it like this:

```
./clone.sh
```

What do you notice? On most computers, you won't have permission to execute the script, and your shell will complain with a message like this:

```
bash: ./clone.sh: Permission denied
```

Use the **ls** command to check file permissions:

```
ls -lah clone.sh
```

which returns the file permissions and ownership of the file:

```
-rw-r--r--  1 coburn  staff    72B Mar  9 19:15 clone.sh
```

There are lots of information presented here, but the most important right now is displayed on the left. This information outlines the read, write, and execute permissions for this file, both for you as the owner and for any other users of your computer:

```
-rw-r--r--
```

Each character here represents some different information about your file. I won't go into the specifics and fine-grained control you have available here. For now, all you need to know is that you only have read and write access to your newly created file – your computer won't let you run it. Change the permissions with the **chmod** command:

```
chmod 775 clone.sh
```

This changes the file permissions. It lets you have read, write, and execute permissions (denoted by the number 7), and it assigns anyone else read and write permissions only (the number 5). If you'd like to learn more about Linux file permissions, then visit *Bri Hatch's* article in "Hacking Linux Exposed": `www.hackinglinuxexposed.com/articles/20030417.html`. Check your permissions again with **ls** and notice how they have changed:

```
-rwxr-xr-x  1 coburn  staff    72B Mar  9 19:16 clone.sh
```

Execute your file again, and you'll see it pull the latest code from Git:

```
./clone.sh
```

Commit your code, and head over to your Pi's terminal. Perform a manual pull, relishing in the fact that this may be the last time you have to do so:

```
git checkout master && git pull
```

Now run your script:

```
./clone.sh
```

Using this bash script, your Pi can update its code base from the master branch. Whenever you'd like to get the latest version of the code onto your Pi, simply run this command. Next you'll use this script to automatically update the code base as part of a wider first-boot installation sequence.

Chapter Summary

This chapter equipped you and your Pi with everything needed to run the Python code for this project. Not only did you install an operating system to the Pi, but you installed Python 3.7 and installed your project dependencies into a virtual environment. You configured SSH and created an update script. You can now remotely access your Pi over your local network and update the code to the head of the master branch from your repository.

The next chapter introduces the code Python module Flask. This open source package provides the core web application routing and logic on which you'll build your application.

CHAPTER 6

Getting Started with Flask

Chapter goal: Get Flask running on your computer. Learn the basics of Flask. Run Flask on the Pi and get it to autostart your application when it boots.

As you learned back in Chapter 4, Flask is a Python microframework – but what does that mean? Essentially, Flask is a web application framework. It makes it easy for you to develop and run complex web applications. Using Flask, you can write Python and have it executed when someone visits your web page. The Flask project resides at https://flask.palletsprojects.com/. It's open source and available on GitHub at https://github.com/pallets/flask. You can create a login and user registration system, web admin panel, student management system, COVID-19 tracker, basic CRUD (create, read, upload, delete) system, or almost anything else you can imagine.

Flask has no opinion. It won't force you to use specific databases or code patterns – it leaves those choices up to you. If you'd like to avoid the decision-making process, Django (www.djangoproject.com/) is a Python framework with an opinion, but this book is based on Flask, and I'll guide you through every step of the way.

© Joseph Coburn 2020
J. Coburn, *Build Your Own Car Dashboard with a Raspberry Pi*,
https://doi.org/10.1007/978-1-4842-6080-7_6

Flask is maintained by an organization called Pallets (`https://palletsprojects.com/`), and if you visit their GitHub profile at `https://github.com/pallets`, you'll see a vast number of exceedingly popular projects. I can personally attest to the usefulness and quality of Python code available from Pallets, and count myself fortunate to contribute to Flask-SQLAlchemy (`https://github.com/pallets/flask-sqlalchemy`). Anyway, I digress.

First Flask Config

Flask is already included in your project. In Chapter 4 you included the source code in your Pipfile. Flask is very simple to use. Begin by navigating to your top-level **Pi-Car** folder in your Terminal, and creating these files and folders:

```
mkdir Pi_Car
cd Pi_Car
mkdir config
touch config/__init__.py
touch config/local_config.py
touch __init__.py
touch app.py
```

Note   By now you should be comfortable with Git and be able to format your code with Black. If you need a reminder, take a look at the Git cheat sheet at the end of Chapter 4. The rest of this book won't explicitly remind you to format and commit your code – remember to do so on a regular basis! A good rule of thumb is any time you have a significant change or working state, or when you're taking a break or have finished coding for the day, commit your work. It's OK to commit broken or incomplete code to feature branches (rarely to master).

There are only two main files here – everything else is either a folder or a Python init. The **local_config.py** file located inside the **config** folder is where you'll store your application configuration. Later on you'll access configurations here from any file in your project. It's a centralized place to store project settings. If you want to change a setting, it's much easier to modify it in one central place, rather than digging through the whole code base and making potentially hundreds of changes. Here's the code you need to get started:

```
# LOCAL DEVELOPMENT CONFIG FILE
# https://flask.palletsprojects.com/en/1.1.x/config/

# Flask-specific values
TESTING = True
APPLICATION_ROOT = "/"
PREFERRED_URL_SCHEME = "http"

# Custom values
# Possible logging levels:
# CRITICAL - FATAL - ERROR - WARNING - INFO - DEBUG - NOTSET
LOGGER_LEVEL = "DEBUG"
LOG_FILE_NAME = "pi-car.log"
```

This config file is a Python file. You can write complex logic in here, but it's best to avoid doing so. You can freely assign, create, delete, or otherwise modify these values. As you can see, there's a mixture of Booleans, strings, and comments. There's nothing special about this code, but it is used to modify the state of the application. Each variable is written in uppercase. This naming convention indicates that these variables are constants – they won't (or should not) change during the execution of the code. On its own this config does nothing. It's only when implemented by your code in other files that they begin to provide value. Here's the breakdown of what each one does.

The **Flask-specific values** section contains configurations for Flask itself. These settings are read by Flask and used to change its behavior. The **TESTING** variable exists to make your life easier as a developer and make your application more secure (when not set). You may not want to use these on a production server, but on your Pi (for personal use), and while developing the code this is fine.

The **APPLICATION_ROUTE** informs Flask where your code lives relative to the folder Flask is running from. The **PREFERRED_URL_SCHEME** tells Flask to use a secure or insecure Hypertext Transfer Protocol – HTTP or HTTPS. Encrypting your application traffic and generating an SSL or TLS certificate is possible locally, but it's not required unless you want to run your code on the Internet. You can learn more about all the possible Flask config options at `https://flask.palletsprojects.com/en/1.1.x/config/`, but these are enough for you to get started.

Cryptographic protocols SSL and TLS exist to establish an encrypted connection between you and the server hosting the website you want to visit. They ensure that any data sent between you and a website is encrypted and not visible to anyone else. These protocols are used by your bank, or websites with a padlock in the URL bar, but a time is coming in the not-too-distant future whereby every website you visit will use some form of encryption. SSL stands for *secure sockets layer*, and TLS stands for *transport layer security*. TLS is the successor to SSL.

The **custom values** section is where you'll find configurations specific to your application. These values won't interfere with Flask itself, and you'll need to explicitly write your code to handle these. **LOGGER_LEVEL** is used to increase or reduce the verbosity of the application logs – which you'll learn about in the following pages. **LOG_FILE_NAME** defines the name of the file to record these logs to. You'll expand on this config file as you develop more code.

The **app.py** file is where the main Flask initialization happens. Here is where you tell Flask how to work. You'll configure different URL routes, logging, security, and much more. It's the central nervous system of your app. This doesn't mean you can smash all your code in here, however. As you'll learn later on, there are ways to split this code into other files to keep it neat and follow OOP practices. For now, the starting code is fine to live here. Here's the code you need to get started:

```python
import logging

from flask import Flask
from logging.handlers import RotatingFileHandler

def create_app(config_file="config/local_config.py"):
    app = Flask(__name__)  # Initialize app
    app.config.from_pyfile(config_file, silent=False)  # Read
    in config from file

    # Configure file-based log handler
    log_file_handler = RotatingFileHandler(
        filename=app.config.get("LOG_FILE_NAME",
        "config/pi-car.log"),
        maxBytes=10000000,
        backupCount=4,
    )
    log_file_handler.setFormatter(
        logging.Formatter("[%(asctime)s] %(levelname)s in
        %(module)s: %(message)s")
    )
    app.logger.addHandler(log_file_handler)
    app.logger.setLevel(app.config.get("LOGGER_LEVEL", "ERROR"))
    app.logger.info("----- STARTING APP ------")
```

```python
@app.route("/")
def hello_world():
    app.logger.info("Running first route")
    return "Hello, World!"

    app.logger.info("----- FINISHED STARTING APP -----")

    return app
```

This may look like a lot of code, but taken one line at a time, it's not as scary as it looks. Let's jump right in. Start by importing some modules:

```python
import logging

from flask import Flask
from logging.handlers import RotatingFileHandler
```

Imports are Python's way of reusing code. Files you want to import are called *modules*, but really they are just folders. You can import a whole module, or smaller sections, and from subfolders. You can import your own code, or code written by other people. All of these imports (so far) are using modules installed previously by *Pipenv*. If Python can't find a module to import, it will complain by raising an error – otherwise known as *throwing an error*, or *throwing an exception*. You can write code to handle errors, but I'll cover that when required.

Next, create a function called **create_app**. This is an application factory, which is a fancy way of saying it is in charge of building the Flask application. Functions (sometimes called *methods*) are blocks of code neatly bundled together with a useful name. They let you recycle code by bunching specific code together. Ideally, functions should not be too long, and should perform one task. You'll refactor this function later as your code grows. Here's the first line:

```python
def create_app(config_file="config/local_config.py"):
```

The keyword **def** lets Python know you'd like to create a new function, and that everything following the keyword is the function. After **def** comes the function name – **create_app** in this case. Python naming convention for functions is all lowercase, with underscores between words.

Next up are your *parameters*. These let you pass data to functions when they are used. This data is accessible inside the function. Using parameters like this lets you change the data every time you use your code. If you don't need to use different data, or your function can "figure out" what it needs, you don't need to use parameters. This function has one parameter called **config_file**. It has a default value of **config/local_config.py**. If you don't provide this parameter, the default value is used instead. Default values are optional – if you don't specify one, your code will crash if you don't supply the parameter. This config file is used inside this function to point your code to your config. It's common to change configs depending on your environment – production, on your computer, on the Pi, and so on.

Finally, the colon indicates the end of the function configuration, and that everything that follows is the function's code. Python uses indentation to assign code to different objects, so ensure everything inside the function lines up.

Here's the first line of code inside the **create_app** function:

```
app = Flask(__name__)  # Initialize app
```

This creates a variable called **app** and instantiates it as a **Flask** object. You can see a **comment** following it – denoted by the hash sign at the start. Comments are ignored by the Python interpreter, and exist to help you and other developers in the future when revisiting code. Comments should be clean and clear – don't just copy what the code does. The comments in these examples are more verbose than may typically be desirable, to really help you out in your understanding.

Before going any further, let's really dig into what this line does. If you think back to Chapter 2 – the software development primer, you learned about object-oriented programming and how classes are really just recipes

which define how a piece of code should work. Here, **Flask** is a class –
and it follows the class naming guidelines of *Pascal Case*. Pascal Case is
where the first letter of every word is uppercase, and the rest of the letters
are lowercase. This Flask class defines how code should work and what
it should do as designed by the Pallets team when creating Flask itself.
Therefore, **app** is a new instance of the **Flask** class.

The parameter __**name**__ is passed to the class. In Flask, this is a
parameter called *import_name*. You don't have to specify this when using
classes or functions – but you can if you'd like to:

```
app = Flask(import_name=__name__)  # Initialize app
```

This **import_name** lets Flask know where the application is running,
relative to your code base. It lets Flask figure out where to find all of its
other code. In Python, __**name**__ is a special variable. This evaluates to
the name of the current module – **Pi-Car.Pi_Car.app** in this file, which
represents the file name, the folder name, and the parent directory
name. Special variables in Python begin and end with *dunder* – double
underscores for both the prefix and suffix.

Next, configure your Flask application by pointing it to the config file
you created previously:

```
app.config.from_pyfile(config_file, silent=False)  # Read in
config from file
```

Notice how the **config_file** variable is passed in here – you defined
this in your function definition, and as of right now, it references the file
in **config/local_config.py**. This helpful function loads all of your config
variables into your Flask app. Any changes you make to the config will get
automatically picked up by Flask whenever you restart the application. The
silent parameter instructs Flask to raise errors if that file does not exist. As
you only have one config file right now, it's a good idea to leave this set to
False. If you wanted to use an optional config file – one which may or may

not exist, then setting **silent** to **True** is a good way to handle this. When true, Flask will happily keep working, even if it can't find the config file.

The next chunk of code handles application logging. Before discussing this, let's look at what logging is and why it's so important.

Logs let you record information during the execution of an application. Essentially they are just messages to yourself, written to aid you during development and deployment. They are an essential metric and provide much-needed visibility into the state of your application.

Logs are often divided into logging levels. Each log is classified into a group depending on its relevance or severity. When looking at logs at a later stage, it's possible to filter these so as to see only the most relevant results. It's also possible to limit the creation of logs based on their level. This is defined in your config file as **LOGGER_LEVEL**.

Logger levels can vary slightly between projects and frameworks, but for the most part, they all work in the same way. Log levels operate in descending order of priority. If you set a log level, your application will output all logs of that level *or higher*. You'll always see logs deemed more important than the current log level, but anything less important will be hidden. From most important to least important, the logging levels available through Flask and this application are

- Critical

- Fatal

- Error

- Warning

- Info

- Debug

The **critical** level indicates there was a serious problem with the code – perhaps a config file or variable is not configured. This should be reserved for problems which prevent the application running at all, or very serious issues which need resolving right now. **Fatal** is very similar to critical (and in the Python core logging library, they are the same). Use fatal when you encounter a problem that cannot be corrected or recovered from in the code.

The **error** logging level is perhaps more common than most. Use this to indicate that a problem has occurred, but not one that prevents the whole application from working. This could be localized to a specific request or function or tied to a specific action. Other requests and functions may still work fine, just this one in particular may be impacted.

When working in a corporate environment, you may be fortunate enough to have an *operations* team, sometimes known as *DevOps* or *ops*. This team is responsible for running the infrastructure needed to execute your code. A good rule of thumb is that critical, fatal, or error levels should be serious enough to get your ops team out of bed, and will require some corrective action. Granted, this car project has far fewer people working on it, and an issue may not warrant immediate corrective action, but you can't fix what you don't know about, so use sensible logs and log levels at every opportunity.

The **warning** log level is much gentler, and often ignored. Use warning levels to indicate that something undesirable happened, or something is unavailable or inaccessible, but the application continues to operate just fine. Perhaps the code is designed to handle this bad condition – but you still want to know when it happens.

The **info** logging level is incredibly useful, but often one that is easy to abuse. This level should be used to inform about the state of the application. A good practice is to put info log statements at the start and end of every function execution. Info could perhaps be used by a nontechnical person to see that every step of a process is followed.

Finally, **debug** is a level that you can use for almost anything. If you want to know the state of a variable at a point in time, or if a particular code block is executed, use debug. Debug log levels exist to help you as a developer understand what is happening in your code, down to a very fine-grained level. You would not generally run applications at this level in production, as it can be too verbose. Occasionally is fine, when troubleshooting or deploying new systems, but when fully operational, a higher log level is often used. I once worked on a Python application where the server bill to store all the logs from running debug in production cost more than the whole application cost to run.

This application uses **log handlers** to output logs to both a file and the *standout output*, known as *stdout*, which is essentially your console. Log handlers are used to configure all kinds of logging settings. You can customize the format, file name, logging level, and more. By default, Flask logging has a log handler which outputs to the console. This is very useful, so let's leave this as is. Create a new file-based log handler, using the **RotatingFileHandler** class, previously imported from **logging.handlers**:

```
# Configure file-based log handler
log_file_handler = RotatingFileHandler(
    filename=app.config.get("LOG_FILE_NAME", "config/pi-car.log"),
    maxBytes=10000000,
    backupCount=4,
)
```

This rotating file handler records all your logs to a file. Once the file gets too large, it creates a new file. Once it reaches four new files, it goes back to the first file and starts again. The **file name** defines what to call the new files created for your logs. **maxBytes** is used to limit the maximum file size in bytes. 10MB is specified here. Finally, **backupCount** specifies the total number of log files to rotate around. Notice how these parameters are named using **CamelCase** – the first letter of every word is uppercase, apart from the first letter of the variable. This is not a Python convention, but as you'll come to find out, software developers all write code in different styles, based on their preferences.

Notice how the file name looks like this:

```
app.config.get("LOG_FILE_NAME", "config/pi-car.log")
```

This reads the config variable **LOG_FILE_NAME** defined in your config file and then loaded into the Flask config object. This is your first introduction to defensive programming. Throughout this application, you should ask yourself, "What happens if this piece of code fails?" In this case, what will happen if **LOG_FILE_NAME** does not exist in your config? **Config** is a dictionary object, and dictionaries support the **get** function. This function *safely* retrieves data from dictionaries. If **LOG_FILE_NAME** is not present in the config, **get** returns None instead of crashing your application. Alternatively, you can specify a default value to use if the **LOG_FILE_NAME** is not found. In summary, if you don't set **LOG_FILE_NAME** in your config, this code will fall back to using **config/pi-car.log**. This makes your code powerful and resilient to failure. It can error-correct itself to continue normal operation.

The alternative to the get function is accessing the dictionary by its key:

```
filename=["LOG_FILE_NAME"]
```

This will return the value defined in your config, but it will crash your application if this key does not exist in the config dictionary. Now this will raise a **KeyError**, which you could correct with a **try/catch** statement (Python's syntax uses the word **Except** here, but the terminology is **Catch**):

```
try:
    filename = ["LOG_FILE_NAME"]
except KeyError:
    filename = "config/pi-car.log"

log_file_handler = RotatingFileHandler(
    filename=filename
    ...
```

Try/catch statements are used liberally in Python (perhaps more so than other languages). This way of handling exceptions is fine in many cases, but in this particular case, it bloats the code when compared to using the **get** function.

This code is another important pattern to learn. If you anticipate errors may happen, wrap your code in a **try/catch** pattern. Any code inside the **try** will let you handle the errors inside the **except**. You can handle specific errors as shown earlier, or you can handle *any* error – although make sure you don't just wrap all your code in a massive try and catch any error. Specific error handling is far more useful than blindly catching all errors. If you want to assign the error itself to a variable, you can **alias** it:

```
try:
    filename = ["LOG_FILE_NAME"]
except KeyError as e:
    filename = "config/pi-car.log"
```

Now, **e** is a variable that contains more information about the problem. You can and should log this with a suitable message, but as you're still configuring the logs at this stage, you may not be able to read the logs yet. Finally, if you want to explicitly ignore an error, you can use the **pass** keyword:

```
try:
    filename = ["LOG_FILE_NAME"]
except KeyError:
    pass
```

A dictionary is an object used to store data in key/value pairs using curly braces. Here's a basic example:

```
my_dict = {
    "A": "Apples",
    "B": "Bananas",
}
```

Items on the left are the keys and items on the right are the values, and you can now access items by their key (and square brackets):

```
my_dict["A"]
```

This will return you the value of "Apples". As you learned about earlier, defensive programming with dictionaries is an excellent way to improve your code.

You can store any data in dictionaries, including complex objects or nested dictionaries.

Back to your log handler, you need to explicitly set the logging level in use by pulling the value out of your config file and using the **setLevel** function:

```
log_file_handler.setLevel(app.config.get("LOGGER_LEVEL", "ERROR"))
```

Notice how this defensively retrieves the config value, or defaults to **ERROR**.

Use the **setFormatter** function to define a format for your logs:

```
log_file_handler.setFormatter(
    logging.Formatter("[%(asctime)s] %(levelname)s in %(module)
    s: %(message)s")
)
```

This injects useful data into your logs, which makes them far more useful when reading at a later date – data such as the date and time they were produced, the log level, and the file they came from. Such a log entry may look like this:

```
[2020-04-04 11:26:38,333] INFO in app: Log message here...
```

Finally, you need to tell Flask about your new log handler, which is done with the **addHandler** function:

```
app.logger.addHandler(log_file_handler)
```

You're now ready to use logs all over your application! Here's how to log to the info level:

```
app.logger.info("----- STARTING APP ------")
```

Notice how you access the **info** attribute of the **logger** object in your app object. Because your app is an instance of the **Flask** class, you have access to **app.logger**, because Flask defined it in the class definition. This is what makes object-oriented code so powerful. The ability to reuse code (built by other people in many cases) can really speed up your development time. You don't need to defensively handle **app.logger** – you can *almost* always rely on functions being available – provided you are certain the object is what you think it is.

To log to the other log levels, replace **info** with the log level you want, all in lowercase:

```
app.logger.critical("This is a critical log message")
app.logger.fatal("This is a fatal log message")
app.logger.error("This is an error log message")
app.logger.warning("This is a warning log message")
app.logger.info("This is an info log message")
app.logger.debug("This is a debug log message")
```

Later on you'll learn how to log complex objects, but for now, play around with logging different messages to different log levels.

Here's the final piece of the Flask puzzle. **Routes** are a foundation of any web app, and Flask is no different. Routes let users and developers use memorable names in the URL, each one *routing* to a different piece of code. Flask needs to know which routes exist, so here's the code that handles this first route:

```
@app.route("/")
def hello_world():
    app.logger.info("Running first route")
    return "Hello, World!"
```

This defines a route accessible at "/". The function is called **hello_world**, but this has no impact on the URL. Inside, you can see some basic logging to the **info** level, and then it returns a string. In Flask, you must return something inside your routes – this is what is shown when you load this page in your browser.

You may be wondering what the **@** sign used for. In Python, this is a **decorator**. Decorators are ways of running functions, and are a common pattern in Python. This essentially provides **hello_world** as a parameter to the **route** function, which is defined in the Flask class, of which your app is an instance of. Decorators keep your code neat, but they can be difficult to write and get confusing when using multiple decorators on the same piece of code.

Finally, as the very last line of code in **create_app**, you need to return your app object:

```
return app
```

As this **create_app** function is an app factory, tasked with making Flask apps, it needs to return the newly built and configured app to whatever code requested it. Any code after this return statement will not run.

That's it for the Flask code. It may be slightly larger than the very core Flask code you need to get started, but you now have an app factory, which implements some very important logging and route functionality. You've learned some core concepts that you can carry with you to any project, and you are now ready to run your app!

From the terminal, make sure you're in a **Pipenv shell** from your top-level project folder (which for me is **Pi-Car**). Configure your environment by telling Flask where to find your app factory:

```
export FLASK_APP=Pi_Car.app
```

This line sets an environment variable called **FLASK_APP** with the value of **Pi_Car.app**. This is your subfolder and your Python file. The **.py** extension is not required. Flask will automatically read this environment variable and go and use your **create_app** function inside **app.py**. Optionally, configure the **FLASK_ENV** variable. Setting this to **development** makes Flask much easier to work with. Flask will monitor your code for any changes and reload the app if it detects any. It's not possible to configure this in your config file, as it needs setting before the app launches:

```
export FLASK_ENV=development
```

Now run your app:

```
flask run
```

Visit http://127.0.0.1:5000/ in your browser. You'll see your "Hello, World!" message on the page, and your console will fill up with your application logs (Figure 6-1)! You'll see several Flask messages about the environment, app name, and so on. You'll also see your application logs. Refresh the page and notice how more logs arrive.

```
(Pi-Car) bash-3.2$ flask run
 * Serving Flask app "Pi_Car.app"
 * Environment: production
   WARNING: This is a development server. Do not use it in a production deployment.
   Use a production WSGI server instead.
 * Debug mode: off
[2020-04-04 11:57:54,202] INFO in app: ------ STARTING APP ------
[2020-04-04 11:57:54,202] INFO in app: ------ FINISHED STARTING APP ------
 * Running on http://127.0.0.1:5000/ (Press CTRL+C to quit)
[2020-04-04 11:58:02,614] INFO in app: Running first route
127.0.0.1 - - [04/Apr/2020 11:58:02] "GET / HTTP/1.1" 200 -
```

Figure 6-1. *Output from running the Flask server*

Open the new **pi-car.log** file and you'll also see your application logs. The logs in your console are temporary and exist to help you out. When running on the Pi, you'll use this log file more often. You don't need to worry about storing this log file in Git – it's already ignored through the **.gitignore** template file GitHub created for you. You can see several sample logs in Figure 6-2. Well done! You are well on your way to becoming a Python expert!

```
[2020-04-04 11:03:05,167] INFO in app: ------ STARTING APP ------
[2020-04-04 11:03:05,167] INFO in app: ------ FINISHED STARTING APP ------
[2020-04-04 11:26:07,686] INFO in app: ------ STARTING APP ------
[2020-04-04 11:26:07,687] INFO in app: ------ FINISHED STARTING APP ------
[2020-04-04 11:26:16,954] INFO in app: ------ STARTING APP ------
[2020-04-04 11:26:16,954] INFO in app: ------ FINISHED STARTING APP ------
[2020-04-04 11:26:23,299] INFO in app: Running first route
[2020-04-04 11:26:31,126] INFO in app: Running first route
[2020-04-04 11:26:38,332] INFO in app: ------ STARTING APP ------
[2020-04-04 11:26:38,333] INFO in app: ------ FINISHED STARTING APP ------
[2020-04-04 11:26:39,479] INFO in app: Running first route
[2020-04-04 11:57:54,202] INFO in app: ------ STARTING APP ------
[2020-04-04 11:57:54,202] INFO in app: ------ FINISHED STARTING APP ------
[2020-04-04 11:58:02,614] INFO in app: Running first route
```

Figure 6-2. *First application logs*

Running Flask on the Pi

Now that you have a working application and know how to run Flask, let's get Flask running on the Pi and access it from your computer over your local network. The start of this process is very similar to running Flask on your computer. You need to get the latest code onto the Pi and boot the server. Start by connecting to your Pi over SSH and navigate to the root project directory:

```
cd Documents/Pi-Car
```

Now use your update script to pull the latest code from the master branch:

```
./clone.sh
```

After updating, start a Pipenv shell:

```
pipenv shell
```

Finally, configure the environment and start the server – Figure 6-3 shows the sample output:

```
export FLASK_APP=Pi_Car.app
flask run
```

Notice the IP address Flask is running on:

```
* Running on http://127.0.0.1:5000/ (Press Ctrl+C to quit)
```

```
(Pi-Car) pi@raspberrypi:~/Documents/Pi-Car $ flask run
 * Serving Flask app "Pi_Car.app"
 * Environment: production
   WARNING: This is a development server. Do not use it in a production deployment.
   Use a production WSGI server instead.
 * Debug mode: off
[2020-04-05 14:08:15,907] INFO in app: ----- STARTING APP ------
[2020-04-05 14:08:15,909] INFO in app: ----- FINISHED STARTING APP -----
 * Running on http://127.0.0.1:5000/ (Press CTRL+C to quit)
```

Figure 6-3. *The Flask server running on the Pi*

This **127.0.0.1** is known as your *localhost* address – sometimes called a *loopback address*. It is an almost universal standard IP address to refer to "this computer." On your Pi, this address is the same. It's the same address on my desktop computer, your laptop, my Pi, or almost any other computer. This is a reserved IP address, and it's used to make developer's lives easier. When running your applications, it doesn't make sense to send packets out over the Internet, only to come back in to access your application. Localhost addresses are often only accessible to the computer that is running something on it – although you can expose them to the Internet via a public-facing IP address.

Herein lies the problem. This localhost address works fine on your computer – Flask runs on this address, and as you're using the computer Flask is running on, you can access it just fine. As the Pi is a different computer to the one you are developing on, you need to tell Flask to run on a different internal IP address, so that you can access it remotely. When running inside your car, this localhost address works perfectly, but while you're still developing this project, it's much easier to access the Pi remotely.

Fortunately, Flask lets you change the IP address when you start the project. Instead of **Flask run**, modify the command to change the IP address, shown in Figure 6-4:

```
flask run --host=0.0.0.0
```

This tells Flask to listen on the IP address **0.0.0.0** – which is another reserved network address. This IP address will never be used by an internal or external network. You can freely use it for purposes such as this. Once again, this is local to your computer or Pi – every computer has its own 0.0.0.0 IP address.

```
(Pi-Car) pi@raspberrypi:~/Documents/Pi-Car $ flask run --host=0.0.0.0
 * Serving Flask app "Pi_Car.app"
 * Environment: production
   WARNING: This is a development server. Do not use it in a production deployment.
   Use a production WSGI server instead.
 * Debug mode: off
[2020-04-05 14:21:27,926] INFO in app: ----- STARTING APP ------
[2020-04-05 14:21:27,928] INFO in app: ----- FINISHED STARTING APP -----
 * Running on http://0.0.0.0:5000/ (Press CTRL+C to quit)
```

Figure 6-4. *Flask server running on port 0.0.0.0*

This IP address listens to all incoming connections. When you connect to your Pi's IP address, your traffic will route to Flask, which is essentially listening to all incoming traffic on the Pi. On your desktop computer, fire up your web browser of choice, and enter your Pi's IP address in the **address bar**:

http://192.168.1.210:5000/

Remember you can get your Pi's IP address by running **ifconfig** on the Pi and looking under the **inet** section for **wlan0**. Now you can access the Flask application running on your Pi from your desktop computer. You can see the logs in real time through your SSH session. For all practical purposes, the Pi is acting as a remote web server, which you are administering over the network. It doesn't matter that the Pi may be on your desk or tucked behind a cupboard – only the IP address changes for a device next to you or 1000 miles away.

IP addresses power every device on the Internet or internal network. The **Domain Name System** (DNS) defines how servers convert memorable domain names such as google.com to hard to remember IP addresses such as 216.58.204.14. There's nothing stopping you from entering IP addresses into your web browser, but letters and words are much easier to remember. When you enter your Pi's IP address into your web browser, you're skipping the domain name lookup process, as you already know the IP address you want.

Notice the **5000** at the end of your IP address? This is the **port** in use by Flask. Ports in networking are communication endpoints. Computers have a maximum of 65535 ports, and each one is associated with a service or application. Certain ports are associated with services by default. Insecure websites use port 80, for example, or TLS connections use port 443. When entering a website, by default, browsers use port 80 or 443 unless told otherwise. As Flask is running on port 5000, trying to connect over port 80 will not work. By using a colon, and specifying the port in the URL, you can connect over the correct port.

Why 65535 ports? Ports are stored as an unsigned 16-bit integer, which provides a maximum of 65535 digits. This means you can theoretically have 65535 applications running on your computer, all listening on a different port from 0 to 65535. Negative ports are not supported in TCP/IP applications.

You *could* configure Flask to run on port 80, but the Pi probably has something already running on that port, and you can't share ports which are in use. For now, let's stick with port 5000.

As for the IP address, you could bookmark this, or write it down, but in the words of Python core developer *Raymond Hettinger*, "there must be a better way!" By using a *hosts* file, you can create an easy-to-remember text-based entry, which will redirect you to the Pi's IP address. This is a bit like running your own DNS server on your computer – you could even redirect google.com to your Pi. Remember though that it's only you who will see this – it's not that easy to hack servers.

You'll need to perform this change on your desktop computer, not the Pi. Start in your console and open the hosts file (it doesn't matter what folder you are currently in), shown in Figure 6-5:

```
sudo nano /private/etc/hosts
```

You'll need to enter your password – the **sudo** command runs this with the necessary privileges required to edit the file. **Nano** is a lightweight console-based text editor, although if you're a fan of *Vi*, *Vim*, or *Emacs*, then you might be screaming at me right now. These alternative software packages also work well, so use whatever you're comfortable with.

```
#
# Host Database
#
# localhost is used to configure the loopback interface
# when the system is booting.  Do not change this entry.
##
127.0.0.1        localhost
255.255.255.255  broadcasthost
::1              localhost
```

Figure 6-5. *macOS default hosts file entries*

Each line in this file represents an independent host entry. The left portion is the address to redirect to, and the right portion is the easy-to-remember name. Notice how there are already several entries:

```
127.0.0.1       localhost
255.255.255.255 broadcasthost
::1             localhost
```

These default entries let you (and other applications) access *127.0.0.1* via the easy-to-remember name of *localhost*. Ensure you don't change these existing entries. Use your keyboard arrow keys to scroll to the bottom of this file, and insert a new blank line with your **return** key. Enter your Pi's IP address on the left and an easy-to-remember name on the right:

```
192.168.1.210   pi-car
```

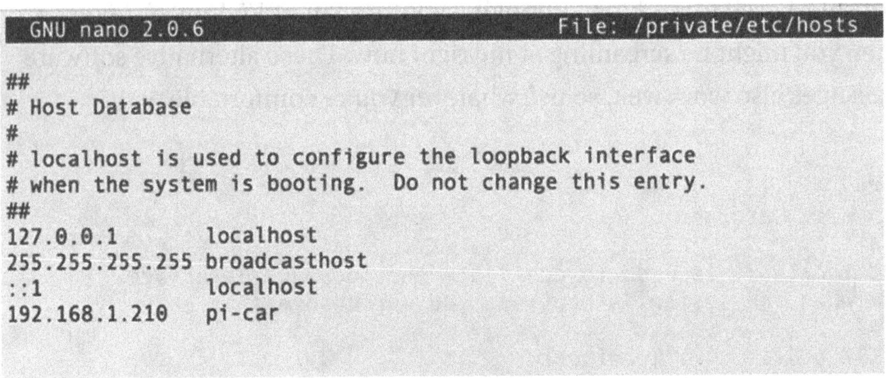

```
  GNU nano 2.0.6                                  File: /private/etc/hosts

##
# Host Database
#
# localhost is used to configure the loopback interface
# when the system is booting.  Do not change this entry.
##
127.0.0.1       localhost
255.255.255.255 broadcasthost
::1             localhost
192.168.1.210   pi-car
```

Figure 6-6. *macOS hosts file with pi-car entry*

Figure 6-6 shows the now modified hosts file. Remember, your internal IP address is different from mine. Press **Ctrl+X** to exit Nano, making sure to type **yes** to save the file (shown in Figure 6-7), and then press **return** to use the existing file name.

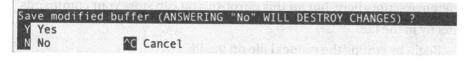

```
Save modified buffer (ANSWERING "No" WILL DESTROY CHANGES) ?
 Y  Yes
 N  No                    ^C  Cancel
```

Figure 6-7. *Nano file saving confirmation message*

Back in your web browser, you can access the Pi via **pi-car** now, instead of **192.168.1.210**. You'll still need to use the port Flask is running on, along with the protocol, like this: `http://pi-car:5000/`. You may need to repeat this process if your Pi's internal IP address changes – which is possible but unlikely.

Autostart Flask When the Pi Boots

Whenever the Pi boots, it needs to run the Flask server. There are many ways to configure autorun behavior such as this on the Pi. Here's how to modify **rc.local** to configure everything you need for Flask to run when the Pi boots. It will

- Ensure the Pi can access your Python 3 interpreter

- Configure the **FLASK_APP** environment variable

- Pull the latest code from your GitHub repository

- Create a virtual environment and install the dependencies

- Run the Flask app

This stands for *run control*, and it exists to let you run commands automatically when the Pi starts up. Commands here get executed by the *root* user, without you having to log in to the Pi. This presents some challenges, as all of your Python installations and files are relative to your user, located in **/home/pi/**. As you'll see shortly, it's a simple process to point the root user to the files necessary to run the server. You can reference scripts here, but for this purpose, you can store your commands directly in the file.

Begin by editing the **rc.local** file on the Pi:

```
sudo nano /etc/rc.local
```

Notice here there's already some code here – several lines of comments followed by a simple IP address retrieval. You can safely remove all of this code. Enter this new code:

```
sleep 15
```

```
export PATH=/home/pi/.pyenv/shims:$PATH
export FLASK_APP=Pi_Car.app
```

```
cd /home/pi/Documents/Pi-Car/
```

```
./clone.sh
pipenv install
flask run --host=0.0.0.0 &
```

```
exit 0
```

Most of this should be familiar to you. Notice how it changes directory into your **/home/pi/** folder, exports the **PATH** into that directory, and runs the Git clone script you created earlier. It also installs the latest requirements from the Pipfile and runs the Flask server on the correct address. You can see this from the Pi's console in Figure 6-8.

```
sleep 15

export PATH=/home/pi/.pyenv/shims:$PATH
export FLASK_APP=Pi_Car.app

cd /home/pi/Documents/Pi-Car/

./clone.sh
pipenv install█
flask run --host=0.0.0.0 &

exit 0
```

Figure 6-8. Basic Pi rc.local configuration

At the start of the file, the **sleep** command delays execution for 15 seconds:

```
sleep 15
```

This ensures that the Pi can access the Internet to clone your latest code. Without it, the Pi may not have finished configuring its network devices and would therefore mean any commands requiring Internet access (such as your Git clone) would fail.

When running the Flask server, pay special attention to the ampersand at the end of the line:

```
pipenv run flask run --host=0.0.0.0 &
```

This isn't a typo. It runs your Flask server in "background mode" as it were. Without it, your server would run just fine, but this script would wait for it to finish execution (which it may never do). By including this special character, the Pi is free to go about any other business it needs to do.

Finally, there is the **exit** command:

```
exit 0
```

This is a *bash exit code*, specifically, the success code. Again, this tells the Pi that everything executed successfully. It's critically important that you retain this line at the bottom of the file. Without it, the Pi would not be able to determine if everything executed successfully, and may prematurely kill off your server.

Save and exit Nano, and restart the Pi:

```
sudo reboot
```

Once the Pi starts up, point your web browser to the Pi's domain and port (`http://pi-car:5000/`), and you'll see your hello world welcome page. Well done, you have now completed possibly the hardest tasks of all. As you progress through these projects, everything else will seem like smooth sailing now that you have all your environments configured and a (mostly) fully automated deployment pipeline.

Chapter Summary

Throughout this chapter, you've installed and configured Flask and built your first application routes. You learned how to run a Flask application server on your local computer and how to do the same on the Pi. You've configured your application logging – both to the standard out and to a rotating log file handler. You configured the Pi to grab the latest code from the repo and start the Flask application when it boots. You can access this over your local network.

In the next chapter, you'll connect a temperature sensor and modify your application to read data from it.

CHAPTER 7

Temperature Monitoring

Chapter goal: Install a temperature sensor and read the values into the application.

Every car needs a temperature sensor. Knowing what the outside temperature is useful for all kinds of purposes. At the basic level, it's useful to know if you should wear a coat and a hat because it's cold, or to leave your coat in the car because it's warm out. On a functional level, it's dangerous to drive in low temperatures, with the risk of icy roads impacting your driving style. By knowing that it's cold outside, you can adjust your driving accordingly. This project is an excellent basis for expansion – you could use it to install additional sensors for your cabin or engine, for example.

Hardware Configuration

Always turn off and disconnect the Pi's power supply when working with electronic circuits. While the low voltage used for these circuits will not kill you and is unlikely to seriously injure you, it's possible to damage both the components and the Pi. It's also possible to start a fire – either by connecting a component wrong or creating a short-circuit, which causes a

© Joseph Coburn 2020
J. Coburn, *Build Your Own Car Dashboard with a Raspberry Pi*,
https://doi.org/10.1007/978-1-4842-6080-7_7

part to overheat and subsequently ignites any nearby fuel sources, such as paper, or the box the Pi came in. Always double-check your circuits before applying power and never risk an accident by taking chances.

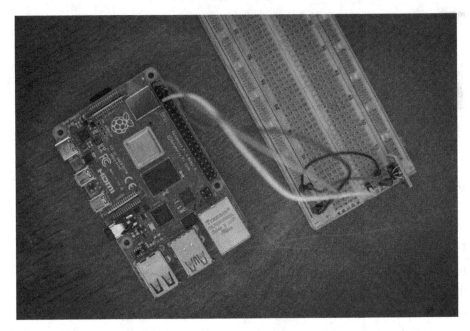

Figure 7-1. DS18B20 temperature sensor wired into the Pi

To sense the temperature, you need to connect the Pi to a temperature sensor – illustrated in Figure 7-1. The *Dallas DS18B20* is perfectly suited for this. It's tiny, low-power, and affordable. This sensor can vary in price, depending on where you purchase it from. It's likely to cost a few cents from an electronic components retailer up to several dollars from Amazon or a big-box store. If purchasing components individually, you'll need to also buy a 4.7k ohm resistor. I'd recommend you buy a complete unit consisting of a DS18B20, 4.7k resistor, and integrated LED. Such a circuit will greatly simplify your build, and costs just a few dollars more. Models such as the *ARCELI DS18B20* or the *DollaTek DS18B20* are all suitable; just make sure that they use the DS18B20 component.

Figure 7-2. *DS18B20 temperature sensor module*

The *DS18B20* is a digital thermometer, shown in Figure 7-2. It can sense temperatures from -55°C to +125°C within an accuracy of 0.5°C. It only requires one connecting cable between it and the Pi – besides power. It's also able to share this single data connection with multiple other units, allowing potentially thousands of different temperature sensors to connect to the Pi over one cable – although this project only requires one. This interface of communication over one wire is called *1-wire*. By default, the Pi's physical pin seven (GPIO4) handles this communication.

Begin by identifying the DS18B20. Notice how one side is curved, while the other has a flat spot. Each of the three legs serves a different function, so make sure to connect everything correctly. Work with the flat spot facing you. From left to right, these legs are as follows:

- Ground (GND) – This is the negative side, or 0 volts.

- Signal – This is where the Pi connects to retrieve the temperature readings.

- Live – This is where your main power input comes in, either 3.3V or 5V.

Look at the illustrated Pi drawing to see the completed circuit. If you're not sure how to read this, trace each wire back from its source, and copy it to link your two components together. Note that this diagram uses the Pi 3, which has a functionally identical pin layout to the Pi 4.

The Pi's pins are numbered in two different ways – by their layout and by their function. Pins are arranged in two rows of 20 and zigzag left to right. The top-left pin is number one, the top-right pin is number two, the pin one down from the top left is number three, and so on. Pins referenced this way are using their *physical* or *board* location. The more popular alternative references pins by their GPIO purpose. As many pins serve specialist purposes, it makes sense to reference the main ones you need to use. This order may appear a little jumbled up, but it greatly emphasizes the GPIO pins over any others. This pin referencing style is called the *Broadcom* layout, or *BCM* for short.

To identify the *general-purpose input/output* (*GPIO*) pins on your Pi, connect over SSH and run the **pinout** command; the output of which is shown in Figure 7-3:

```
pinout
```

```
J8:
     3V3  (1)  (2)   5V
   GPIO2  (3)  (4)   5V
   GPIO3  (5)  (6)   GND
   GPIO4  (7)  (8)   GPIO14
          (9)  (10)  GPIO15
  GPIO17 (11)  (12)  GPIO18
  GPIO27 (13)  (14)  GND
  GPIO22 (15)  (16)  GPIO23
     3V3 (17)  (18)  GPIO24
  GPIO10 (19)  (20)  GND
   GPIO9 (21)  (22)  GPIO25
  GPIO11 (23)  (24)  GPIO8
         (25)  (26)  GPIO7
   GPIO0 (27)  (28)  GPIO1
   GPIO5 (29)  (30)  GND
   GPIO6 (31)  (32)  GPIO12
  GPIO13 (33)  (34)  GND
  GPIO19 (35)  (36)  GPIO16
  GPIO26 (37)  (38)  GPIO20
         (39)  (40)  GPIO21
```

Figure 7-3. *Pi 4 GPIO pinout output of the pinout command*

This command tells you the exact purpose of every GPIO pin on your Pi – they vary slightly between older Pi models. Looking at the Pi 4 from above, with the USB ports at the bottom and the GPIO pins on the top right, the three pins you need for this project are as follows:

- 1 (physical) or 3v3 power (BCM) – 3.3V

- 6 (physical) or ground (BCM) – Ground or GND

- 7 (physical) or 4 (BCM) – GPIO4

The 3.3V and GND pins provide the electricity the sensor needs to function. GPIO4 is a general-purpose data connection, which the Pi can use to communicate with the outside world. Here's where you'll connect the middle leg of your sensor.

Connect the DS18B20 to your Pi via the 4.7k ohm resistor. This resistor serves a very important function. It prevents the sensor or the Pi from creating a short-circuit and getting destroyed, and it's called a *pull-up* resistor. If connected to the ground instead of the positive voltage, its name changes to a *pull-down* resistor. Figure 7-4 shows the wiring diagram between the Pi, a breadboard, and the DS18B20 temperature sensor.

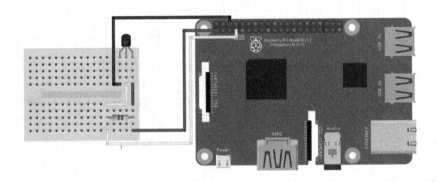

Figure 7-4. *Breadboard wiring diagram for the temperature sensor*

It also ensures that the readings from the sensor are accurate and not muddled up with spurious readings. It helps to ensure the Pi can tell the difference between the real sensor values and noise from the environment. This noise isn't audible; it's interference from all around you – mains power, other data signals, your wireless network, or various other things that exist to interfere with your temperature reading. The Pi has built-in resistors on every GPIO pin, but this sensor needs a slightly different value to operate correctly.

Once connected, go back and double-check your work before applying power.

Pi Configuration

Open an SSH connection to your Pi. To begin using the Pi's GPIO pin with the temperature sensor, you need to configure it. The **config.txt** file located inside the **/boot/** folder configures several aspects of the Pi. HDMI resolution, video quality, pin settings, and more are handled here. Begin by opening this file in your command-line editor of choice:

```
sudo nano /boot/config.txt
```

Add this line at the bottom of the file, taking care to keep all remaining values:

```
dtoverlay=w1-gpio
```

Save and exist, and then restart the Pi:

```
sudo reboot
```

Once restarted, the Pi will have access to its GPIO pins using the 1-wire protocol. This config option is a *device tree overlay*. It's a bit like a driver in Microsoft Windows systems. It lets the Pi's Linux kernel have access to many different hardware configurations, without getting into the complex guts of operating system logic required to support such a variety of hardware.

Flask Temperature Sensor Logic

Back on your computer, you need to instruct the Pi (through Python) to read the temperature values from the sensor. For this section of the project, you'll create a **Sensors** class, which will handle all current and future communication with the Pi's sensors. You'll also learn about *blueprints*. This Flask pattern lets you store your application code outside of the *create_app* function.

177

It's possible to write 100% of the code to read these values, but it's much easier to use an open source library to handle the heavy lifting. While it's not *too* difficult to handle this yourself, it detracts from the main focus of this project, and it isn't as simple as you'd imagine. To facilitate this process, the Python package *W1ThermSensor* (`https://github.com/timofurrer/w1thermsensor`) needs installing. This works on both the Pi and your desktop computer.

From inside a **pipenv shell**, install W1ThermSensor and regenerate the **Pipfile.lock**:

```
pipenv install W1ThermSensor
pipenv lock
```

Create a folder to store your blueprints, along with a new blueprint file called **data**. This should live inside your **Pi_Car** directory:

```
touch Pi_Car/data.py
```

This **data.py** file will contain your main Flask route. It will collate the date from all the sensors, and serve it up, ready for the application to consume later on. Create the **sensors** file, which will house your **Sensors** class:

```
touch Pi_Car/sensors.py
```

Here's the code you need for your **sensors** file:

```
from flask import current_app as app

try:
    from w1thermsensor import W1ThermSensor
except Exception:
    W1ThermSensor = None
```

```python
class Sensors:
    @staticmethod
    def get_external_temp():
        """

        Safely read the external temperature
        :return: Integer of current temperature
        """

        app.logger.info("Starting to read temperature sensor")

        try:
            sensor = W1ThermSensor()
            temperature = sensor.get_temperature()
        except TypeError as e:
            app.logger.warning(
                f"Unable to use primary temperature sensor in
                this environment: {e}"
            )
            temperature = 0
        except Exception as e:
            app.logger.error(
                f"Unknown problem with primary external
                temperature sensor: {e}"
            )
            temperature = 0

        app.logger.info("Finished reading temperature sensor")
        app.logger.debug(f"Temperature: {temperature}")
        return int(temperature)
```

That may look like a lot of code, but much of it should be familiar by now. Notice the copious use of logging, at various different levels. There are only three lines needed to read a temperature – the library does much of the work for you:

```
from w1thermsensor import W1ThermSensor
sensor = W1ThermSensor()
temperature = sensor.get_temperature()
```

Begin by importing the library into your code. Create a new sensor object, based on the **W1ThermSensor** class. Finally, use the **get_ temperature** function to read the current temperature.

The rest of this logic is logging, and defensive handling. All of this ensures the Pi can keep on working even if the temperature sensor is removed. If you're driving a car, it wouldn't make sense for the radio to break if the temperature sensor fails, and the same is true here. If this logic is allowed to fail, the Pi cannot continue its work with all the other (possibly more important) sensors. Notice how the temperature variable is set to zero if any errors occur. This ensures that the temperature sensor can fail entirely, and you'd only lose this data. No other aspect of the system is impacted, which is how code should be designed almost all of the time.

Notice the exception handling around the library import:

```
try:
    from w1thermsensor import W1ThermSensor
except Exception:
    W1ThermSensor = None
```

Generally speaking, you should try to avoid *generic* exception handling. This code handles *any* error, rather than certain specific errors. It's a bit of a brutish approach, but it works in this use case because of one specific flaw in the library. By performing this import, the **W1ThermSensor** library begins to run its code. Just importing it is enough for it to configure the device to read the sensor. This sounds like a good thing, but it's another anti-pattern. In Python and object-oriented programming languages, it's good to explicitly run your logic. Running code on import is an *implicit* action – and you may not even know it's happening.

It's not possible to log this failure at the point of import. The Flask logger is not accessible until you are in a class – imports get evaluated before the app boots, so Flask hasn't started configuring the app or the logger when this code executes.

In this case, this import fails when running locally on your computer. It only works on the Pi or other devices which support the 1-wire protocol. This library provides custom exceptions you can handle, but again, just importing these runs the config code, and fails again.

By setting **W1ThermSensor** to **None** upon error, you can safely run this module on devices other than the Pi – such as your computer. Later on, the exception handling around the temperature object creation also handles this:

```
except TypeError:
    app.logger.warning("Unable to use primary temperature
    sensor in this environment")
    temperature = 0
```

Trying to access the library code when it has failed and been set to **None** raises a **TypeError**, which is safely handled (and logged appropriately) here.

This library does provide the ability to prevent this behavior, but in my opinion, it just pushes the same problem to a different part of your code. This library is still one of the best for this purpose, and this minor issue isn't enough to completely derail the experience. It makes unit testing more difficult, but you'll notice there are no tests for this portion of the code. While you could *technically* write some tests, they would deliver very little value, as most of the work is handled by the library. In an ideal world, you would write these tests, but software development is often performed in an imperfect environment, and as such, the time to implement tests on this code (while considering the workarounds needed with the imports) outweighs the benefits.

Finally, the value of **temperature** is cast to an integer using the **int** function – which is part of Python's core library. This ensures that it is always a number and rounds it to the nearest whole number. How many cars have you seen which display the precise temperature, to several decimal places? It's not necessary, and as the sensor is only accurate to within half a degree anyway, you're not losing critical information.

Inside **data.py**, here's the code you need:

```python
from flask import Blueprint, jsonify
from .sensors import Sensors
from flask import current_app as app

data_blueprint = Blueprint("data", __name__)

@data_blueprint.route("/")
def show():
    app.logger.info("Starting to retrieve core data")
    temperature = Sensors.get_external_temp()

    result = {"temperature": temperature}

    app.logger.info("Finished retrieving core data")
    app.logger.debug(f"Core data: {result}")
    return jsonify(result)
```

There are very few lines here. Much of it should be familiar from the "Hello, world!" Flask route you created inside **app.py**.

Let's start with this import:

```python
from flask import current_app as app
```

Inside Flask, you can access the running app through **current_app**, which is aliased to the shorter **app**. This lets you access your configs, your logger object, and anything else configured by your **create_app** function.

This **app** object is used to write the application logs in this file, which route to the correct log handlers.

Blueprints are Flask's way of letting you move application routes outside of your **create_app** and into their own individual files. By creating an instance of the **Blueprint** class called **data_blueprint**, you're building everything Flask needs to know about – using the **decorator** to tell Flask that everything inside your function is part of the **data** blueprint:

```
@data_blueprint.route("/")
```

This forward slash is your URL route. It can be anything you like – it's what you'll type in your browser's URL bar. Note the call to your **Sensor** class:

```
temperature = Sensors.get_external_temp()
```

You defined this function as a *static method*. It requires no access to any other parts of the class, which means you don't need to define an instance of the class first, you can just access the object directly.

Finally, the data is returned as JSON using the **jsonify** function. This converts it from a Python dictionary object to a JSON object – which is essentially a string. Flask only allows specific shape objects or strings as valid return types from routes, as it has to render these in the browser.

Back inside your **app.py**, you need to tell Flask about your new route. Begin by importing it at the top of the file:

```
from .data import data_blueprint
```

Now remove your "Hello, World!" route from inside **create_app**, and replace it with a *blueprint registration*:

```
app.register_blueprint(data_blueprint)
```

This is functionally equivalent to creating routes inside **create_app**, but it keeps your logic very tidy, and compartmentalized into their own files, each with a specific purpose. This is what your complete **app.py** file now looks like:

```python
import logging

from flask import Flask
from logging.handlers import RotatingFileHandler
from .data import data_blueprint

def create_app(config_file="config/local_config.py"):
    app = Flask(__name__)  # Initialize app
    app.config.from_pyfile(config_file, silent=False)  # Read
    in config from file

    # Configure file-based log handler
    log_file_handler = RotatingFileHandler(
        filename=app.config.get("LOG_FILE_NAME", "config/pi-
        car.log"),
        maxBytes=10000000,
        backupCount=4,
    )
    log_file_handler.setLevel(app.config.get("LOGGER_LEVEL",
    "ERROR"))
    log_file_handler.setFormatter(
        logging.Formatter("[%(asctime)s] %(levelname)s in
        %(module)s: %(message)s")
    )
    app.logger.addHandler(log_file_handler)

    app.logger.info("----- STARTING APP ------")
    app.register_blueprint(data_blueprint)
    app.logger.info("----- FINISHED STARTING APP -----")

    return app
```

Start Flask and load up your route in your web browser of choice. Notice how your logs fill up with warnings, and there is no temperature displayed. With no temperature sensor on your computer, it's impossible to read the temperature! The code is working perfectly – it continues to run just fine without access to the temperature sensor. Commit your code and perform a build on the Pi by restarting.

```
[2020-04-10 20:08:26,044] INFO in app: ――――― STARTING APP ―――――
[2020-04-10 20:08:26,044] INFO in app: ――――― FINISHED STARTING APP ―――――
[2020-04-10 20:08:30,907] INFO in data: Starting to retrieve core data
[2020-04-10 20:08:30,907] INFO in sensors: Starting to read temperature sensor
[2020-04-10 20:08:30,908] WARNING in sensors: Unable to use primary temperature sensor in this environment
[2020-04-10 20:08:30,908] INFO in sensors: Finished reading temperature sensor
[2020-04-10 20:08:30,908] DEBUG in sensors: Temperature: 0
[2020-04-10 20:08:30,908] INFO in data: Finished retrieving core data
[2020-04-10 20:08:30,909] DEBUG in data: Core data: {'temperature': 0}
127.0.0.1 - - [10/Apr/2020 20:08:30] "GET / HTTP/1.1" 200 -
```

Figure 7-5. *Application logs for the temperature sensor*

Visit your Pi's URL, and bask in the overwhelming glory that is your network-connected temperature sensor. The sample application logs are shown in Figure 7-5, and Figure 7-6 shows the JSON output served to your web browser. It may not look pretty, but it's perfectly functional. Later on in this book, you'll learn how to make all the data you're collecting look much nicer, but for now, all you need to care about is functionality. I'll never forget a phrase I was told in my first programming job: "Make it work, and then make it look pretty. It's all well and good having flashy lights and bright colors, but if it's core function doesn't work, nobody can use your code." It's stuck with me ever since.

```
{"temperature":20}
```

Figure 7-6. *JSON output of temperature sensor*

Finish testing your sensor by warming it up – either with your breath or holding it (briefly) near a radiator or other heat source. Reload your app to see the increased temperature displayed.

If you're struggling to see these changes on your Pi, then open up your application logs, visible in **/home/pi/Documents/Pi-Car/pi-car.log**. What do you notice about them? Are there any errors or stack traces visible? If so, go back and double-check your code. Test it first by running it on your computer. You may need to change your logging level to something more verbose first. Check your sensor is installed correctly (making sure to shut down and unplug the Pi first).

Chapter Summary

In this chapter you learned how to connect a digital temperature sensor module to the Pi and defensively program your application to read this data and expose it to the network through your Flask server. You also learned how to write your code such that it can handle a total sensor failure – either through incorrect wiring, a broken sensor, or any number of other hardware faults that could prevent the sensor from working.

In the next chapter, you'll continue to expand the system by building a boot sensor.

CHAPTER 8

Boot Sensor

Chapter goal: Install a boot sensor, and read its state into your application.

The boot sensor serves an important function – it lets you know if the boot is open! You'll use a momentary switch for this purpose. If so desired, you could expand or change this project to encompass car doors or even a bonnet sensor.

Hardware Configuration

Remember to disconnect the Pi's power supply when connecting or disconnecting any circuits.

This circuit uses a miniature momentary tactile switch. These cost a few cents and measure roughly a quarter of an inch in diameter. They are designed to bridge the gap between a solderless breadboard – as visible in Figure 8-1 – or for integrating into your own circuits. Each button has four legs, arranged in two pairs. Orient the button such that the legs are facing horizontally, as if it was installed on a breadboard with the dividing channel running vertically. The top-left and top-right legs are connected as one pair. The bottom right and bottom left are also connected as the second pair. This arrangement allows the buttons to span the gap in a breadboard and connect two otherwise unconnected sides.

© Joseph Coburn 2020
J. Coburn, *Build Your Own Car Dashboard with a Raspberry Pi*,
https://doi.org/10.1007/978-1-4842-6080-7_8

Figure 8-1. Boot sensor completed circuit on a breadboard

When the button is pressed, the pairs join up. Current is allowed to flow from the top to the bottom pairs, and complete whatever circuit you are using the button in. These buttons are only momentary acting. The circuit is only completed when you hold the button down. Release the button, and the connection is closed. You'll need to handle any latching action in the code (but that isn't required for this project).

For this project, you won't need a pull-down or pull-up resistor. The Pi has built-in resistors for this purpose. The resistor used in the previous circuits exists to help protect the sensor. As this is an extremely cheap component, and it only serves one simple mechanical purpose, the Pi's built-in resistor is more than sufficient.

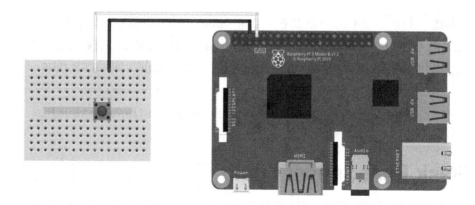

Figure 8-2. *Wiring diagram for the boot sensor*

You only need two pins for this project – the Pi's ground and the GPIO pin, which will detect the change. Figure 8-2 shows the wiring diagram for this circuit. Connect the following:

- 6 (physical) or ground (BCM) – Ground or GND

- 8 (physical) or 14 (BCM) – GPIO 14

The GPIO pin will supply the current necessary to detect the button press. When you are not pressing the button, GPIO pin 14 detects the Pi's internal voltage through its in-built pull-up resistor. This value is seen as *HIGH*, *1*, or *ON*. When you complete the circuit by pressing the button, the signal changes to the ground. This state changes to *LOW*, *0*, or *OFF*. This is basic binary logic – each pin can have one of two states: on or off, high or low, one or zero. Changes between these states are detected by the Pi.

> **Note**   The Pi uses a mixture of pull-down and pull-up resistors for its GPIO pins. While you can reconfigure each one to serve your specific needs, always double-check the Pi's default values for pins.

After double-checking your work, apply power and boot up your Pi.

Flask Boot Sensor Logic

This project requires no changes to the Pi's operating system – it's handled entirely by Flask and your application logic. Most modern installations on the Pi come with the required GPIO library preinstalled, but should that not be the case on your Pi (for whatever reason), you'll specify an additional Python package in your Pipfile to avoid issues.

This button is used by your boot. When installed, the boot should rest on the button, effectively completing the circuit. Therefore, when the button is pressed, the boot is closed. When the boot is open, it's no longer pressing the button. By coding for these states accordingly, you'll have a functional boot sensor.

Begin by entering your project's **Pipenv shell** and installing the two packages used to interface Python and the GPIO pins. **GPIOZero** is a modern wrapper for several older GPIO modules. It makes GPIO communication in Python easier than ever. It's well supported and has a large community following. This internally uses several other libraries for GPIO communication. If a certain library is not available on your Pi, it's capable of *failing over* to another library – and it can do this several times. By default, the first GPIO communication library GPIOZero uses is **RPi.GPIO** – which is the default library on Raspbian. **PiGPIO** is one of the fail-over libraries, so by installing it, you have the best possible chance of avoiding issues, regardless of your Pi's operating system. Install the two Python packages:

```
pipenv install gpiozero
pipenv install pigpio
```

PyPI is the default Python package repository. Whenever you download a package using **PIP** or **Pyenv**, your Python interpreter searches PyPI. Why am I telling you this now? Packages hosted on PyPI are not case sensitive. It's a common practice to use case-insensitive package names on PyPI (although it makes no difference). It's important to clarify this fact, as both of these packages use mixed-case naming conventions, yet the installation commands are all in lowercase.

Once again, when running the application on your computer, the Pi's GPIO pins are not available. It's possible to access them remotely through one of the Python GPIO communication libraries, but it's not necessary. With your build process, and the speed at which the Pi can install new changes, you can write code on your computer and ensure it *runs* and then run it on the Pi to ensure it works *fully*.

Begin by modifying the **Sensors** class (inside **sensors.py**) by importing the previously installed library:

```
from gpiozero import Button, exc
```

This imports the **Button** class, and the **exc** class from the **gpiozero** module. It's not necessary to import **pigpio** – **gpiozero** uses this internally if there are errors with any other GPIO libraries it needs.

Create a new static method called **get_boot_status**. This function will handle all aspects of the boot sensor. It will return a string outlining the status of the boot. This function returns three different strings. If there was a problem (such as the GPIO pins not existing, in the case of your local development computer), the function returns "Unknown". When the boot is closed (the button is pressed), the function returns "Closed". Finally, when the boot is open and the button is no longer held down, this function returns "Open".

Here's the code you need:

```python
@staticmethod
def get_boot_status():
    """
    Safely read the boot sensor and calculate the state - open/
    closed/unknown
    :return: String - boot status
    """

    app.logger.info("Starting to read boot sensor")
    result = None
    status = None

    try:
        button = Button(pin=14)
        status = button.is_pressed
    except exc.BadPinFactory as e:
        app.logger.warning(f"Unable to use boot sensor in this
        environment: {e}")
        result = "Unknown"
    except Exception as e:
        app.logger.error(f"Unknown problem with boot sensor:
        {e}")
        result = "Unknown"

    if not result:
        if status:
            result = "Closed"
```

```
    else:
        result = "Open"

app.logger.debug(f"Boot: {result}")
app.logger.info("Finished reading boot sensor")
return result
```

Once again, notice the liberal use of logging at various levels. Even in the case of a total failure, the function still continues to work. The overall application may provide a diminished experience, but it still works. Failure with the boot sensor *should not* and *will not* cause other sensors or the whole system to fall over.

There are two main lines of code here. Create a new button, based on the **Button** class from the **gpiozero** library:

```
button = Button(pin=14)
```

The **pin** parameter is the GPIO pin you connected your button to. Pin 14 is the BCM naming convention for the GPIO pin 14 you connected to earlier. Now detect your button status using the **is_pressed** attribute:

```
status = button.is_pressed
```

This isn't a function – it's a variable from your **button** object. It's updated by the library whenever the button changes state. It's a Boolean value – True or False.

These objects are wrapped in a **try/catch** block, to handle any exceptions. The **Button** class raises an **exc.BadPinFactory** exception if there is a problem with the underlying GPIO libraries. This is a custom exception implemented by GPIOZero. After handling this exception, a generic **Exception** is handled. Handling generic exceptions like this is *not* a bad practice, providing you have handled at least one specific error. Just blindly wrapping code in generic exception handling is not a smart move, but it's perfectly fine to do once you've considered the most likely errors.

In either error condition, the status is logged, and the final value is set to "Unknown".

At this point, the function could return – it's finished its work, there's no point running any more code. Well, to ensure the final log statements run, the function continues to its completion. Notice how the button value checking is wrapped inside the check for **result**. If the result is **None**, then there are no errors, and the final logic can execute.

Inside your **data.py** Flask route, add your new boot sensor call to the **show** function:

```
boot_status = Sensors.get_boot_status()
```

Modify the resulting dictionary to contain the new value:

```
result = {"temperature": temperature, "boot": boot_status}
```

Your existing imports and logging are already sufficient for this new change.

Start Flask on your computer, and load the main route in your web browser. Your JSON payload should now contain information from the boot sensor, like this:

```
{"boot":"Unknown","temperature":0}
```

Your logs will contain errors and warnings about pin libraries and other boot sensor–related problems, yet the application continues to run, despite a full failure in the boot sensor. These logs are polluted as there is no boot sensor on your computer, and even if there was, the GPIO libraries are designed to work on a Pi, so will need configuring on your computer. This is the beauty of defensive programming. Despite running in an unsuitable environment without access to the GPIO pins, your application continues to work in "limp mode" – it may have reduced usefulness, but it refuses to let a major error hold it back. Figure 8-3 shows the application logs for a failing sensor.

```
[2020-04-14 18:55:35,884] WARNING in sensors: Unable to use boot sensor in this environment: Unable to load any default pin factory!
[2020-04-14 18:55:35,885] DEBUG in sensors: Boot: Unknown
[2020-04-14 18:55:35,888] INFO in sensors: Finished reading boot sensor
[2020-04-14 18:55:35,888] INFO in data: Finished retrieving core data
[2020-04-14 18:55:35,888] DEBUG in data: Core data: {'temperature': 0, 'boot': 'Unknown'}
127.0.0.1 - - [14/Apr/2020 18:55:35] "GET / HTTP/1.1" 200 -
127.0.0.1 - - [14/Apr/2020 18:55:36] "GET /favicon.ico HTTP/1.1" 404 -
```

Figure 8-3. *Boot sensor application logs, with a failed boot sensor*

Commit your code and restart the Pi to pick up the latest changes. Visit the Pi's main application route, and observe the new sensor status:

```
{"boot":"Open","temperature":0}
```

As the button is not held down, your code is detecting this as an open boot. In the real world, the boot will hold down this button. Hold the button with your finger, and reload the page. The status should change to "Closed":

```
{"boot":"Closed","temperature":0}
```

If you don't see this status, don't panic. Go and check your application logs – what do they say? Has the Pi completed its restart procedure? Have the new libraries installed and is the latest code on the Pi? You can check this through SSH. Navigate to the **Pi-Car** directory and check the status of Git:

```
cd home/pi/Documents/Pi-Car
git pull
```

If up to date, git should inform you of the fact:

```
Already up to date.
```

Turn the Pi off and triple-check your wiring. Are the wires fully inserted into the breadboard? Are you connected to the correct pins, ensuring your pins match either the physical or Broadcom pin layout specific earlier?

First Unit Tests

Way back in the software development primer, I discussed *test-driven development* (TDD) and how writing unit tests before application logic produces better code. You may be wondering where the unit tests are then? That's a fair question, and it's one with a simple answer – there are none yet! I'm a firm believer in unit testing, but up until this point, you're still getting your feet wet with Python, Flask, and this application. It's difficult to write fully TDD code if you don't yet understand what the code will do or how it should behave. Unit tests can help you determine this, but for simplicity, these first two projects have omitted the tests thus far. The projects following this chapter utilize test-driven development, but for this project, let's write your first tests.

Let's begin by breaking down what needs unit tests. Unit tests serve to test small independent components. The Flask route inside **data.py** has little logic to unit test. It ties together logic from the **sensor** class. This file would be a good candidate for integration testing, as it ultimately displays data to the outside world. **App.py** does little outside of Flask config and implementing logging. There's little purpose unit testing other code which is already unit tested. As a general rule, you can rely on third-party libraries to work and (hopefully) have unit tests. You don't need to test these libraries.

Therefore, **sensors.py** is the core file left. This is starting to grow and implement your business logic. It's the perfect file to write unit tests for. As covered in the previous chapter, the **get_external_temp** function is not getting tests in this project. The benefits from testing its tiny amount of logic are far outweighed by the difficulties of working with the temperature library. The **get_boot_status** function, however, is perfect. It implements its own logic, with several simple conditions. Any reliance on third-party logic is easy to replace in the tests, and it serves one purpose.

This function returns the status of the boot sensor as a string. There are three possible conditions:

- Open
- Closed
- Unknown

These conditions are determined by the error handling logic, or the output of **button.is_pressed**. To tightly control the conditions inside this test, you need to understand *mocking*. Mocking is the process of replacing a component inside your code. This component is not the piece under test at a given moment in time. This could be an API call, which costs you $1 every time it runs, a function to launch a missile, or some other expensive logic to run. You can imagine the trouble that may arise from running expensive or dangerous logic regularly in your tests. For this reason, mocking external dependencies (external to the code under test) is an essential part of unit testing.

For these tests, you'll use the *Pytest* unit testing framework. This is an extension to the older *unittest* library. Both are excellent and well-used choices, although Pytest is fast becoming the go-to library for unit testing in Python. It's possible to unit test without a framework such as Pytest, but it's a lot more work. Pytest handles running the tests, ensuring they all pass, showing you the error message for failures, and lots more. There's no need to reinvent the wheel and write your own test framework.

Inside your **tests** folder, delete the **test_practice.py** file. This fake test is no longer required now that you are writing a real test. Tests and test files should reflect the logic they are testing as far as possible. It's OK to have long names for unit test functions, providing they provide clarity to you and other developers. Create a new file inside **tests** called **test_sensors.py**:

```
touch tests/test_sensors.py
```

This file will contain all the tests for the **sensors** class, but it won't work just yet. Create two more files:

```
touch tests/conftest.py
touch Pi_Car/config/test_config.py
```

Conftest.py is a Pytest configuration file. Here's where you can store code and common test variables, accessible to all unit tests. The config file **test_config.py** is another configuration file, just like your **local_config. py**. This config file stores configs for when your app is running tests. You may not always need the same configuration for tests as when running the application. Start with the **test_config.py**. Here are the three lines you need:

```
TESTING = True
LOGGER_LEVEL = "DEBUG"
FILE_LOGGING = False
```

You don't need any other configuration options when running tests. You may notice a new config item at the bottom of this file called **FILE_LOGGING**. This is a new config item. Pytest will tell you what the problem is and show the logs from STDOUT when the tests fail, so it's a bit redundant writing these to a log file as well. Making this a new config item lets you disable file logging for tests and enable it again for the normal application uses.

Add this new logging option to your **local_config.py**:

```
FILE_LOGGING = True
```

Now you need to implement it in your **create_app** app factory. Add an **if** statement to your **app.py**:

```
if app.config.get("FILE_LOGGING"):
```

Wrap all of the file based log handling inside this if. When this config option is True, the file-based logs will get written. When False, the logs will not get written. Here's the new and improved **create_app** function:

```python
def create_app(config_file="config/local_config.py"):
    app = Flask(__name__)  # Initialize app
    app.config.from_pyfile(config_file, silent=False)  # Read
    in config from file

    if app.config.get("FILE_LOGGING"):
        # Configure file based log handler
        log_file_handler = RotatingFileHandler(
            filename=app.config.get("LOG_FILE_NAME", "config/
            pi-car.log"),
            maxBytes=10000000,
            backupCount=4,
        )
        log_file_handler.setFormatter(
            logging.Formatter("[%(asctime)s] %(levelname)s in
            %(module)s: %(message)s")
        )
        app.logger.addHandler(log_file_handler)

    app.logger.setLevel(app.config.get("LOGGER_LEVEL", "ERROR"))

    app.logger.info("----- STARTING APP ------")
    app.register_blueprint(data_blueprint)
    app.logger.info("----- FINISHED STARTING APP -----")

    return app
```

Back in your unit tests, here are the contents of **conftest.py**:

```python
import pytest
from Pi_Car.app import create_app

@pytest.fixture(scope="session", autouse=True)
def build_testing_app():
    """
    Builds a testing app with basic application context
    """
    app = create_app(config_file="config/test_config.py")
    app.app_context().push()

    yield app
```

This introduces several Pytest patterns. The **build_testing_app** function is a *Pytest fixture*. Fixtures let you share code between tests. This fixture builds a Flask app using your application factory (**create_app**). To run tests against Flask code, or code which uses Flask features, you need an application running. This logic builds an app. The **app_context** is a Flask object that gets populated when Flask runs. This gets populated with all kinds of information which Flask needs to work. By pushing a new context, you're configuring Flask with everything it needs to handle normal operations during your tests.

The **yield** statement is essentially the same as a **return** statement right now, but yield serves a powerful purpose. Pytest will run this code until the yield statement – it will build and return a Flask app. Once the tests have finished executing, Pytest will return and run any code after the yield statement. This lets you write logic to build requirements for tests, and then more logic to destroy or reset these requirements. The yield statement is a great way to reduce boilerplate code and get on with writing useful, valuable code.

Finally, the **Pytest fixture** decorator tells Pytest to use this function as a fixture:

```
@pytest.fixture(scope="session", autouse=True)
```

Pytest fixtures are blocks of code that you can use in your tests. The **scope** parameter configures when to run this code. The **session** value means Pytest will run this code once at the start of your tests (and at the end). Other scopes exist such as running code for every test, every class, and more. Finally, the **autouse** parameter tells Pytest to run this code automatically, rather than explicitly waiting for you to call the function. Your conftest is now ready to start assisting your tests.

Back in your **test_sensors.py**, here are the first tests you need:

```
from unittest.mock import patch
from Pi_Car.sensors import Sensors
from gpiozero import exc

class TestSensors:
    @patch("Pi_Car.sensors.Button")
    def test_get_boot_status_bad_pin_factory(self,
    mock_button):
        mock_button.side_effect = exc.BadPinFactory
        result = Sensors.get_boot_status()
        assert result == "Unknown"

    @patch("Pi_Car.sensors.Button")
    def test_get_boot_status_other_pin_error(self,
    mock_button):
        mock_button.side_effect = TypeError
        result = Sensors.get_boot_status()
        assert result == "Unknown"
```

```
@patch("Pi_Car.sensors.Button")
def test_get_boot_status_closed(self, mock_button):
    mock_button.return_value = type("Button", (),
    {"is_pressed": True})
    result = Sensors.get_boot_status()
    assert result == "Closed"

@patch("Pi_Car.sensors.Button")
def test_get_boot_status_open(self, mock_button):
    mock_button.return_value = type("Button", (),
    {"is_pressed": False})
    result = Sensors.get_boot_status()
    assert result == "Open"
```

Run these from your console using the **Pytest** command:

```
pytest
```

If you'd like to see the logs as well, use the **-s** flag (although Pytest will only show logs when the tests fail):

```
pytest -s
```

There are four tests here, each with a unique and detailed name. Pytest automatically runs any test files inside the **test** folder. Files beginning with the word "test", along with classes and functions, are run as tests. Any function, file, or class which does not begin with "test" will not run.

```
Joes-iMac:Pi-Car coburn$ pytest -s
================================================================ test session starts =======
platform darwin -- Python 3.7.6, pytest-5.3.5, py-1.8.1, pluggy-0.13.1
rootdir: /Users/coburn/Documents/Pi-Car
plugins: cov-2.8.1
collected 4 items

tests/test_sensors.py ....

================================================================ 4 passed in 0.03s =======
Joes-iMac:Pi-Car coburn$
```

Figure 8-4. *Successful unit test run*

Note how Pytest provides you a test status – number of tests run and the total number of passes. If they are all successful, the Pytest status bar goes green (Figure 8-4). If there are any failures, Pytest indicates this with a red status bar (Figure 8-5) and by pointing out the exact number of failures and the condition.

```
Joes-iMac:Pi-Car coburn$ pytest -s
================================================================ test session starts =========================
platform darwin -- Python 3.7.6, pytest-5.3.5, py-1.8.1, pluggy-0.13.1
rootdir: /Users/coburn/Documents/Pi-Car
plugins: cov-2.8.1
collected 4 items

tests/test_sensors.py ...F

=========================================================== FAILURES ==============================
_____ TestSensors.test_get_boot_status_open _____

self = <tests.test_sensors.TestSensors object at 0x10c58a650>, mock_button = <MagicMock name='Button' id='4502102672'>

    @patch("Pi_Car.sensors.Button")
    def test_get_boot_status_open(self, mock_button):
        mock_button.return_value = type("Button", (), {"is_pressed": False})
        result = Sensors.get_boot_status()
>       assert result == "Ope"
E       AssertionError: assert 'Open' == 'Ope'
E         - Open
E         ?    -
E         + Ope

tests/test_sensors.py:29: AssertionError
------------------------------------------------------------- Captured log call -----------------------------
INFO     Pi_Car.app:sensors.py:39 Starting to read boot sensor
DEBUG    Pi_Car.app:sensors.py:59 Boot: Open
INFO     Pi_Car.app:sensors.py:60 Finished reading boot sensor
=========================================================== 1 failed, 3 passed in 0.06s ==================
Joes-iMac:Pi-Car coburn$ ▌
```

Figure 8-5. *Failing unit test run*

Play around with your sensor code by changing it to fail the tests – change return types, and exception handling, and notice how the tests fail. This is what makes well-written unit tests so powerful. By covering the edge cases and core functionality, you can be confident that your tests will pick up any existing functionality you may break when implementing new features.

After importing the testing libraries, and some of the modules to test, there are four test functions residing inside the **TestSensors** class. Each function tests a specific condition of the **get_boot_status** function. These four conditions are as follows:

1. Bad pin factory – The GPIO library cannot read the pins.

2. Other pin error – The exception handling caught an error when reading the GPIO pins.

3. Closed – The function returns "Closed" when the button is pressed.

4. Open – The function returns "Open" when the button is not pressed.

Each test functions in a similar way. They begin by configuring the conditions required for the code under test to reach a certain state. They then run the code and use **assert** statements to verify that the output of the function is as expected when the code runs under the predefined conditions.

Each test uses the **patch** decorator to *mock* the sensor library:

```
@patch("Pi_Car.sensors.Button")
```

This function is part of the **unittest** library, which Pytest extends. This is a *mock*. As mentioned earlier, mocking lets you replace parts of your code to make it run a certain way under test. Tests should be as repeatable as possible. Right now, your defensive programming kicks in and manipulates the logic when certain libraries are not available. This is great for ensuring your logic still works when running in different environments, but it's not consistent enough for a reliable test suite.

By mocking the GPIO library, you can control when, what, and how this library works, to achieve the desired result. The first two functions use *side effects*, with the **side_effect** property. This is a way to make your code raise specific errors. As your function returns "Unknown" in two error conditions, mocking these functions to raise both **exc.BadPinFactory** and **TypeError** ensures these conditions are met during the tests.

The final two tests use the **return_value** attribute to force the **Button** class to return a specific value for the **is_pressed** attribute. Remember, you're not testing that the external libraries work, you're testing your specific logic operates under given conditions. Because **is_pressed** is an attribute and not a function (that is to say, it's a variable assigned to instances of the **Button** class), the **return_value** attribute lets you force a function or attribute to return what *you* say it should.

You may be wondering why you can't set the return value like this:

```
mock_button.is_pressed.return_value = True
```

Ordinarily, this would work. For functions, you can specify what they should return exactly like this. However, as the **is_pressed** attribute is a variable and not a function, it needs a little more assistance. By using the **type** function (part of the Python core library), it's possible to construct entire fake objects to really manipulate your code under test:

```
mock_button.return_value = type("Button", (), {"is_pressed":
False})
```

The third parameter passed to this function is a dictionary. This dictionary is essentially the name and return values for any attribute you want to mock. You can see that **test_get_boot_status_closed** and **test_get_boot_status_open** return different values for **is_pressed**, according to their test requirements.

Asserts are a special utility in Python. Any assert statement is used by tests or test-like logic to ensure that a condition meets the criteria. It's a bit like an *if* statement but uses far less lines of code, and it is automatically picked up by test frameworks such as Pytest. Assert statements are like saying "make sure this thing returns some specific value." This logic checks that whatever **Sensors.get_boot_status()** returns is a string with a value of "Open":

```
result = Sensors.get_boot_status()
assert result == "Open"
```

If this condition is not met, the tests will fail.

It's very important to ensure that you only use assert statements inside test code. They may look like a shortcut to improve your code, but they are not designed to run inside production code and *will* come back to hurt you at some point in the future. It's possible to disable assert statements altogether in Python. This nets you a modest performance increase, and as you shouldn't use them for production code, it *shouldn't* be a problem. With asserts disabled, they will not evaluate, so any code actually relying on them will fail.

As you progress with these projects, I'll show you some Pytest tricks to reduce the lines of test code you need to write. I'll also cover writing tests in a fully TDD way, which can improve your overall code quality.

Chapter Summary

In this chapter you installed and developed the code for a simple boot sensor. You can expand this project to cover your car doors, bonnet, or any other opening. You developed your first unit tests using Pytest and learned how to write assertions, along with when not to use them. Once again, you developed this code defensively, such that the application can continue to work even with a total sensor failure.

In the next chapter, you'll expand on your unit testing skills by developing a light sensor.

CHAPTER 9

Light Sensor

Chapter goal: Install a light sensor and read its state into your application. Begin test-driven development and enhance your unit testing skills.

For this project, you'll use a light sensor to read in the available light, and make an assessment – daytime or nighttime. This is another quick project, but it serves a valuable purpose. Not only is it useful for your car to inform you that it's getting dark outside, but it is the valuable foundation for any of your own future projects. You could expand this to switch on your headlights automatically or turn on the cabin lights if it's dark and you open the door.

The code covered here may look familiar to the previous chapter, which serves to reinforce your learning, but it also introduces you to several unit-testing time savers. In this chapter you'll learn how to begin *test-driven development*, whereby you write unit tests before your application code. You'll also learn how to avoid test duplication and quickly test multiple conditions using Pytest's *parametrize* decorator.

Hardware Configuration

Remember to disconnect the Pi's power supply when connecting or disconnecting any circuits.

© Joseph Coburn 2020
J. Coburn, *Build Your Own Car Dashboard with a Raspberry Pi*,
https://doi.org/10.1007/978-1-4842-6080-7_9

To complete this project, you will need a *photoresistor*, sometimes called a *light-sensing resistor*, *light-dependent resistor*, or *LDR*. LDRs cost a few cents up to a dollar or two depending on the store. They are small, lightweight, and fairly universally available within electronics stores. You can buy LDRs from Amazon, or your local electronics store. You only need one for this project, but buy several, as they are easy to lose. You won't need a stand-alone resistor for this project. Figure 9-1 shows the LDR wired up to the Pi on a breadboard.

Figure 9-1. *Light-sensing circuit complete on a breadboard*

LDRs work like resistors – they limit the flow of electricity. What's special about this component is that the resistance varies depending on the amount of available light. When there's more light, the resistance increases. When there's less light, there is less resistance. The Pi can detect these changes in resistance and convert this to a signal between zero (total darkness) and one (bright daytime), and anywhere in between. You'll use the Pi's built-in pull-up resistor on its GPIO pin to facilitate this circuit. LDRs have no polarity – it does not matter which way round they are connected.

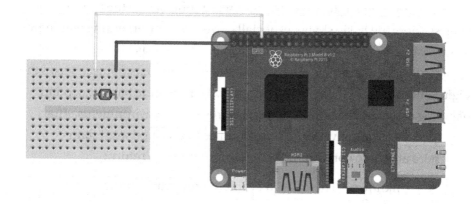

Figure 9-2. *Wiring diagram for the light-sensing circuit*

You only need two pins for this project – the Pi's 3.3v and the GPIO pin, which will sense the resistance. Figure 9-2 shows the wiring diagram:

- 1 (physical) or 3.3v (BCM) – 3.3v

- 10 (physical) or 15 (BCM) – GPIO 15

Connect GPIO pin 15 to one side of the LDR. Connect the other side to the Pi's 3.3v pin. After double-checking your work, apply power and boot up your Pi.

Test-Driven Development Light Sensor Tests

Test-driven development (TDD) is the art of writing your unit tests before fleshing out your code. By considering the edge cases, and the criteria you need for your tests, you end up with better, cleaner code, which is less bloated. By writing just enough code to pass the tests, you avoid adding unnecessary features which are not required. You also gain a better understanding of what exactly the code should do, and a full set of unit tests as well. With a full suite of unit tests, you can be confident in any future changes or refactoring, as the tests ensure the core logic still works.

Naturally, you'll often have to write *some* code before the tests, so you at least know the basic shape, especially if you're experimenting with new features, but for now, let's start with the completed tests.

This light-sensing logic is very similar to the boto sensor logic. It uses the **LightSensor** class of the **gpiozero** module. There's some basic exception handling to ensure the application still works in bad environments. After that, the core logic converts the sensor values to a string-based status.

There are three conditions your new function can return:

- Unknown – There was a problem preventing the sensor from working.

- Daytime – It's bright outside.

- Nighttime – It's dark outside.

Begin by writing two tests to cover the core exception handling:

```
@patch("Pi_Car.sensors.LightSensor")
def test_get_light_status_bad_pin_factory(self, mock_light_
sensor):
    mock_light_sensor.side_effect = exc.BadPinFactory
    result = Sensors.get_light_status()
    assert result == "Unknown"

@patch("Pi_Car.sensors.LightSensor")
def test_get_light_status_other_pin_error(self, mock_light_
sensor):
    mock_light_sensor.side_effect = TypeError
    result = Sensors.get_light_status()
    assert result == "Unknown"
```

These tests are very similar to the tests for the boot status function. They use the **patch** function from the **unittest** library to mock certain aspects of the GPIO modules, to tightly control the test conditions, and to emulate a real failure. These tests use the **get_light_status** function, which doesn't exist yet! Your tests would totally fall over if you were to run them now, but it's important to think about the logic that's happening here. They assert that if there was an error (either a bad pin factory or some other exception), the function returns an "Unknown" status. This is a valuable test – it ensures your application doesn't fall over due to a bad environment or circuit.

The LDR returns a value between zero and one inclusive. You can use this to determine if it's day or night. Values greater than 0.5 are daytime, and anything else is nighttime (or an error occurred). It's not necessary to test every possible value – there could be tens of thousands of possible options! Often, you only need to test the edge cases – conditions where it's more likely you'll have an error. There are eight different edge cases, so these eight values should return the following values:

1. 1 – Daytime

2. 0.9 – Daytime

3. 0.55 – Daytime

4. 0.5 – Daytime

5. 0.49 – Nighttime

6. 0.4 – Nighttime

7. 0 – Nighttime

8. None – Unknown

Here's the unit test to verify these conditions:

```
@pytest.mark.parametrize(
    "sensor_value, expected_result",
    [
        (1, "Daytime"),
        (0.9, "Daytime"),
        (0.55, "Daytime"),
        (0.5, "Daytime"),
        (0.49, "Nighttime"),
        (0.4, "Nighttime"),
        (0, "Nighttime"),
        (None, "Unknown"),
    ],
)
@patch("Pi_Car.sensors.LightSensor")
def test_get_light_status_values(
    self, mock_light_sensor, sensor_value, expected_result
):
    mock_light_sensor.return_value = type("Button", (),
    {"value": sensor_value})
    result = Sensors.get_light_status()
    assert result == expected_result
```

Notice how this is only one unit test, yet it asserts all eight conditions. It begins by mocking the sensor return value to the desired state and then asserts the return string meets the expected result. You *could* write eight different tests for these conditions, or manually code up every one in the same test, but that's a lot of work for essentially the same test. By using the **parametrize** decorator function from Pytest, you can easily repeat the same test with different data. This utility function makes it very easy for you to test multiple edge cases, without having to fill up your tests with repetitive logic. This function looks like this, and it sits above your test function:

```
@pytest.mark.parametrize(
    "sensor_value, expected_result",
    [
        (1, "Daytime"),
        (0.9, "Daytime"),
        (0.55, "Daytime"),
        (0.5, "Daytime"),
        (0.49, "Nighttime"),
        (0.4, "Nighttime"),
        (0, "Nighttime"),
        (None, "Unknown"),
    ],
)
```

You can see that most of it contains your edge cases. Each pair of **sensor_value** and **expected_result** represents one test run. Pytest will automatically run the test eight times, changing the data every time.

Flask Light Sensor Logic

Now that you understand the criteria your code needs to meet, you can begin coding. Inside your **Sensors** class, expand your imports by importing the **LightSensor** class from the **gpiozero** module. You already have this module installed from the boot sensor project:

```
from gpiozero import Button, exc, LightSensor
```

Create a new *static method* called **get_light_sensor**. Here's the code you need:

```
@staticmethod
def get_light_status():
    """
    Safely read the available light and calculate a status -
    daytime/dusk/nighttime/unknown
    :return: String - light status
    """
    app.logger.info("Starting to read available light")
    status = -1

    try:
        sensor = LightSensor(pin=15)
        status = float(sensor.value)
    except exc.BadPinFactory as e:
        app.logger.warning(f"Unable to use light sensor in this
        environment: {e}")
    except Exception as e:
        app.logger.error(f"Unknown problem with light
        sensor: {e}")

    if status == -1:
        result = "Unknown"
    elif status >= 0.5:
        result = "Daytime"
    else:
        result = "Nighttime"

    app.logger.debug(f"Light: {status} - {result}")
    app.logger.info("Finished reading available light")

    return result
```

Because this function uses the same **gpiozero** library as the boot sensor logic, some of the exception handling and configuration looks very similar. Instead of creating a **Button** object, this function creates a **LightSensor** object called **sensor**. This sensor is pointed to your BCM GPIO pin 15, which is the pin you connected your LDR to. The sensor value is read using the **value** attribute. This is cast to a **float** data type, to ensure that it's always in the correct shape and to remove any unnecessary characters and the extremely precise number of decimal places.

Floats store high-precision numbers, with lots of decimal places. It's not possible to store decimal values in integers.

Toward the bottom of the function is the core logic. This converts the sensor values to a human-readable status:

```
if status == -1:
    result = "Unknown"
elif status >= 0.5:
    result = "Daytime"
else:
    result = "Nighttime"
```

You may be wondering why there is a third condition checking for a value of minus one. This is because of **none** types. In Python, **none** is a special type. Often, it's used like **null** – there is no value set. The **status** variable needs a default value. If there is an error with reading the sensor, the **status** never gets set, so it needs to fall back to something. You could fall back to a value of **none**, but that presents a problem. You can't do arithmetic checks on **none** values. As the sensor will only ever return values between zero and one, a default value of minus one means that there is no real value from the sensor, so the logic converts this to the "Unknown" status.

Once the code is in place, run your unit tests with Pytest:

```
pytest
```

If your tests fail, double-check your logic is correct. You can see the logs for the tests with the **-s** flag:

```
pytest -s
```

Once satisfied that all 14 tests pass, modify your main route inside **data.py** to implement your new light sensor function:

```
light_status = Sensors.get_light_status()
result = {"temperature": temperature, "boot": boot_status,
"light": light_status}
```

Run your app locally and validate everything still works. Check your logs don't show any major issues. Remember, without access to the GPIO pins on your computer, there will be warnings in the logs, but everything should still work. When you're ready, commit your code and perform a build on the Pi.

Access the Pi's main page from your web browser, and verify that you can see the new sensor feeding back data like this:

```
{"boot":"Open","light":"Daytime","temperature":0}
```

Now perform a functional test. Cover the sensor, or otherwise turn off the lights and close the curtains to emulate nighttime. Now reload your page. You should see the sensor value change from "Daytime" to "Nighttime". Put the lights back on or uncover the sensor again and perform a final validation check – the page should return "Daytime" again. Well done! You now have a working light sensor, which you developed using *test-driven development!*

Chapter Summary

In this chapter you connected and coded the logic for an analog light sensor. You wrote code to convert the light readings to human-readable strings. You learned a new way to think about testing in the form of test-driven development, and you learned some Pytest time savers, along with mocking. These skills are valuable regardless of the programming language you use.

In the next chapter, you'll build two circuits to sense your car's reversing and fog lights.

CHAPTER 10

Fog and Reverse Sensors

Chapter goal: Detect when the fog lights are on, or when the car is in reverse. Refactor sensors class to reduce duplication.

This project implements two further sensors to detect when the car is in reverse gear, or the fog lights are on. These are two independent sensors, but they are both identical in terms of code and hardware. By detecting when the reversing light is enabled, it's possible to identify when the car is in the reverse gear. Later on, you'll use this sensor to change the display to provide more value for reversing. For the fog light sensor, this is only needed for informational purposes – the completed dashboard will show a fog light status image to the user. Not all cars have front-facing fog lights, but most countries mandate operational rear fog lights for the vast majority of vehicles.

Hardware Configuration

Remember to disconnect the Pi's power supply when connecting or disconnecting any circuits.

© Joseph Coburn 2020
J. Coburn, *Build Your Own Car Dashboard with a Raspberry Pi*,
https://doi.org/10.1007/978-1-4842-6080-7_10

The vast majority of cars manufactured in the last ~30 years (at least) use a 12v electric system powered by a lead-acid battery. Some very old cars may differ from this voltage, and there may be exceptions. Double-check your car voltage in one of the three ways:

- Open the bonnet and look at the battery label.

- Search online for information about your make and model of car.

- Read the manufacturers handbook.

While it's very likely that your car runs on a 12v system, always double-check! Failing to do so and making assumptions could lead to a potentially fatal incident, with a best-case scenario being a burnt-out Pi and worst-case scenario being a burnt-out car. Keep in mind that with this project, a short-circuit from the car could destroy your Pi – even with the current-limiting resistors and safety fuses in place.

As most car circuits operate at 12v, and the Pi runs at 3.3v, you'll need to install a resistor to protect the Pi from burning out just from basic operation. If you don't care about the physics, then use two 23k ohm, 0.25W resistors – one for each sensor circuit.

If your car has a voltage system other than 12v, or you're interested in the equations, then there are three calculations required to determine the resistor size to use. Begin by calculating the voltage drop. This is the difference between the car's voltage and the Pi's.

The formula for voltage drop is a simple one – subtract the Pi's voltage from the car's voltage:

$$\textbf{Vdrop} = \textbf{14.7v} - \textbf{3.3v}$$

This gives you a voltage drop of 11.4v (14.7 - 3.3). You may be wondering where 14.7v has come from, as I just discussed cars running at 12v. For cars that run on 12v battery systems, the actual voltage is slightly higher when the engine is running – and it varies slightly depending on the age of the battery, the condition, and the operating conditions at the time of the measurement. A 12v car battery system often ranges between 12v and 14.7v. For the next calculation, this voltage drop of 11.4v is known as **V** - the *force voltage*.

Next, calculate the required resistance using *Ohm's law*, and the formula for resistance:

R = V / I

Resistance (**R**) in ohms equals force (**V**) in volts divided by the current (**I**) in amps. You need the resistance, you have the voltage, so the only missing component is the current (measured in amps). The Pi requires 0.5 milliamps (mA) of current. To achieve this, substitute your new figures into the equation:

11.4 / 0.0005 = 22800

The voltage drop of 11.4 volts divided by the required current of 0.5mA (0.0005A) equals a total of 22800 ohms, roughly 23k ohms. Perfect - with two calculations, you know the required resistance necessary to protect the Pi and allow it to detect when the bulbs are on. Using these values, you can calculate the required power, to ensure the resistor can handle the power coming from the car. The greater the power, the more work the resistor has to do to convert electrical energy into heat (and the more heat generated). To safely handle higher loads, resistors are specifically designed and rated to work correctly. Ohm's formula for power is as follows:

P = I²R

Power in watts equals current in amps (squared) multiplied by resistance in ohms:

0.0005 x 0.0005 x 22800 = 0.0057

This formula states that the resistor power rating should be equal to 0.006W. As resistors are often manufactured in 0.25W increments, it's not practical to purchase anything smaller than 0.25W. It's perfectly safe to use a higher-rated resistor than what's required. Using a lower-rated resistor is not recommended, as it may not be able to handle the power provided.

As I mentioned in previous project chapters, the Pi uses a mixture of pull-down and pull-up resistors. The two pins specified here both have pull-down resistors enabled by default – which work just fine for this use. Connect pin 15 (physical) or 22 (BCM) to the +12v line supplied to your car's reverse light. Connect pin 16 (physical) or 23 (BCM) to the +12v line supplied to your car's fog light. Ensure that the resistor sits between the car's circuits and the Pi's GPIO pin. Connect the Pi's ground to the car's ground – either the chassis or the 0v connector on the bulb sockets themselves. Figure 10-1 shows the wiring diagram for this circuit.

When the lights are on, the GPIO pin sees +12v and, thus, detects the bulb as on. When the lights are off, the GPIO pins get pulled to ground by the built-in resistor and therefore are detected as off.

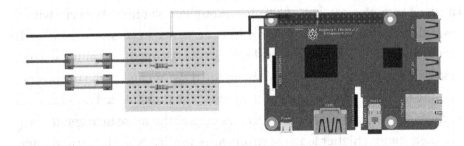

Figure 10-1. *Light sensor wiring diagram*

To test this on your breadboard, you can connect either a switch or temporarily connect to the Pi's 3.3v (without the resistor). When connecting to the car, ensure you follow the safety advice in the following chapters and include an inline fuse – one per GPIO pin. This fuse should be as small as you can find – 250mA or lower. This will protect the Pi in the event of a power surge, short-circuit, or other issue with the car's systems.

In the event of a surge or other failure from the car, you may break a GPIO pin, but your Pi should continue to function. Cars use high-current circuits, with thick wires. By using a fuse, not only do you protect your Pi, but you can also use thin wires (such as your breadboard jumper leads) between the Pi and the fuse, making it much easier to work with.

Fog and Reverse Sensors Logic

Before jumping fully into this code, let's do some refactoring! The process of refactoring involves improving (often by modifying) existing code in some way. This project is essentially the same logic as the previous button sensors. The Pi detects car lighting systems turning on or off exactly the same as a button opening or closing a circuit. For this reason, it makes sense to reuse some of the existing button logic. This keeps your code smaller, reduces duplication, and makes it easier to use and easier to introduce new features.

Much of the code inside **get_boot_status** is exception handling and button object creation. By pulling this specific logic out into its own function, you can easily reuse it for any other button projects.

Create a new static method called **get_bool_pin**. This function is responsible for reading a button or button-like pin state and returning True, False, or none in the case of an error. Almost all of this code exists in the **get_boot_status** function:

```
@staticmethod
def get_bool_pin(pin):
    """

    Defensively read boolean pin as a button
    :param pin: GPIO pin (in BCM layout) to read
    :return: Boolean result -- pressed on not, or none
    """

    app.logger.info(f"Starting to read boolean value from pin:
{pin}")
```

223

```
try:
    button = Button(pin=pin, pull_up=False)
    result = button.is_pressed
except exc.BadPinFactory as e:
    app.logger.warning(f"Unable to use boot sensor in this
    environment: {e}")
    result = None
except Exception as e:
    app.logger.error(f"Unknown problem with boot sensor:
    {e}")
    result = None

app.logger.info(f"Finished reading boolean value from pin:
{pin}")
return result
```

There is a subtle change here to the **button** object instantiation. A new parameter **pull_up** is passed through as **False**. By default, the gpiozero library converts all pins to use pull-up resistors. It also (confusingly) inverts the logic, such that a state change results in a *high* signal, even if the circuit is going to ground, and should be a *low* signal. This works fine for the previous circuits but needs disabling for all the following circuits. This change is backward-compatible with all the previous circuits – those pins will revert to their default state of pull-up. All the GPIO pins in use going forward default to pull-down and are required to pull down the circuits to work. When gpiozero sets these to pull-up, it's a breaking change to the logic.

When the car bulbs are off, the Pi uses the pull-down resistors to detect ground – no signal, the bulbs are off. When the bulbs are on, the Pi detects +12v (14.7v in reality) as high.

Now modify the **get_boot_status** to use this new function. You'll need to convert this function from a **static method** to a **class method**. Class methods can access other functions within a class, but still don't require *instance-level* access to objects. This function doesn't need access to specific data from the class, which may change depending on the object instantiated, but it does need access to other shared utility functions. Here's the new and revised code:

```
@classmethod
def get_boot_status(cls):
    """
    Safely read the boot sensor and calculate the state - open/
    closed/unavailable/unknown
    :return: String - boot status
    """
    app.logger.info("Starting to read boot sensor")
    button_status = cls.get_bool_pin(pin=14)

    if button_status is None:
        result = "Unknown"
    else:
        if button_status:
            result = "Closed"
        else:
            result = "Open"

    app.logger.debug(f"Boot: {result}")
    app.logger.info("Finished reading boot sensor")
    return result
```

Notice how much smaller it is? Most of the exception handling is now handled by the utility function **get_bool_pin**. By passing in the pin to read, this new function is accessible by any function, and **get_boot_status** continues to operate as normal. Run your unit tests again and they should all pass – the changes made to this function haven't altered its use. This is the real benefit of unit tests – you can refactor and otherwise change or improve code with the confidence that it still works as it did before your changes.

Create two new unit tests for your **get_bool_pin** function. These are very similar to the other tests, differing only in that they expect **none** as a value when there is an error:

```
@patch("Pi_Car.sensors.Button")
def test_get_bool_pin_bad_pin_factory(self, mock_button):
    mock_button.side_effect = exc.BadPinFactory
    result = Sensors.get_bool_pin(pin=None)
    assert result is None

@patch("Pi_Car.sensors.Button")
def test_get_bool_pin_other_pin_error(self, mock_button):
    mock_button.side_effect = TypeError
    result = Sensors.get_bool_pin(pin=None)
    assert result is None
```

Now you're ready to write your new sensing functions, happy in the knowledge that half the code is already written and waiting for you to use! Because these new sensors are essentially just reading button states, you could just use the new **get_bool_pin** function to handle all the work for you, but to enhance your application with a little more logging, let's create two simple functions which wrap this utility function. Inside **sensors.py** create two functions. These don't need unit tests – they simply call **get_bool_pin** with a suitable GPIO pin and log some data around the function call:

```
@classmethod
def get_reverse_status(cls):
    """

    Safely read the reversing sensor
    :return: Boolean - reversing or not, or None
    """
```

```
app.logger.info("Starting to read reverse sensor")
result = cls.get_bool_pin(pin=22)
app.logger.debug(f"Boot: {result}")
app.logger.info("Finished reading reverse sensor")
return result

@classmethod
def get_fog_light_status(cls):
    """

    Safely read the fog light sensor
    :return: Boolean - fog lights on or not, or None
    """

    app.logger.info("Starting to read fog light sensor")
    result = cls.get_bool_pin(pin=23)
    app.logger.debug(f"Fog: {result}")
    app.logger.info("Finished reading fog light sensor")
    return result
```

Finally, implement these new functions into your main application route inside **data.py** (notice how **Black** has cleaned up the **result** dictionary; now it's starting to get longer than one line):

```
reverse_light = Sensors.get_reverse_status()
fog_light = Sensors.get_fog_light_status()

result = {
    "temperature": temperature,
    "boot": boot_status,
    "light": light_status,
    "reverse": reverse_light,
    "fog": fog_light,
}
```

The resulting main route now looks like this:

```python
@data_blueprint.route("/")
def show():
    app.logger.info("Starting to retrieve core data")
    temperature = Sensors.get_external_temp()
    boot_status = Sensors.get_boot_status()
    light_status = Sensors.get_light_status()
    reverse_light = Sensors.get_reverse_status()
    fog_light = Sensors.get_fog_light_status()

    result = {
        "temperature": temperature,
        "boot": boot_status,
        "light": light_status,
        "reverse": reverse_light,
        "fog": fog_light,
    }

    app.logger.info("Finished retrieving core data")
    app.logger.debug(f"Core data: {result}")
    return jsonify(result)
```

Once committed and deployed, fire up your Pi's application page from your computer, and observe the sensor data. Simulate the car's lights by pressing the buttons and watching the values change.

Chapter Summary

In this chapter you built two similar circuits to detect your car's reverse or fog lights. This is the easiest way to detect when the car is in the reverse gear or has the fog lights switched on. Later on you'll expand the application to perform additional tasks based on the reverse state. The fog light sensor is used to augment the driver's experience, and you can apply this circuit and application logic to any other car lighting component.

The next chapter covers the installation and software development of a reversing camera, using the official Pi Camera module.

CHAPTER 11

Reversing Camera

Chapter goal: Configure the Pi Camera to act as a reversing camera. Stream this video feed to the application.

For this project, you'll connect the Pi Camera to the Pi and stream the video feed to a web page. You'll learn how to configure the camera and settings and get the best possible image quality. In later chapters, you'll use this camera in conjunction with several of the other reversing sensors to build a complete reversing module, which automatically kicks in when you engage the reverse gear.

The Pi Camera is unlike other cameras you may have used. There is no button to take a picture, and there's no memory card to save photos to. There's no battery, and it's a fragile looking circuit which won't survive one trip to the beach. This Pi Camera is a camera *module*. It connects to the Pi and relays camera data for the Pi to process. The camera module handles reading the sensor stream, streaming data, adjusting light, and more, but the Pi has to tell it what to do and perform some processing of its own, to convert the raw stream into usable image formats.

It's possible to complete this project with a USB webcam (and many of the steps remain the same), but due to the vast number of different makes, models, styles, and price tags of USB webcams, the number of variations and slight changes needed for every model would not be possible to cover in a sensible number of chapters.

© Joseph Coburn 2020
J. Coburn, *Build Your Own Car Dashboard with a Raspberry Pi*,
https://doi.org/10.1007/978-1-4842-6080-7_11

Figure 11-1. *The Pi Camera V2.1*

For this project, you'll need to purchase the official Raspberry Pi V2 camera module, shown in Figure 11-1. Introduced in April 2016, this module is developed and built by the Raspberry Pi Foundation. It costs roughly $25 and is available on Amazon, or from any other store which sells Raspberry Pis. Similar clones of the camera module are available, as are the earlier V1 versions, but for the simplest experience following this chapter, you'll have less issues with the V2 model.

Camera Connection

Always turn off and disconnect the Pi's power supply when working with electronic circuits.

The Pi Camera connects to the Pi using a *ribbon* cable and the *camera serial interface*, or *CSI* port. This thin cable is included with the camera. Not only does it allow the Pi to communicate with the camera, but it also supplies power to the camera. If you've been using an inadequate power supply for your Pi, then the increased current draw required by the camera may mandate the need for a suitable power supply. The 3A supply specified in the *Project Overview – Equipment List* is sufficient for both the Pi and the camera.

Figure 11-2. *Pi Camera ribbon cable installed on the Pi*

With the exception of the *Pi Zero*, every single Pi has the camera connection port. This proprietary connection is cheap to manufacture, although it's not very durable. It's not so fragile that you should be afraid of using it, or using the Pi or connecting other peripherals or components to your GPIO ports; just don't go overboard by stressing the connector.

Begin by powering down the Pi and removing the power supply. The camera module comes with the ribbon cable already connected – you only need to connect the other end to the Pi itself – shown in Figure 11-2. Locate the camera module port, which is a narrow, 1-inch long connector behind the LAN port. Gently pull the connector's plastic cover up, roughly 1/8th of an inch. It won't fully detach.

Figure 11-3. *Pi Camera ribbon cable installed on the Pi*

Now gently insert the ribbon cable, with the exposed "pins" facing away from the Pi's I/O section, toward the HDMI and power connections – as shown in Figure 11-3. Don't force it. If you're struggling, double-check your cable is the correct orientation and that you're inserting it square on, and not at an angle. Once seated 1/8th of an inch, gently push the plastic cover back down, clamping down on the cable. Visually inspect the cable, and *gently* tug it, to ensure it's seated properly. When ready, apply the power and boot up the Pi.

Pi Camera First Time Configuration

Connect to the Pi over SSH. To begin using the camera, you need to tell the Pi it's connected. You can do this with the **raspi-config** utility. The output from this command is shown in Figure 11-4:

```
sudo raspi-config
```

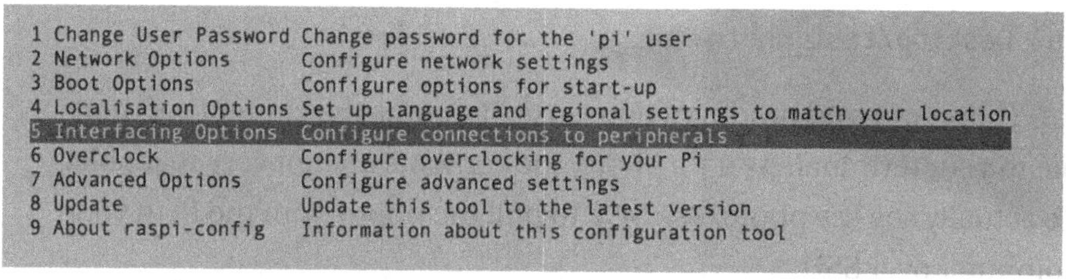

```
1 Change User Password Change password for the 'pi' user
2 Network Options      Configure network settings
3 Boot Options         Configure options for start-up
4 Localisation Options Set up language and regional settings to match your location
5 Interfacing Options  Configure connections to peripherals
6 Overclock            Configure overclocking for your Pi
7 Advanced Options     Configure advanced settings
8 Update               Update this tool to the latest version
9 About raspi-config   Information about this configuration tool
```

Figure 11-4. *The Pi configuration utility menu*

Use the arrow and enter keys to navigate around this tool. Scroll down and choose **Interfacing Options**. Figure 11-5 shows the *Interfacing Options* menu. Choose **P1 Camera**, and select **yes** when asked to enable the Pi Camera. Choose OK when the Pi confirms the camera is enabled. Now use your **right** arrow key to select **finish**, and choose **yes** when the Pi asks to restart.

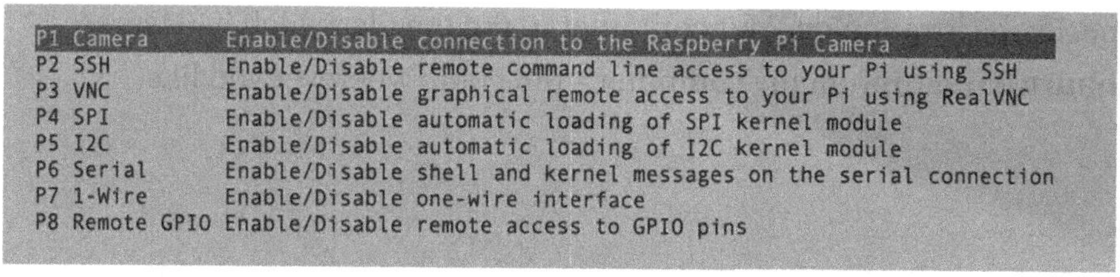

```
P1 Camera        Enable/Disable connection to the Raspberry Pi Camera
P2 SSH           Enable/Disable remote command line access to your Pi using SSH
P3 VNC           Enable/Disable graphical remote access to your Pi using RealVNC
P4 SPI           Enable/Disable automatic loading of SPI kernel module
P5 I2C           Enable/Disable automatic loading of I2C kernel module
P6 Serial        Enable/Disable shell and kernel messages on the serial connection
P7 1-Wire        Enable/Disable one-wire interface
P8 Remote GPIO   Enable/Disable remote access to GPIO pins
```

Figure 11-5. *Interfacing Options menu of the Pi configuration utility*

Once restarted, you can test your camera. The **raspistill** utility is a command-line tool to work with the Pi Camera, and it's included with your Raspbian install. Use it to save a test photo to your Pi's desktop, called "test_photo.jpg":

```
raspistill -o Desktop/test_photo.jpg
```

You can inspect the contents of this photo file using the **cat** command:

```
cat Desktop/test_photo.jpg
```

This command produces nonsense. It dumps the contents of the file to your terminal. As it's a photo, the contents are not very readable. To actually see the photo, use **SCP** to pull the photo from the Pi to your computer over SSH:

```
scp pi@192.168.1.210:Desktop/test_photo.jpg /Users/coburn/
Desktop/
```

SCP stands for *secure copy*. It lets you copy files from one remote location to another. This command is split into three sections. Begin with the **scp** keyword. This invokes the secure copy tool. The next section is the remote address and file location – separated by a colon. This looks for the file in location **Desktop/test_photo.jpg** on the remote **pi@192.168.1.210** – your IP address will vary, or you could use your **pi-car** alias here. Finally, specify the location on your computer to put the file, which is **/Users/coburn/Desktop/** on my computer – put yours wherever you like.

Figure 11-6. *Early, uncorrected Pi Camera photo*

Open your photo and look at it. It may not be perfect – my photo is blurry and upside down and visible in Figure 11-6. For now, providing that you have *something*, then that will do. You'll improve the quality and make it usable later on, but right now, this test is about ensuring the module works properly. If you can't copy the file, double-check your **scp** command. Does the file exist at all on the Pi? Was there a problem **raspistill** raised saving the photo at all? Double-check your work and, if necessary, your wiring.

Camera Live Stream Configuration

To work with this camera feed, the Pi will read in the camera data, interpret it, process it, and stream it to the network over its TCP port. This section isn't configured in Python. There are many Python libraries available, but

237

a solution which is both simple to configure and that works reliably (or can be defensively programmed around) is difficult to achieve in Python.

For this section, you'll use the **Motion** (`https://motion-project.github.io/`) library to handle the stream. This is a Debian package for working with the Pi Camera. It's mainly designed around motion detection and video recording (which would be an interesting extension project), yet it has excellent streaming capabilities, and is configured with a config file. It can run as a daemon, so the Pi can configure the stream itself when it boots.

Update the Pi's package list, and install Motion onto the Pi itself as a package:

```
sudo apt-get update
sudo apt-get install motion
```

Configure the Motion daemon – this allows motion to start when the Pi boots. Edit the **motion** file:

```
sudo nano /etc/default/motion
```

Change the **start_motion_daemon** option to **yes**, such that the whole file looks like this:

```
# Set to 'yes' to enable the motion daemon
start_motion_daemon=yes
```

Save and exit this file. Modify the file so it's executable by all users, and restart the Pi:

```
sudo chmod 777 /etc/default/motion
sudo reboot
```

When the Pi restarts, Motion will automatically start and begin streaming. Use the **service** command to check on the status:

```
sudo service motion status
```

You can also use this command to stop, start, or restart services such as motion, which you'll do shortly:

```
sudo service motion start
sudo service motion stop
sudo service motion restart
```

Motion is now running, but you can't see it. You can see *evidence* in the motion logs:

```
cat /var/log/motion/motion.log
```

This is good, but application logs are no substitute for a camera feed – they won't stop you reversing into a tree! To configure motion further, edit the **motion.conf** file, which defines all the possible settings for motion:

```
sudo nano /etc/motion/motion.conf
```

There are lots of options here, the vast majority of which you can safely ignore and leave as is. Table 11-1 covers the core features you need to change and what they do.

Table 11-1. *Motion config changes required*

Option	Value	Description	Full config line
width	800	Width of the video in pixels.	width 800
height	480	Height of the video in pixels.	height 480
framerate	30	Number of frames (individual images) to stream per second.	framerate 30
stream_quality	100	Percentage quality of video stream.	stream_quality 100
stream_localhost	off	Restrict the video stream to the Pi only, or allow access over the network.	stream_localhost off

(continued)

Table 11-1. (*continued*)

Option	Value	Description	Full config line
ffmpeg_output_ movies	off	Record videos to the Pi's memory card in addition to streaming.	ffmpeg_output_ movies off
stream_ maxrate	30	The maximum framerate to stream.	stream_maxrate 30
rotate	180	Rotate the video feed in degrees, only works in increments of 90.	rotate 180

When configured, save and exit the config file, and restart the motion service:

```
sudo service motion restart
```

Now load the Pi in your web browser, and use Motion's default streaming port of **8081**:

```
http://pi-car:8081/
```

Verify that you see the feed from the camera. Move around and observe as it changes. Note the timestamp in the bottom-right corner of the video. The stream is now ready to pull into your Flask application. You may need to revisit these configuration settings as the project progresses. Perhaps when you install the project into your car, the camera is rotated upside down, or you need to change the quality. Figure 11-7 shows the rotated image stream, complete with timestamp in the lower-right corner.

Figure 11-7. *Rotated and refined Pi Camera photo*

Pi Camera Focus Adjustment

Like any camera, the Pi Camera V2 has a lens with adjustable focus.
There's no autofocus, it's purely manual – a mechanical lens adjustment. If
your video feed is blurry, and providing you haven't increased the output
dimensions to huge numbers (which will reduce the quality), then you
may need to adjust the lens focus.

All cameras use a *plane of focus* (PoF). This imaginary line defines what
is and is not in focus at a given time. Adjusting the focus on a lens moves this
plane forward or backward. Everything parallel to the lens at a given distance
is in focus, and moving nearer or further from or to the lens gets increasingly
out of focus. An object 1M away could be in focus, and something right next
to the lens would be out of focus. For these reasons, you won't be able to get
everything the camera sees in focus – it will be a compromise, which may
need adjusting once the camera is mounted on your car.

To adjust the Pi's focus, identify the sensor and lens module on the front of the Pi Camera module. The small black square in the middle of the module houses the lens. Within this square, the lens features a hexagonal casing, known as the *lens barrel*. By rotating this barrel, you can adjust the plane of focus.

Figure 11-8. *Tools needed for Pi Camera lens focus adjustment*

Use a small pair of pliers to grip the outer lens housing – shown in Figure 11-8. Use a small screwdriver to nudge the lens barrel, and use the indentation to grip your tool. Be very careful not to apply too much pressure. Slipping here could damage the lens itself or risk pulling the entire lens assembly away from the module itself. Treat this lens and this maintenance step as you would a pair of glasses, or when putting contact lenses in.

Remember, this focus will need adjusting when the camera is installed in your car.

Camera Flask Code

For this code section, you'll create a new Flask route to serve the image. Later on, you'll expand this route to make use of the reversing sensors, but for now, it simply serves the camera feed. This is a simple code change – the Pi is already handling the hard work of the video.

Create the files needed for this section:

```
touch Pi_Car/reverse.py
mkdir Pi_Car/templates
touch Pi_Car/templates/reverse.html
```

The **reverse.py** file is the new route for this reversing screen. The template file **reverse.html** is the markup to render this stream. It lives inside the **templates** folder, which is a Flask pattern for storing markup files.

Here's the code you need for **reverse.py**:

```python
from flask import Blueprint, render_template
from flask import current_app as app

reverse_blueprint = Blueprint("reverse", __name__)

@reverse_blueprint.route("/reverse/")
def reverse():
    app.logger.info("Starting to load reverse route")
    stream_port = app.config.get("STREAM_PORT", 8081)
    host = "pi-car"
    stream_url = f"http://{host}:{stream_port}"
    app.logger.debug(f"Camera streaming url: {stream_url}")
    app.logger.info("Finished loading reverse route")
    return render_template(template_name_or_list="reverse.
html", base_url=stream_url)
```

This is a new blueprint file. It defines a new route /**reverse**/ and handles the logic to connect to the stream. There's lots of logging (as is standard across this project). This file uses the **render_template** function from Flask. This function renders the contents of a template to the browser – **reverse.html**. Notice how you don't need to specify the **templates** folder, as Flask already knows this is where to look for templates. By using a render template, you can keep your code neater, as all the HTML and markup-specific logic lives in the template itself, ready for reuse by any of your application logic.

You can also pass data to templates. This route passes the **stream_url** to the template. This stream URL is where the browser can find the video feed. It's a *Fully Qualified Domain Name*, or *FQDN*. It consists of the protocol (http), host (pi-car), and stream port. Notice how the stream port is pulled from the config even though it does not exist. This defensive logic falls back to the 8081 stream port if the config is not set. This lets you easily change the port in the future, just by modifying the config file. You don't have to dig through the code, which could use this port in numerous locations in a bigger code base.

Here's the code you need for the **reverse.html** template:

```
<img src="{{ base_url }}">
```

This isn't valid HTML, but I cover that in detail in the tidying up chapter toward the end of this book. For now, it's sufficient. This tag tells the browser to render an image. It points the browser toward the live stream URL you built in the **reverse.py** file. Notice the dual curly braces around the variable:

```
{{ base_url }}
```

This is **Jinja**, the templating language included with Flask. This renders the value "http://pi-car:8081", as specified in your back-end logic.

Finally, inside **app.py**, import your new blueprint:

```
from .reverse import reverse_blueprint
```

and then register the route:

```
app.register_blueprint(reverse_blueprint)
```

Your whole **app.py** file now looks like this:

```
import logging

from flask import Flask
from logging.handlers import RotatingFileHandler
from .data import data_blueprint
from .reverse import reverse_blueprint

def create_app(config_file="config/local_config.py"):
    app = Flask(__name__)  # Initialize app
    app.config.from_pyfile(config_file, silent=False)  # Read
    in config from file

    if app.config.get("FILE_LOGGING"):
        # Configure file-based log handler
        log_file_handler = RotatingFileHandler(
            filename=app.config.get("LOG_FILE_NAME", "config/
            pi-car.log"),
            maxBytes=10000000,
            backupCount=4,
        )
        log_file_handler.setFormatter(
            logging.Formatter("[%(asctime)s] %(levelname)s in
            %(module)s: %(message)s")
        )
        app.logger.addHandler(log_file_handler)
```

```
app.logger.setLevel(app.config.get("LOGGER_LEVEL", "ERROR"))

app.logger.info("----- STARTING APP ------")

app.register_blueprint(data_blueprint)
app.register_blueprint(reverse_blueprint)

app.logger.info("----- FINISHED STARTING APP -----")

return app
```

Start Flask on your computer, and visit the new URL route at http://127.0.0.1:5000/reverse/. Providing the Pi is on and the **Motion** service is streaming the video feed, you'll see the real-time video. Commit your changes, and perform a build on the Pi. Visit the Pi's URL and verify the route also works there at http://pi-car:5000/reverse/ (shown in Figure 11-9).

Figure 11-9. *Flask application streaming the live video feed*

Notice how you're using port 5000 to access the application, but if you look at the code rendered by the reverse route (by **right-clicking** and choosing **inspect** to bring up your console developer tools), you'll see the stream is coming from `http://pi-car:8081`. This is due to ports, as discussed in earlier chapters. The application runs on port 5000, but the stream runs on port 8081. You don't need to merge or combine the two – they are independent data feeds coming out of the Pi.

Chapter Summary

This chapter introduced to you the Pi Camera module. You learned how to connect it to the Pi and fine-tune the settings to achieve the best possible quality. You configured the Pi to stream the camera feed over the network and created a basic template to pull this stream into your application. This is the basis for your entire reversing module, which you'll continue to expand upon later on.

The next chapter shows you how to develop a reverse beeper, to indicate the presence of a rear obstacle.

CHAPTER 12

Reversing Beeper

Chapter goal: Connect a piezo element and configure the application to beep on command.

A beeper is an essential element of a modern car's reversing system. When used in conjunction with a distance sensor (see the next project chapter), a system which beeps when you get near an object is an incredibly useful utility. This project introduces a piezo element to produce beep sounds, and the associated logic and application routes to do so.

Piezo Connection

This project uses a *piezo* element to produce the beep sound. Piezo, or piezoelectric elements, generate a charge from electrical energy. This charge produces a squeezing or stretching of the material and generates a noise. The size of the material and the amount and duration of electricity supplied all impact the resulting output. Piezo elements are used in your desktop computer to produce the startup beep after passing through the POST stage of the startup sequence – although this is less common now than it used to be. Another common use is as microphones in some instruments. You can see this completed circuit in Figure 12-1.

© Joseph Coburn 2020
J. Coburn, *Build Your Own Car Dashboard with a Raspberry Pi*,
https://doi.org/10.1007/978-1-4842-6080-7_12

Figure 12-1. *Piezo wired into the Pi*

POST   stands for power-on self-test. It's a series of tests carried out by your computer before booting into the operating system. It tests that your RAM, keyboard, drives, and other devices are working correctly. Piezo elements were the perfect choice to indicate these tests have passed – small, cheap, and easy to use!

You can buy piezo elements from Amazon, or your local electronics store. To avoid confusion with piezos designed for musical instruments, search for "5v piezo," or elements designed for electronic circuits, or Arduino/Pi projects. You can expect to pay around one dollar for a single element, although they are often sold in bulk packs for a lower price per unit. Many piezos work with a variety of different voltages – try to get one designed for 3v.

Piezos have a polarity – they will only work one way round. Often they come with pre-soldered positive and negative wires, but if not, one leg is often marked as negative. You won't cause any damage by installing a piezo in reverse – it just won't work properly, if at all.

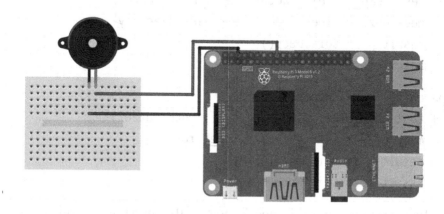

Figure 12-2. *Piezo wiring diagram*

Connect the negative leg to the Pi's ground. Connect the positive leg to physical pin 18 (GPIO pin 24). That's it. Piezos don't need any complex hardware to run – you apply power and they emit a noise. The longer the power is applied for, the longer and more intense the sound is. Figure 12-2 shows the wiring diagram for this circuit.

Piezo Flask Logic

This piezo logic will live inside your **Sensors** class. You could argue semantics that a piezo element *is not* a sensor – but it will respond to sensor data. This project uses the **Buzzer** class from the gpiozero library. Once configured, you'll apply power to the element, wait for a set duration, and then remove power. Begin with your unit tests. Add your two now standard tests for bad pin factory and other errors. These tests and associated logic ensure your function will still work when not running on the Pi itself. Inside **test_sensors.py**, expand the **TestSensors** class:

```
@patch("Pi_Car.sensors.Buzzer")
def test_beep_bad_pin_factory(self, mock_buzzer):
    mock_buzzer.side_effect = exc.BadPinFactory
    result = Sensors.beep()
    assert result is None

@patch("Pi_Car.sensors.Buzzer")
def test_beep_other_pin_error(self, mock_buzzer):
    mock_buzzer.side_effect = TypeError
    result = Sensors.beep()
    assert result is None
```

Inside **sensors.py**, add a new import for the **time** library, and import **Buzzer** from gpiozero, such that all of your imports now look like this:

```
import time

from flask import current_app as app
from gpiozero import Button, exc, LightSensor, Buzzer

try:
    from w1thermsensor import W1ThermSensor
except Exception:
    W1ThermSensor = None
```

The **time** library is used to wait for the beep to complete. Now expand the **Sensors** class with a new static method called **beep**:

```
@staticmethod
def beep(duration=1):
    """

    Issue a single "beep" sound
```

```
:param duration: Time to sustain beep for, in seconds
:return: None
"""

app.logger.info("Starting beep")
app.logger.debug(f"Beep duration: {duration}")

try:
    buzzer = Buzzer(pin=24)
    buzzer.on()
    time.sleep(duration)
    buzzer.off()
except exc.BadPinFactory as e:
    app.logger.warning(f"Unable to issue beep in this
    environment: {e}")
except Exception as e:
    app.logger.error(f"Unknown problem with beep: {e}")

app.logger.info("Finished beep")
```

Much of the code here should look familiar. The error handling, logging, and docstring are used throughout the other sensor functions. The core of this code begins by creating a new **buzzer** object based on the **Buzzer** class. This uses GPIO pin 24. After turning the buzzer on using the **on** function, the **sleep** function from the **time** library is used to wait one second. This **duration** variable defaults to one second, but you can override it when you call this function.

The **off** function turns the buzzer off. In many cases, using **time. sleep** like this is not a perfect pattern. The Pi has to wait for this action to complete – it *blocks* the Pi from doing any other work. In this case, the main dashboard will call this function in a background-like operation, so the fact it blocks is not an issue. You could use the **beep** function from the **Buzzer** class, along with the **background** parameter to avoid blocking here, but it's not going to cause a problem not doing so.

Finally, call your beep function (temporarily) from your main application route inside **data.py:**

```
Sensors.beep()
```

Your completed route so far should look like this:

```
@data_blueprint.route("/")
def show():
    app.logger.info("Starting to retrieve core data")
    temperature = Sensors.get_external_temp()
    boot_status = Sensors.get_boot_status()
    light_status = Sensors.get_light_status()
    reverse_light = Sensors.get_reverse_status()
    fog_light = Sensors.get_fog_light_status()

    result = {
        "temperature": temperature,
        "boot": boot_status,
        "light": light_status,
        "reverse": reverse_light,
        "fog": fog_light,
    }

    Sensors.beep()
    app.logger.info("Finished retrieving core data")
    app.logger.debug(f"Core data: {result}")
    return jsonify(result)
```

Using this beep is just temporary, as the Pi has to wait the one second for the beep to complete. It will delay the loading of your data by one second. This is just a test for now, and I'll show you how to optimize this function during the cleaning up chapter. Once running locally, commit your code and perform a build on the Pi. Load the Pi's application page at http://pi-car:5000 and listen for the beep. If you don't hear one, double-check your logic. Is the piezo element wired in reverse? What do the Pi's application logs show?

This simple project is quick to implement, yet provides a very valuable feature for your overall project.

Chapter Summary

This simple chapter showed you how to use a piezo element to emit a "beep" sound on command. You learned how different size piezo elements can alter the sound, as can different code parameters. This application logic is once again ready to implement into your whole reversing module.

The next chapter shows you how to install a rear distance sensor, which is used in conjunction with this chapter to produce a sound when a rear obstacle appears.

CHAPTER 13

Distance Sensor

Chapter Goal: Install an IR distance sensor and detect when an object is in range.

A distance sensor is an incredibly useful tool that many modern cars (and few older or budget cars) have. When reversing (and in conjunction with an audible beep sound), immediate feedback as to the distance of an object seriously helps prevent an accident. This could be a child, another car, a wall, or anything. This distance sensor is often called a parking sensor, or parking assist, and it's the final component of your reversing module. While complex in nature, the sensor circuit handles all the hard work for you, making this project one of the simplest.

Distance Sensor Theory

There are several different ways to detect an object in close proximity to a car. The theory is the same for most of the techniques. Sensors emit some kind of signal. This could be sound, light, or electromagnetic pulses. This signal bounces off nearby objects, and another sensor reads this returning signal. The longer it takes to return, the further away the object is. In practice, it's a lot more complex than this, but that's the basic principle. Many cars use a combination of sensors, to detect objects around most of the car. This project only covers one simple sensor, but you could expand it if you so desire.

© Joseph Coburn 2020
J. Coburn, *Build Your Own Car Dashboard with a Raspberry Pi*,
https://doi.org/10.1007/978-1-4842-6080-7_13

A common hobby sensor is the ultrasonic range-finder, number HC-SR04P. This cheap component uses soundwaves to detect objects. These work well, and if you'd like to use one, the *DistanceSensor* class of gpiozero (`https://gpiozero.readthedocs.io/en/stable/api_input.html#distancesensor-hc-sr04`) handles the work for you. To use this sensor requires three GPIO pins and several resistors arranged together as a voltage divider.

To keep things simple, I've chosen to implement an infrared (IR) range sensor using the *KY-032* module. Everything you need is included in the hardware module, and it's extremely simple to wire up and code – especially if you've completed the previous project chapters. These sensors cost a few dollars and are available from Amazon or your local electronics store.

This sensor emits an infrared light, which bounces off nearby objects back into the infrared detector. It's already fine-tuned to the specific wavelengths required and comes with its own integrated circuit to handle the transmission for you. It has a maximum range of roughly 15 inches – which may not match commercial car sensors – but it's about on par with the ultrasonic range-finder and is fairly standard for consumer sensors in this price range.

Distance Sensor Hardware

Always turn off and disconnect the Pi's power supply when working with electronic circuits.

To build this project, you'll need a KY-032 IR sensor module. These come in several minor variants. You'll run this at 3.3v, but almost all of the modules available operate at 3.3v–5v. Make sure you double-check. Running at a lower voltage than required won't break it, but it may not work correctly, if at all. Most units come with four connection pins and a jumper header to reconfigure the circuit. Alternatively, a three-pin model also exists, which provides the exact same functionality.

Begin by studying your IR module, shown in Figure 13-1. Holding it
with the circuit toward you and the pins facing down there are four key
sections. At the top is the IR transmitter and receiver pair. This emits
and detects the signal. In the middle is the circuitry required to make
this module work, with the customization header toward the lower-right
side. To the left and right are two status LEDs. Below this are the two
potentiometers used to fine-tune settings, and finally the header pins are
at the bottom.

Figure 13-1. *KY-032 IR sensor module*

The left status LED is labelled as "PLED". This stands for *power LED*. It lights up to indicate that the module has power. The LED on the right is labelled as "SLED", which stands for *status LED*. This lights up when there is an obstruction detected by the sensor. When clear, it turns off again.

These configuration potentiometers serve two independent purposes. The potentiometer on the left adjusts the range. All the way counterclockwise allows the sensor to operate at maximum range. All the way clockwise limits the sensor to its minimum range. Use a small screwdriver or your nail to adjust this fully counterclockwise. The right potentiometer adjusts the frequency of the IR signal. This is preset at the factory and does not need adjusting.

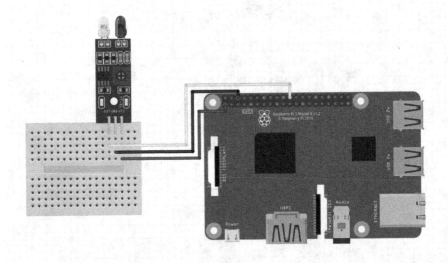

Figure 13-2. *KY-032 IR sensor wiring diagram*

From left to right, the pins at the bottom are labelled as

- GND

- +

- Out

- EN

Connect the Pi's ground to **GND**. Connect the Pi's 3.3v to **+**. Connect physical pin 22 (GPIO pin 25) to **Out**. This is where the Pi will read the sensor state. The final pin, marked **EN**, is an *enable* pin. You can optionally use this to trigger sensor pings. By default, the module automatically sends out sensor pings, configured using the jumper on the lower right. You can ignore this pin. The wiring diagram is shown in Figure 13-2.

Once ready, connect the power supply and boot the Pi.

Distance Sensor Flask Code

This sensor is very easy to code for. It produces a HIGH or LOW signal, depending on object detection – much like a button. If an object is detected within range, the *SLED* status LED lights up, and the sensor returns a HIGH value. If no object is detected, the Pi's pull-down resistor is detected by the GPIO pin as LOW. For this reason, you can use the **Button** class and your existing logic to read this data.

Create a new function to read this sensor called **get_rear_distance_ sensor**. Place it inside your **Sensors** class:

```
@classmethod
def get_rear_distance_sensor(cls):
    """

    Safely read the reversing sensor
    :return: Boolean - reversing or not, or None
    """

    app.logger.info("Starting to read distance sensor")
    result = cls.get_bool_pin(pin=25)
    if result:
        result = False
```

```
else:
    result = True
app.logger.debug(f"Rear distance sensor: {result}")
app.logger.info("Finished reading distance sensor")
return result
```

This function uses your **get_bool_pin** function to handle the processing as a button. Because the gpiozero library inverts the state of pins (depending on their configuration at runtime), you need to invert the value. The simple logic here flips the values from True > False and False > True:

```
if result:
    result = False
else:
    result = True
```

Finally, add the new sensor call to your main route inside **data.py**:

```
rear_distance = Sensors.get_rear_distance_sensor()
```

Make sure you update your **result** dictionary as well, such that your whole route looks like this:

```
@data_blueprint.route("/")
def show():
    app.logger.info("Starting to retrieve core data")
    temperature = Sensors.get_external_temp()
    boot_status = Sensors.get_boot_status()
    light_status = Sensors.get_light_status()
    reverse_light = Sensors.get_reverse_status()
    fog_light = Sensors.get_fog_light_status()
    rear_distance = Sensors.get_rear_distance_sensor()
```

```
result = {
    "temperature": temperature,
    "boot": boot_status,
    "light": light_status,
    "reverse": reverse_light,
    "rear_distance": rear_distance,
    "fog": fog_light,
}

Sensors.beep()
app.logger.info("Finished retrieving core data")
app.logger.debug(f"Core data: {result}")
return jsonify(result)
```

Once verified on your machine, commit your code and perform a build. Load the main page at http://pi-car:500 and check the result under the **rear_distance** key. Reload the page several times while covering and uncovering the sensor.

Chapter Summary

In this chapter you build a rear distance sensor using an IR module. You learned the differences between several different rear sensing techniques and the pitfalls of consumer-level sensors. You coded around some potentially confusing logic introduced by a third-party library and continued to expand your application with clean, documented, and easy-to-read code.

Well done! You now have everything in place to finish configuring your car dashboard system. In the next chapter, I'll cover bringing everything together into a functional and usable system and performing final polishing and system tuning.

CHAPTER 14

System Polishing

Chapter goal: Use HTML and CSS to make the dashboard usable and pretty. Fine-tune the system and shape it into a working dashboard.

Up to this point, you've been working mainly with Python and Bash. You've been writing sensor components and building circuits, with little thought to the style or usability. You've been following my mantra of "make it work, then make it pretty." Well now the time has come to make it pretty. This is one chapter where you have a lot of flexibility. Want to make it bright pink? Fill the screen with cat photos, or a sentient AI able to perceive your every move? That's all possible, and totally up to your creativity. Don't worry if you're not creative – I'll show you how to make a minimalistic dashboard, which you can use as a basis to expand on into something unique.

For this chapter, you'll use several libraries to help make this dashboard pretty. You'll use Bootstrap (`https://getbootstrap.com/`) for most of the styling and layout. You'll also use Font Awesome (`https://fontawesome.com/`) for some fantastic (and open source) icons. Font Awesome has a paid-for, Pro service, but the free tier is more than good enough for this project.

For most websites, a *content delivery network* (CDN) lets you quickly and easily pull in these external assets. CDNs greatly speed up the user experience on any website, and free public CDNs exist to host the required

© Joseph Coburn 2020
J. Coburn, *Build Your Own Car Dashboard with a Raspberry Pi*,
https://doi.org/10.1007/978-1-4842-6080-7_14

resources for you. However, because the Pi is going in your car, it may not always have (nor should it need to rely on) an Internet connection. This makes public CDNs a no-go. I'll show you how to download these resources and serve them up locally from the Pi.

Public-facing websites also need to cater to a variety of users – from very old browsers, small screens, and Internet connections to browsers built-into games consoles, ultrafast modern computers, or even ancient systems such as OS/2. On the Internet, you get it all, and it's your job as a developer to ensure that most visitors can see your website as you intended. Fortunately, this dashboard is only for you to use. The Pi has a known web browser, with a fixed-size screen. Every time you visit the page, the Pi renders the content in the same way. This makes development and testing slightly easier. At the expense of cutting corners, you can be happy enough if it looks good on the Pi. You don't need to worry about other users or browser compatibility.

Basic Dashboard Layout

Let's begin by designing the basic dashboard (ignoring the reversing screen for now). This will start as a "static" page. It won't update based on the data from the Pi; you're just getting a feel for the design.

Start by downloading the assets for Bootstrap and Font Awesome. Visit the Bootstrap download page (https://getbootstrap.com/docs/4.4/getting-started/download/). The current version of Bootstrap is v4.4 – but this is likely to change in the future, as new releases come out. Double-check you're on the latest version by clicking the "v4.4" on the top-right corner of the screen and choosing the "latest" option from the version drop-down menu (Figure 14-1). Scroll down to the "Compiled CSS and JS" section, and choose **download source**. This will download a compressed file, containing all the files Bootstrap needs to work – which is a lot.

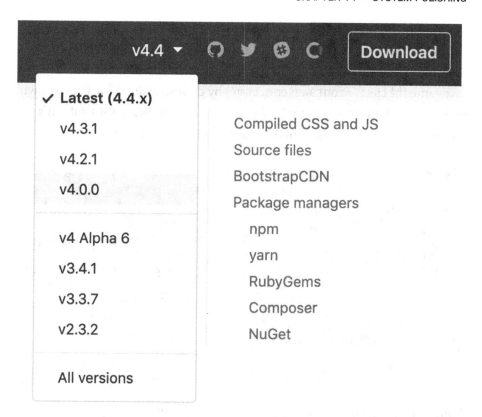

Figure 14-1. *Changing Bootstrap version before download*

Double-click this file to extract it. You now have a Bootstrap folder called something like **bootstrap-4.3.1-dist** (your version number may differ). Back in your project terminal, create a folder called **static**, inside your **Pi_Car** folder:

```
mkdir Pi_Car/static
```

Now move the entire bootstrap folder into this static folder – either through finder/your GUI tool of choice or over the command line:

```
mv /Users/coburn/Downloads/bootstrap-4.3.1-dist /Users/coburn/
Documents/Pi-Car/Pi_Car/static
```

Modify the paths to suit your folder structure.

Bootstrap is now ready to use in your application, so let's get Font Awesome ready in much the same way. Create an account at Font Awesome (https://fontawesome.com/) by choosing **Start for Free** shown in Figure 14-2. Enter your email address and choose **Send Kit Code**. It's not possible to download Font Awesome without signing up.

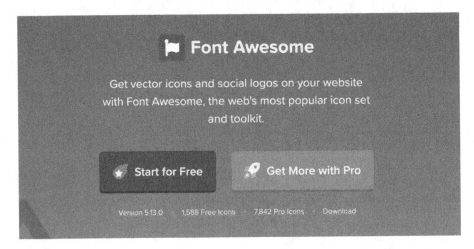

Figure 14-2. *Font Awesome getting started screen*

After confirming your email address, visit the "Other Methods" page (https://fontawesome.com/start#other-methods) and choose **download** (Figure 14-3). From the next page, choose **Download Font Awesome Free for the Web**. Confirm you have a new file downloaded called something like **fontawesome-free-5.13.0-web**. This version number is subject to change in the future, but Font Awesome will serve you the new files as they become available.

Download

Serve Font Awesome yourself.

Figure 14-3. *Font Awesome download button*

Once again, **double-click** to extract the compressed files, and move them into your **static** folder:

```
mv /Users/coburn/Downloads/fontawesome-free-5.13.0-web /Users/
coburn/Documents/Pi-Car/Pi_Car/static
```

Let's create the core dashboard now. Inside your **templates** folder, create a new file called **main.html**:

```
touch templates/main.html
```

Here's the code you need:

```
<!doctype html>

<html lang="en">

<head>
    <meta charset="utf-8">
    <meta name="viewport" content="width=device-width, initial-
    scale=1, shrink-to-fit=no">

    <title>Pi Car</title>
    <meta name="description" content="Raspberry Pi based car
    system">
    <meta name="author" content="Joe Coburn">
    <link href="static/fontawesome-free-5.13.0-web/css/all.css"
    rel="stylesheet">
```

```
<link rel="stylesheet" type="text/css" href="static/
bootstrap-4.3.1-dist/css/bootstrap.min.css">
<link rel="stylesheet" type="text/css" href="static/css/
style.css">
</head>

<body>
    <div class="container text-center text-light">
        <h1>Hello.</h1>
        <h2>Wednesday 8th January 2020</h2>
        <div class="row">
            <div class="col text-left">
                <i class="fas fa-clock"></i>15:50
            </div>
            <div class="col text-right">
                <i class="fas fa-snowflake"></i> 20° C
                <br />
                <i class="fas fa-moon"></i>
                <i class="fas fa-sun"></i>Daytime
            </div>
        </div>
        <div class="row">
            <div class="col text-middle">
                <i class="fas fa-car icon-huge"></i>
            </div>
        </div>
        <div class="row">
            <div class="col text-middle">
                <i class="fas fa-exclamation"></i><span
                class="exclamation">Boot is open</span>
```

```
            <br>
            <i class="fas fa-lightbulb"></i>Fog lights are on
        </div>
    </div>
</div>
</body>

</html>
```

This may look like a lot, but it's much simpler than it may first appear. This isn't code as such, it's markup. Hypertext Markup Language, or HTML, is the Internet standard markup language for websites. It can't perform calculations or logic, it's simply instructions for the browser to interpret. HTML is a *markup language*. With it, you can define tables, boxes, text, images, and so on. Your browser understands these commands and does its best to draw the elements you specify. Each browser interprets these slightly differently, however, making cross-platform web development more like a game of whack-a-mole if you're not careful.

HTML does not render pretty colors or define the sizes of things aside from a few browser defaults. *Cascading Style Sheets*, or CSS, almost always accompanies HTML to make things pretty, but I'll cover that after breaking down this HTML.

HTML is a simple language, and your page will continue to work even if you make a mistake – it might look a bit odd though, depending on the error. HTML contains *tags*. A tag is an instruction and can contain other text and other tags inside it. Tags need a matching tag to *close* them, although there are exceptions, and self-closing tags. Think of HTML as defining a series of boxes for text of images to sit in. This basic tag is a **H1** element:

```
<h1>Hello.</h1>
```

It has an opening and a closing tag and contains the text "Hello".

Starting at the top of the file, there are some tags to tell the browser this is HTML and the language to use.

```
<!doctype html>
<html lang="en">
```

The **doctype** is a bit like a *shebang* in Bash scripts – it doesn't need closing. This **HTML** tag is closed at the end of the file. Therefore, everything in this file is enclosed in the **HTML** tag.

Next is the **head** tag, with associated nested tags:

```
<head>
    <meta charset="utf-8">
    <meta name="viewport" content="width=device-width, initial-
    scale=1, shrink-to-fit=no">

    <title>Pi Car</title>
    <meta name="description" content="Raspberry Pi based car
    system">
    <meta name="author" content="Joe Coburn">
    <link href="/static/fontawesome-free-5.13.0-web/css/all.
    css" rel="stylesheet">
    <link rel="stylesheet" type="text/css" href="/static/
    bootstrap-4.3.1-dist/css/bootstrap.min.css">
    <link rel="stylesheet" type="text/css" href="/static/css/
    style.css">
</head>
```

The head tag is used for page metadata. Things such as the page title, character encoding (**charset**), and other metadata are defined here. Toward the bottom you can see the **link** tags. These pull in your Bootstrap and Font Awesome **CSS** files you downloaded earlier. This makes them accessible on the page. This also references a **style.css** file. This doesn't exist yet, but it's where you'll write any custom CSS needed to style this page.

Moving on, the **body** tag is where the bulk of your page content lives. You can see this is full of **div** tags, which are containers to store other elements. **H** tags (**H1**, **H2**, etc.) are used for titles or larger text. You can see these tags have multiple **classes** attached:

```
<div class="col text-right">
```

Classes are used to point HTML elements to a CSS style. This lets you reuse CSS without copying and pasting it all over the place and lets you target specific elements to style. The classes listed here are defined by Bootstrap, with a little custom CSS.

Finally, there are the **i** tags:

```
<i class="fas fa-lightbulb"></i>
```

These elements use the Font Awesome classes to render the icons you can see on the dashboard.

There are lots of different HTML elements, tags, and techniques, but the premise is mostly the same across them all – different tags, each supporting attributes such as **class**, each one with specific purpose. Some tags have historical relevance, and some are no longer valid, as they are deprecated due to their age or incompatibility.

Remember, this HTML is static right now – it's hard-coded to always display the same information – and isn't tied into your sensor data.

Moving onto the CSS – most of this is handled for you by Bootstrap. As far as CSS files go, this is quite a small file, at 33 lines long. Create a new folder called **CSS** inside your **static** folder:

```
mkdir Pi_Car/static/css
```

Create a CSS file called **style**:

```
touch Pi_Car/static/css/style.css
```

This file will contain your custom CSS – any changes you need which Bootstrap doesn't handle for you. Here's the code you need:

```css
html,
body {
      font-size: 25px;
      background-color: var(--gray-dark);
      text-shadow: 2px 2px #000000;
      cursor: none;
      padding: 0;
}

i {
      margin-right: 10px;
}

.icon-huge {
      font-size: 350px;
      font-weight: bold;
      text-shadow: 4px 4px #000000;
}

.fa-snowflake {
      color: var(--blue);
}

.fa-sun {
      color: var(--yellow);
}

.fa-moon {
      color: var(--cyan);
}
```

```
.fa-exclamation,
.exclamation {
    color: var(--red);
}
```

CSS lets you change a huge number of stylistic and layout elements. You can animate elements; change the size, color, and position of almost anything; hide elements; and more. The changes here mostly impact the size, and color of the text and icons.

Core HTML elements are targeted with their name – such as **html**. Everything inside the curly braces is applied to elements that meet the criteria. You can target multiple elements, high-level elements, or only elements that exist inside a different element. Some of the colors use the bootstrap variables. This uses the Bootstrap variable called "--blue":

```
.fa-snowflake {
    color: var(--blue);
}
```

The **cursor** attribute ensures you won't see the mouse cursor on the screen. Not very useful for a website, but incredibly useful for a Pi project such as this:

```
cursor: none;
```

Now that you have your HTML and CSS all ready, modify your application route inside **main.py** to load the **main.html** template, using the **render_template** function from Flask. Import the function:

```
from flask import Blueprint, jsonify, render_template
```

Then temporarily modify your route to ignore the data:

```
@data_blueprint.route("/")
def show():
```

```
app.logger.info("Starting to retrieve core data")
temperature = Sensors.get_external_temp()
boot_status = Sensors.get_boot_status()
light_status = Sensors.get_light_status()
reverse_light = Sensors.get_reverse_status()
fog_light = Sensors.get_fog_light_status()
rear_distance = Sensors.get_rear_distance_sensor()

result = {
    "temperature": "temperature",
    "boot": "boot_status",
    "light": "light_status",
    "reverse": "reverse_light",
    "rear_distance": "rear_distance",
    "fog": "fog_light",
}

Sensors.beep()
app.logger.info("Finished retrieving core data")
app.logger.debug(f"Core data: {result}")
#return jsonify(result)
return render_template("main.html")
```

Run the app on your computer and visit it in your web browser of choice, found at http://127.0.0.1:5000/.

Figure 14-4. *Static dashboard styling*

Observe what it looks like (shown in Figure 14-4). The background has a dark color, the text is white (with a slight shadow), and there are various elements displaying (fake) data. There are icons next to some of the items. There are currently too many icons – not all of these will be visible when it's hooked into your main dataset, but for now, commit the code and perform a build on the Pi. Visit the Pi's application at `http://pi-car:5000/` and verify the build. Resize your browser window and observe how the layout reflows to fit. It may not always fit at all sizes, but that's OK – the Pi has a fixed-size screen.

Bootstrap is configured on this page for a *responsive* layout. That is to say, as the size of your web browser changes, so does the layout of the page. Figure 14-5 shows this dashboard on a different sized screen. This doesn't really matter for this project, as the Pi will always have the same screen size, but it's a good practice to get into (and Bootstrap does it all for you).

Figure 14-5. *Dashboard resized to the screen*

Right now, the Pi boots up. It downloads the latest code, installs the dependencies, and spins up the Flask server (accessible over the network). It doesn't have a screen, and it doesn't open the web browser and load the page for you – let's fix that next.

Autoload the Pi's Web Browser

For a truly interaction-free startup process, the Pi needs to open a web browser and visit the application it's already running. Your installation of Raspbian on the Pi comes with a web browser. It's perhaps not as full featured as your desktop computer browser, but it's sufficient for this project.

If it's not currently connected, then plug in your Pi's mini LCD display using the full-size HDMI to micro-HDMI cable. Connect to the Pi over SSH.

It's perfectly possible to start a browser from the root user account, perhaps in your rc.local, but that's an imperfect solution. Right now, your Pi boots to the *Lightweight X11 Desktop Environment* (LXDE) desktop. This provides your GUI desktop interface, which so far you have ignored in favor of a remote terminal session. This LXDE environment has control over the HDMI display. It's difficult to launch a browser which uses this display through the existing boot scripts. Enter *LXDE-pi/autostart*. Commands inside this file run when the desktop loads, for any user. Begin by opening the file:

```
sudo nano /etc/xdg/lxsession/LXDE-pi/autostart
```

Under the existing options in here, add the following command:

```
/usr/bin/chromium-browser --no-first-run --noerrdialogs
--start-fullscreen --start-maximized --disable-notifications
--disable-infobars --kiosk --incognito http://localhost:5000
```

Save and exit the file. What does this do? It starts the *Chromium* browser, located at **/usr/bin/chromium-browser**. It points it to your localhost address and port of your Flask server, and it passes in several options to the browser. These options start the browser without any distractions. Fullscreen, *kiosk* mode prevents you from showing the URL address bar or bookmarks and hides lots of alerts and warnings – perfect for an integrated system such as this.

Restart the Pi and observe as the browser starts after booting to the desktop environment. You may notice that the address cannot be found, but after several minutes, it eventually arrives. This is because Flask is still booting when the browser starts. Shortly I'll show you how to speed this up once you're no longer actively developing the system.

For me, the Pi is running my display horizontally – and it won't switch automatically just by rotating the Pi. For my system, I know I want a vertical display, so I need to configure that. If you're happy with your display as is, then you don't need to worry about this step. Begin by editing the displayed config file, called **dispsetup.sh**:

```
sudo nano /usr/share/dispsetup.sh
```

Now add this line *before* the **exit 0**, which must remain at the bottom of the file:

```
DISPLAY=:0 xrandr --output HDMI-1 --rotate left
```

This tells the Pi to configure the *primary* display (**DISPLAY=:0**), connected to **HDMI 1**. It rotates it 90 degrees to the left. To rotate different directions, change **left** to one of the following:

- Left
- Right
- Inverted
- Normal

Now restart the Pi to see these changes take effect – shown in Figure 14-6.

Figure 14-6. *The almost completed dashboard*

Show Sensor Data

Up until now you have two fairly independent modules. The template shows a nice-looking dashboard with hard-coded data, and the back-end Python code reads all the sensors. Let's link the two together. All the hard work is already done, so it's almost a simple case of pointing the templates to the data. Modify your main route inside **main.py**.

Change the return to use Flask's **render_template**, and pass the sensor data to the **main.html** template. I've removed the beep and reverse function calls, as these are not needed just yet. Here's the revised code:

```python
from flask import Blueprint, render_template
from .sensors import Sensors
from flask import current_app as app
from datetime import datetime

main_blueprint = Blueprint("main", __name__)

@main_blueprint.route("/")
def show():
    app.logger.info("Starting to retrieve core data")
    sensors = Sensors()

    temperature = sensors.get_external_temp()
    boot_status = sensors.get_boot_status()
    light_status = sensors.get_light_status()
    fog_light = sensors.get_fog_light_status()

    today = datetime.now()
    time = today.strftime("%H:%M")
    date = today.strftime("%A %d %B %Y")

    result = {
        "temperature": temperature,
        "boot": boot_status,
```

```
        "light": light_status,
        "fog": fog_light,
        "time": time,
        "date": date,
    }

    app.logger.info("Finished retrieving core data")
    app.logger.debug(f"Core data: {result}")

    return render_template("main.html", data=result)
```

Notice how the sensor data is passed to the template through the name **data**. It's a dictionary called **result**, but on the template itself, you'll access it through its new name of **data**. I've modified this to include the current date and time – a useful change, which is simple with the Python core library:

```
today = datetime.now()
time = today.strftime("%H:%M")
date = today.strftime("%A %d %B %Y")
```

The **strftime** function converts the datetime object into a readable format.

Over inside the **main.html** template, you can access this data through Jinja2 variables, like this:

```
{{ data.date }}
```

By using simple logic, or just spitting out the data, you can control what's shown to the screen. For example, here's how to show the snowflake icon *only* if it's cold:

```
{% if data.temperature <=4 %}
    <i class="fas fa-snowflake"></i>
{% endif %}
```

Here's the revised code for your **body** tag:

```
<div class="container text-center text-light">
    <h2>Hello.</h2>
    <h3>{{ data.date }}</h3>
    <div class="row">
        <div class="col text-left">
            <i class="fas fa-clock"></i>{{ data.time }}
        </div>
        <div class="col text-right">
            {% if data.temperature <=4 %}
                <i class="fas fa-snowflake"></i>
            {% endif %}
            {{ data.temperature }}° C
            <br />
            {% if data.light == 'Daytime' %}
                <i class="fas fa-sun"></i>
            {% else %}
                <i class="fas fa-moon"></i>
            {% endif %}
            {{ data.light }}
        </div>
    </div>
    <div class="row">
        <div class="col text-middle">
            <i class="fas fa-car icon-huge"></i>
        </div>
    </div>
    <div class="row">
        <div class="col text-middle">
            {% if data.boot == 'Open' %}
```

```
        <i class="fas fa-exclamation"></i><span
        class="exclamation">Boot is open</span>
     {% endif %}
     <br>
     {% if data.fog %}
        <i class="fas fa-lightbulb"></i>Fog lights are on
     {% endif %}
     </div>
  </div>
</div>
```

Remember the golden rule when working with templates – simple logic to show/hide data or minor UI tweaks are fine. Complex logic or calculations should live inside the Python classes!

Finally, let's get this data to update in near-real time. Inside the **head** tags, add this new meta tag:

```
<meta http-equiv="refresh" content="0.25">
```

This HTML tag instructs the browser to reload the page every quarter of a second. It doesn't actually do it that quickly, but it's fairly fast. Now, the page constantly reloads, getting fresh data every time. Commit your code and push to the Pi. Once booted, observe the dashboard. Make some changes such as holding down buttons, covering the light sensor, or warming up the temperature sensor. Notice how the dashboard updates to reflect these changes? Very nice – it's almost complete now.

Reversing Module Completion

Several of the stand-alone projects included components and sensors for the reversing module. The Pi camera, beeper unit, and rear distance sensor all require integrating into this dashboard.

Let's begin with the reverse sensor. Check this every time the main page loads – if it's triggered (the car is in reverse gear), switch to the reverse camera feed page. Starting with the Python code inside **main.py**, shuffle the code around such that the reverse sensor is checked before any other sensors – no point checking the temperature if the reversing screen will run. Use a simple **if** to route to the **reverse** code if the sensor is detected:

```
reverse_light = sensors.get_reverse_status()
if reverse_light:
    return reverse()
```

The **reverse** name needs importing from the **reverse.py** file:

```
from .reverse import reverse
```

Now, whenever the main page detects the reverse sensor, it will redirect and run the reverse route code. If you run this code on the Pi, there's one big problem. The video feed is loading from http://pi-car:8081. This host does not resolve on the Pi – you only configured it on your computer, so let's fix that. Using a hosts entry like this means the video feed can work on the Pi, or when accessing the Pi over the network – it's a far more flexible approach. On the Pi, edit your hosts file:

```
sudo nano /etc/hosts
```

Add a new entry to route **pi-car** to your **localhost** address:

```
127.0.0.1 pi-car
```

Now save and restart. When booted, hold down the reverse sensor button (or otherwise trigger the sensor). You should see the Pi switch to the video feed page – it's not pretty yet, but it should work (providing you configured the Pi camera and video stream in the previous projects).

Let's improve this reversing page. It needs to call the beep and distance sensor functions, the camera needs fitting to the page, and it needs some styling. Here's the revised HTML to go inside **reverse.html**:

```
<!doctype html>

<html lang="en">
    <head>
        <meta charset="utf-8">
        <meta name="viewport" content="width=device-width,
        initial-scale=1, shrink-to-fit=no">

        <title>Pi Car</title>
        <meta name="description" content="Raspberry Pi based
        car system">
        <meta name="author" content="Joe Coburn">
        <link rel="stylesheet" type="text/css" href="/static/
        css/style.css">
    </head>

    <body>
        <img src="{{ base_url }}">
    </body>
</html>
```

You could argue that you don't need to "follow the rules" as it were. This HTML adds little functionality, and as your dashboard isn't on the Internet, you don't need to follow standards. That's understandable – feel free to skip this, but it's a good practice to follow the standards. Shortly you'll modify this to include some essential code to read the sensors and issue the beep.

Notice how most of this HTML in the **head** section is identical to the main page – with a few stylesheets removed. In any big system, or website with more than three or four pages, it makes sense to centralize this logic to reduce duplication. For example, changing the name of your CSS file requires updating the same tag in two files now. In this project with only two basic templates, that's an acceptable compromise. If you're interested in reducing this duplication, then look into *Jinja macros* (`https://jinja.palletsprojects.com/en/2.11.x/templates/#macros`) – an excellent way to reuse code.

You may need to rotate your camera again, based on your final screen orientation. As with the first rotation, edit your **motion** config file to handle this:

```
sudo nano /etc/motion/motion.conf
rotate 90
```

Revisit the reversing camera chapter for full motion config breakdown.

When you're ready, commit your code and restart the Pi. Trigger the reverse light sensor, and watch as your dashboard switches over to the live camera feed – it's really taking shape now. It's not there yet, however. The reversing page doesn't switch back to the main dashboard when the reverse gear is disengaged, and it doesn't yet issue the beep or IR distance-sensing reverse assist, so let's fix that.

For this file, constantly restarting the page as was the case with the main index page is too disruptive to the live video feed. It works, but the video feed ends up slightly jittery. To accomplish this, you'll use *JavaScript*. JavaScript is a front-end programming language. It's executed by your web browser, and website visitors can often read the code itself. It's not the same thing as *Java*, and it's perfect for running tasks "in the background" using *Asynchronous JavaScript and XML* (AJAX). AJAX is used with JavaScript to create asynchronous client-side applications. You could use it on the previous page to update all the data, but it would require a fair amount of JavaScript code, for little benefit.

Almost all of the modern Internet uses JavaScript in some way. It doesn't need installing either, as it's part of the instructions your browser can understand by default. Let's not get too carried away though, as

JavaScript is horribly inconsistent (even with itself) and it's much slower than Python to execute. Still, it's more than good enough for this small task.

For this task, JavaScript will essentially load another web page, which will route to Flask, ping the distance sensor, and issue a beep if an object is nearby. JavaScript doesn't need to change any data, or even look for a successful response – it just hits this page and carries on as normal.

Create a new Flask route inside **reverse.py** called **reverse_beep**. This needs a route of **/reverse/beep/**, which is the URL address your JavaScript will load. Here's the code:

```
@reverse_blueprint.route("/reverse/beep/")
def reverse_beep():
    sensors = Sensors()
    rear_distance_item = sensors.get_rear_distance_sensor()
    if rear_distance_item:
        sensors.beep()
    return "Success"
```

There are no surprises in this code. It calls the **get_rear_distance_ sensor** function from your **Sensors** class. If that returns **True**, it issues a beep using the **beep** function. If you visit this new route from your browser, you can see it in action (http://pi-car:5000/reverse/beep/). There is no logging in this function – and for good reason. There's enough logging in the sensor code itself to handle this, and as this code could potentially run four times every second, your logs will quickly fill up with too much noise and become almost unusable.

Let's write JavaScript to call this endpoint. Over in **reverse.html**, create a **script** tag, which needs to live *inside* the **head** tag:

```
<script type="text/javascript">

</script>
```

Any JavaScript your write *must* be within a **script** tag. The script type of **text/javascript** tells your browser that this script contains JavaScript. Here's your JavaScript AJAX code:

```
var runSensors = function() {
  var xhttp = new XMLHttpRequest();
  xhttp.open("GET", "/reverse/beep/", true);
  xhttp.send();
}
window.onload = function() {
  setInterval(runSensors, 250);
}
```

This code performs three core functions. It creates a function called **runSensors**, following the JavaScript naming convention of *CamelCase*. This function uses the **XMLHttpRequest** object to send an AJAX request to your new /**reverse**/**beep**/ route. Next, it uses the **setInterval** function to call your new **runSensors** function. **SetInterval** runs code regularly on a schedule, defined by the number – 250 milliseconds in this case. Every quarter of a second, JavaScript pings the /**reverse**/**beep**/ route to sense objects and issue beeps. This does not care about the response, or the duration.

The final argument to **xhttp.open** is set to **true**. This is the *asynchronous* parameter – it instructs the browser to run this code in the background while doing other tasks. No matter how slow this endpoint is, it will still issue the next command, and the next, and so on. Remember, this endpoint waits one second while issuing the beep.

Finally, **window.onload** ensures your code is loaded when the page loads. Without this, your code would never execute at all.

Commit your code and perform a build. Trigger the reverse sensor to load the reverse page. Now cover the distance sensor, and observe the beeps. Now move your hand and listen – the beeps stop. If you open your application logs, you'll see the beep and distance sensor logs corresponding to the AJAX requests every quarter of a second.

Finally, let's write some code to check the reverse sensor. If it's no longer detecting the reverse bulb, JavaScript needs to switch back to the main dashboard, and let that take over.

Back in Python, modify the **reverse_beep** function to call the main reverse sensor, and return a status of **Exit** if it's no longer detected:

```python
@reverse_blueprint.route("/reverse/beep/")
def reverse_beep():
    sensors = Sensors()
    reverse_light = sensors.get_reverse_status()
    if not reverse_light:
        return "Exit"

    rear_distance_item = sensors.get_rear_distance_sensor()
    if rear_distance_item:
        sensors.beep()

    return "Success"
```

Finally, modify the JavaScript **runSensors** function to check the result returned from the Python, and redirect to the dashboard if it equals **Exit**. This uses the **onreadystatechange** function, and it checks the **readyState** variables equals four – the operation is complete. Here's the complete JavaScript code:

```javascript
var runSensors = function() {
  var xhttp = new XMLHttpRequest();
  xhttp.open("GET", "/reverse/beep/", true);
  xhttp.onreadystatechange = function() {
    if (xhttp.readyState === 4) {
      result = xhttp.response
```

```
    if (result === "Exit") {
      window.location.href = "/";
    }
  }
}
xhttp.send();
}
window.onload = function() {
  setInterval(runSensors, 250);
}
```

You can learn more about the different ready state options at https://developer.mozilla.org/en-US/docs/Web/API/XMLHttpRequest/readyState.

Load the Pi's main dashboard. Play around with triggering the reverse sensor, and see it redirect to the reversing camera (with distance sensing and beeps). Now remove power from the sensor and watch it send you back to the dashboard. Excellent – the whole system is nearly finished now.

Final Pi Improvements

Your system is now practically complete. The Python is done, there's no more code to write, and it's fully working – pending installation in your car. There are two tasks left to finish this system. You may have noticed your Pi going to sleep to save energy. After five minutes or so, the display turns off and your dashboard disappears. It's still around – it's accessible over SSH and it operates just fine, but the screen is off. The Pi has switched off its display output to save energy. This energy saving is a useful feature for occasional use, but it's a nuisance for a car dashboard project. While the Pi has power and is running the application, it should send data to the display. Let's fix this.

Modify the Debian display configuration file **lightdm.conf**:

```
sudo nano /etc/lightdm/lightdm.conf
```

This file contains configuration options for all kinds of system-level display features. Scroll down to the **[Seat:*]** section. Uncomment the **xserver-command=X** line by removing the hash symbol. Extend this line to prevent the display from sleeping – shown in Figure 14-7:

```
xserver-command=X -s 0 dpms
```

Save and exit this file, taking care not to disrupt any other config lines. Now restart your Pi and wait some time – roughly five to ten minutes should be enough. Watch and see that your display now remains on forevermore – if the Pi is on, so is the display.

```
[Seat:*]
#type=local
#pam-service=lightdm
#pam-autologin-service=lightdm-autologin
#pam-greeter-service=lightdm-greeter
#xserver-backend=
xserver-command=X -s 0 dpms
#xmir-command=Xmir
#xserver-config=
#xserver-layout=
#xserver-allow-tcp=false
#xserver-share=true
#xserver-hostname=
#xserver-display-number=
#xdmcp-manager=
#xdmcp-port=177
#xdmcp-key=
```

Figure 14-7. *Sample Debian display configuration file*

The final change is to prevent the Pi from auto-updating its code base from Git. This is slow – you have to code a delay into the script to ensure the Internet connection exists, and it's ugly. By waiting, downloading, and then installing the latest dependencies and code, the LXDE has already booted and started the browser. This leads to an ugly few minutes whereby the browser is ready to go, but the server isn't running yet. Besides, full CI/CD perhaps isn't the best paradigm for a car – having to wait for an update before you can begin your journey isn't the best experience – ever been frustrated waiting for video game updates before?

Head back into your **rc.local** file from previous chapters, and comment out all the slow stuff – the sleep, clone script, and pipenv install. Here's the final script contents:

```
#sleep 15

export PATH=/home/pi/.pyenv/shims:$PATH
export FLASK_APP=Pi_Car.app

cd /home/pi/Documents/Pi-Car/
#./clone.sh
#pipenv install
pipenv run flask run --host=0.0.0.0 &

exit 0
```

By commenting these lines out, you can easily reinstate them in the future. A fun expansion project would be to *push* updates to the Pi, or integrate your build chain to deploy to a small number of cars, and continue the rollout once it's stable and there are no reported issues over a given period of time. If there are issues, automatically roll back to the previous version. This is beyond the scope of this book, and it's straying into *devops* territory. For those interested, *Ansible* (www.ansible.com/) is a great tool for this job.

Restart your Pi and bask in your own brilliance. Watch the sheer speed at which the Pi can start now that it's no longer burdened by auto-updates. It doesn't need an Internet connection to work – it has everything it needs in a self-contained package. Any sensor failures won't hold it back, as you programmed it defensively to operate in almost any environment. Naturally, if lots of sensors fail, it may enter into *limp mode* – with diminished functionality. That's still far better than a total failure, and often at times it's not possible to work normally if there's a huge system failure.

This chapter cleans up the system and turns it into a functional and pleasant dashboard. By building on the application logic developed in all the previous chapters, there's a lot of margin for customization here. All the previous chapters develop the core logic, and so much of this chapter is open to your interpretation. You learned how to switch between the rear view camera and the main display and how to speed up the entire application's startup time. You learned about CDNs, CSS, JavaScript, and HTML, along with AJAX and Chromium.

Throughout this book, you have learned how to write software. It's my hope that you really understood what's happening at every level and tediously typed out every line of code, instead of blindly loading up the repository and doing a copy-paste job. I'd love to hear from you if you enjoyed this book. Visit this book's GitHub repository at `https://github.com/CoburnJoe/Pi-Car` and say hello. Create a pull request and enhance the code, or join any discussions around topics (either in this repo, or anywhere else on GitHub). While GitHub doesn't support direct messages anymore, you can see my latest projects and contact details on my profile: `https://github.com/CoburnJoe`.

Here are some possible expansion projects, all based on the hardware and software you've used so far:

- Door sensors

- Boot sensor

- Headlight sensor

- Engine temperature sensor

- Random "message of the day" (perhaps based on the time of day)

- Climate control options

- Dashboard "debug" overlay/reporting of sensor failure to the dashboard

- Apple CarPlay/Android Auto support

- Multiple reversing sensors

- Report errors over the Internet

Last of all, remember that code is for humans. Computers will understand almost any jumbled mess of spaghetti code, so make your code simple and clear, such that anyone in the future can easily understand its intent. Complex, clever, or otherwise convoluted code makes modifications or troubleshooting more complex for everyone involved.

Index

A

Acceptance testing, 42

Adapter pattern, 27

Amazon Web Services (AWS), 51, 110

Ambulance-dispatch system, 34

ApplePiBaker
  macOS, 122, 123
  main screen, 123
  NOOBS, 125

apt-get command, 135

ARCELI DS18B20/DollaTek
  DS18B20, 172

Asynchronous JavaScript and XML
  (AJAX), 288, 290, 295

Autostart Flask
  exit command, 170
  nano, 170
  Pi boots, 167
  Pipfile, 168
  rc.local file, 168
  sleep command, 169

B

Basic dashboard layout
  bootstrap, 266, 267, 273, 278
  cursor attribute, 275
  custom CSS, 274, 275

designing, 266

doctype, 272

Font Awesome
  download button, 269
  started screen, 268

HTML, 271

render_template function, 275

resized screen, 278

route modification, 275

run application, 276

static folder, 267, 273

style.css file, 272

styling, 277

tags, 271

template folder, 269, 270

Beeper
  piezo/piezoelectric
    elements, 249, 251
  reversing system, 249

Black package, 88

Black-box testing, 43

Black Check step, 114

Blacklists, 36

Booleans, 18

Boot Sensor, Flask
  application logs, 194
  Button class, 191
  code, 192

J. Coburn, *Build Your Own Car Dashboard with a Raspberry Pi*,
https://doi.org/10.1007/978-1-4842-6080-7

Printed in the United States
By Bookmasters